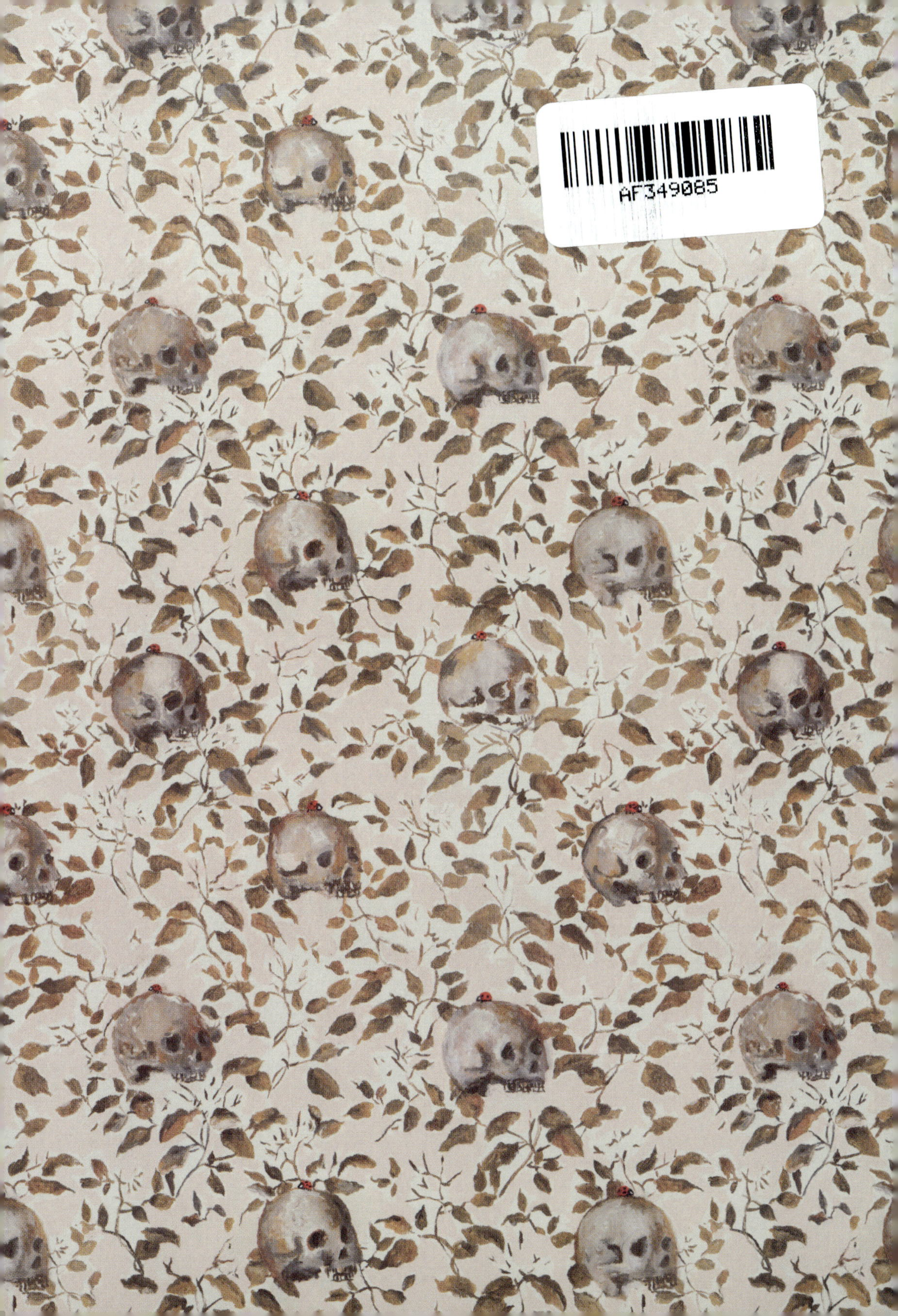
AF349085

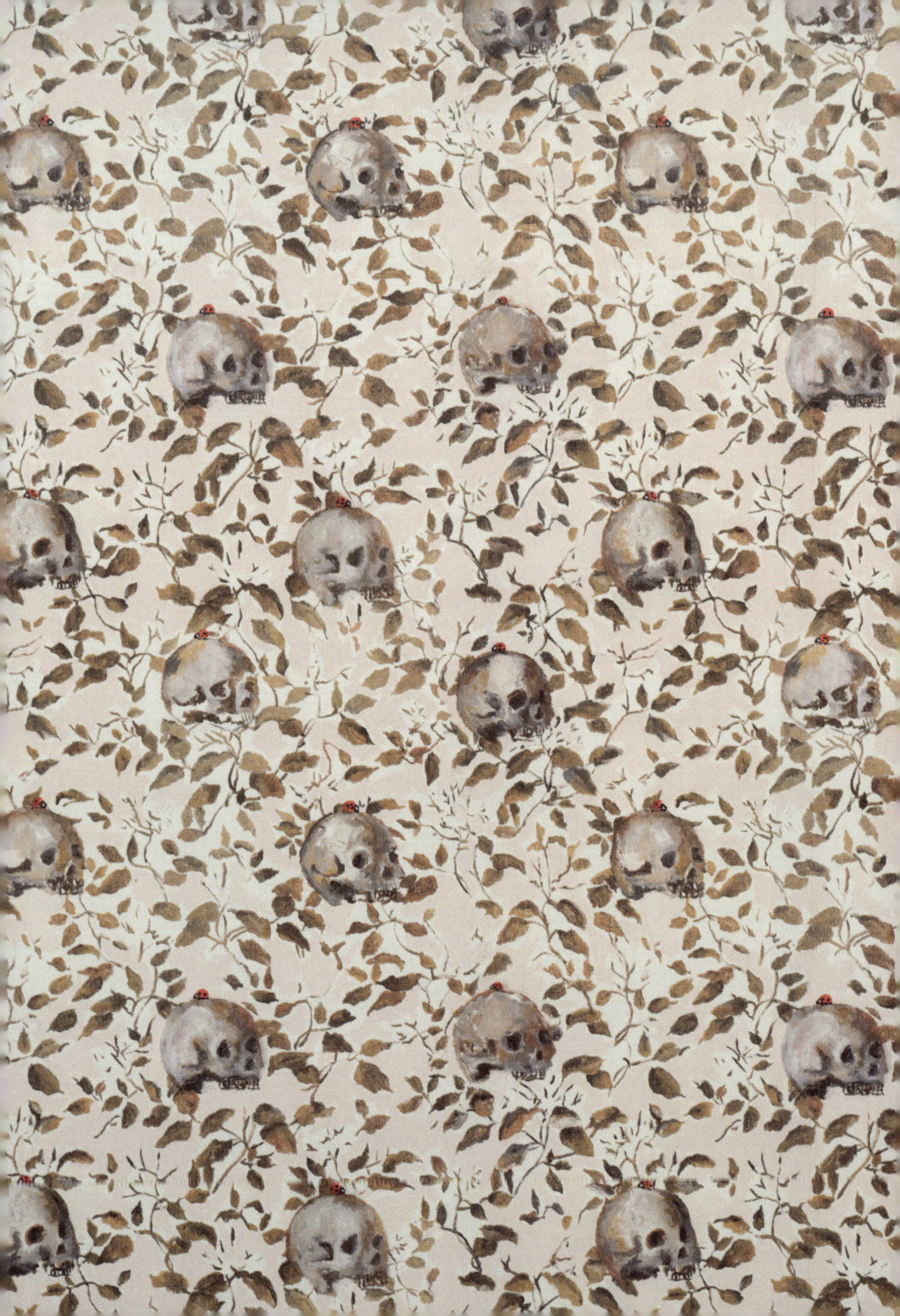

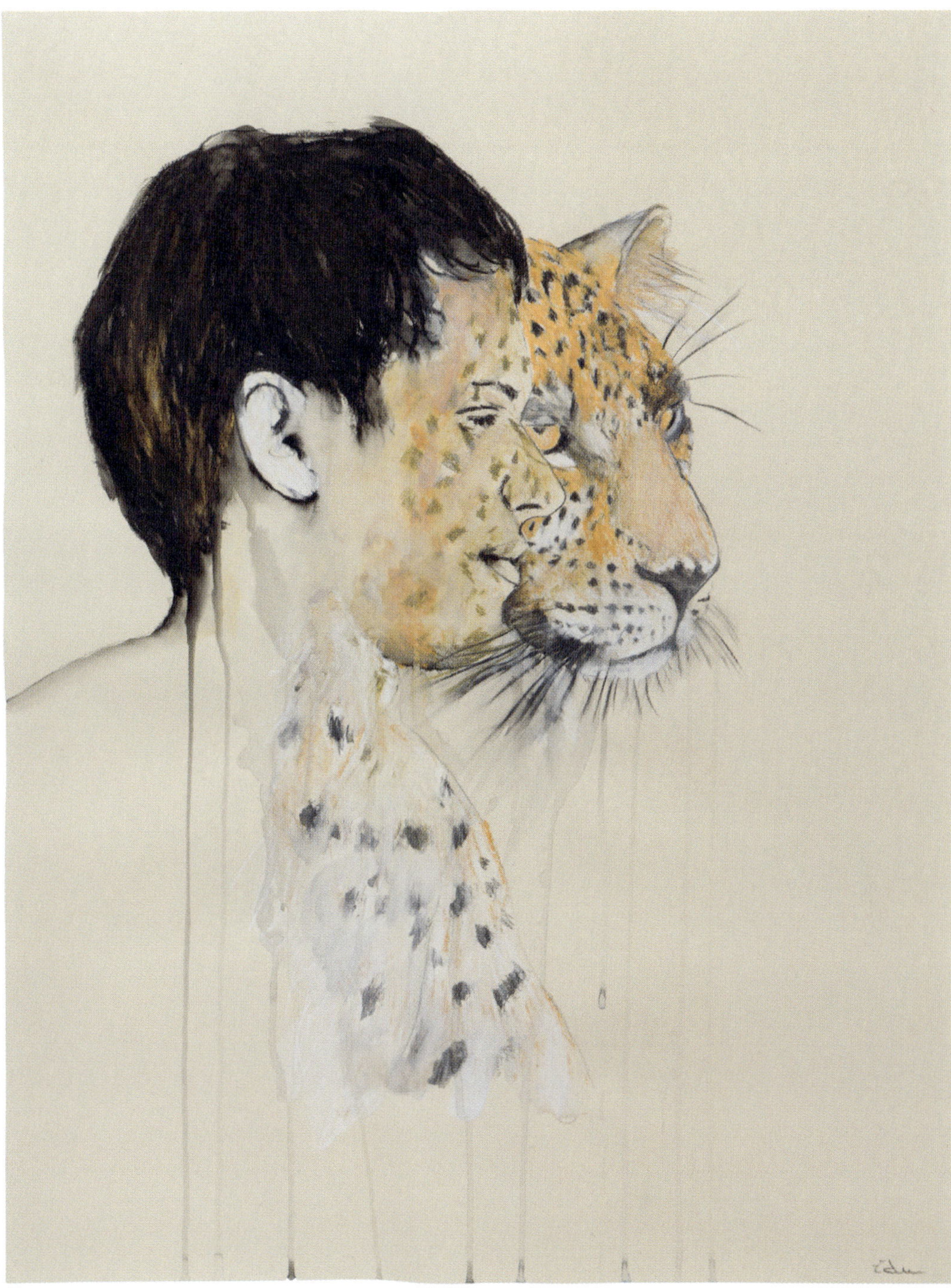

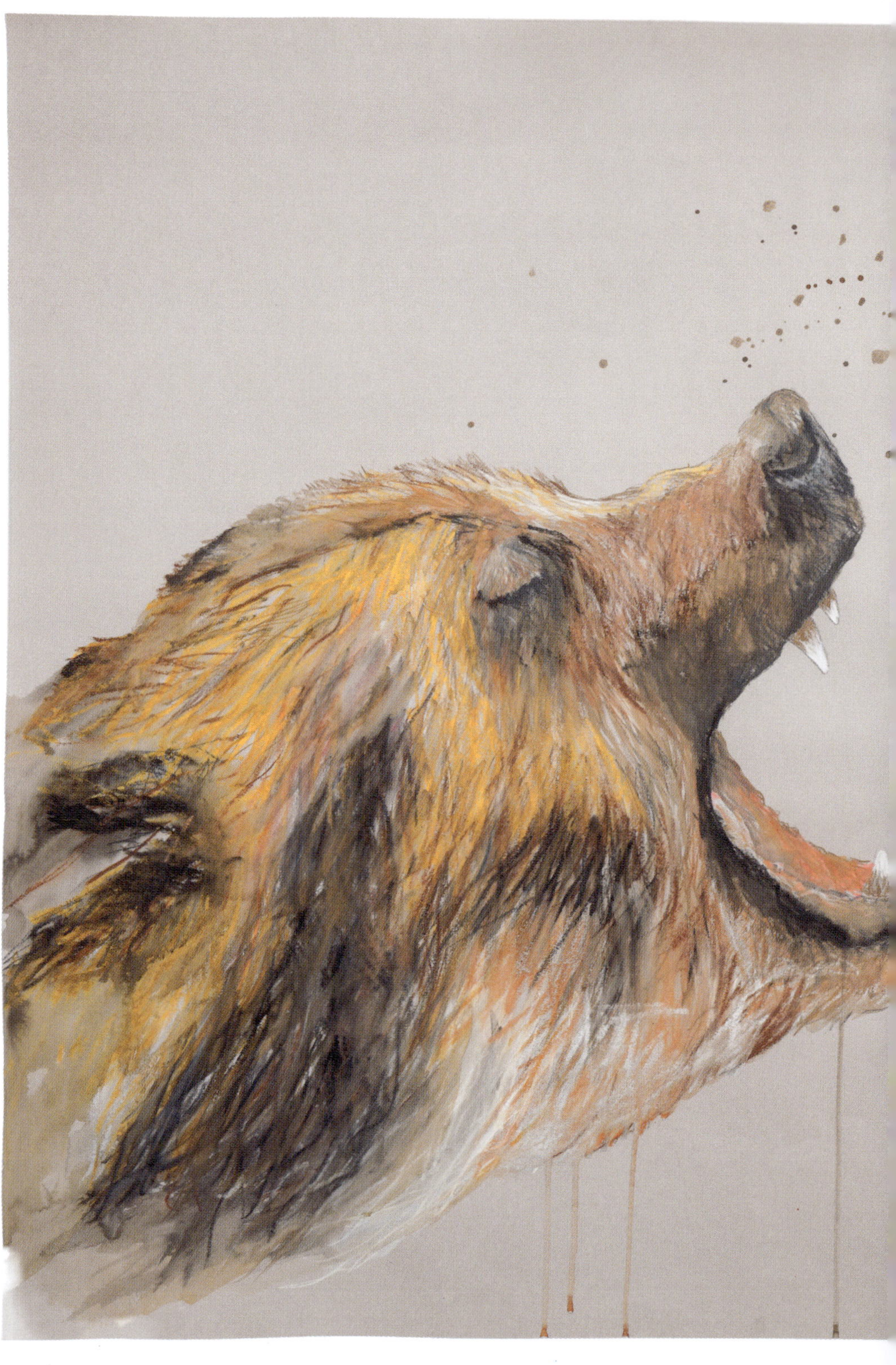

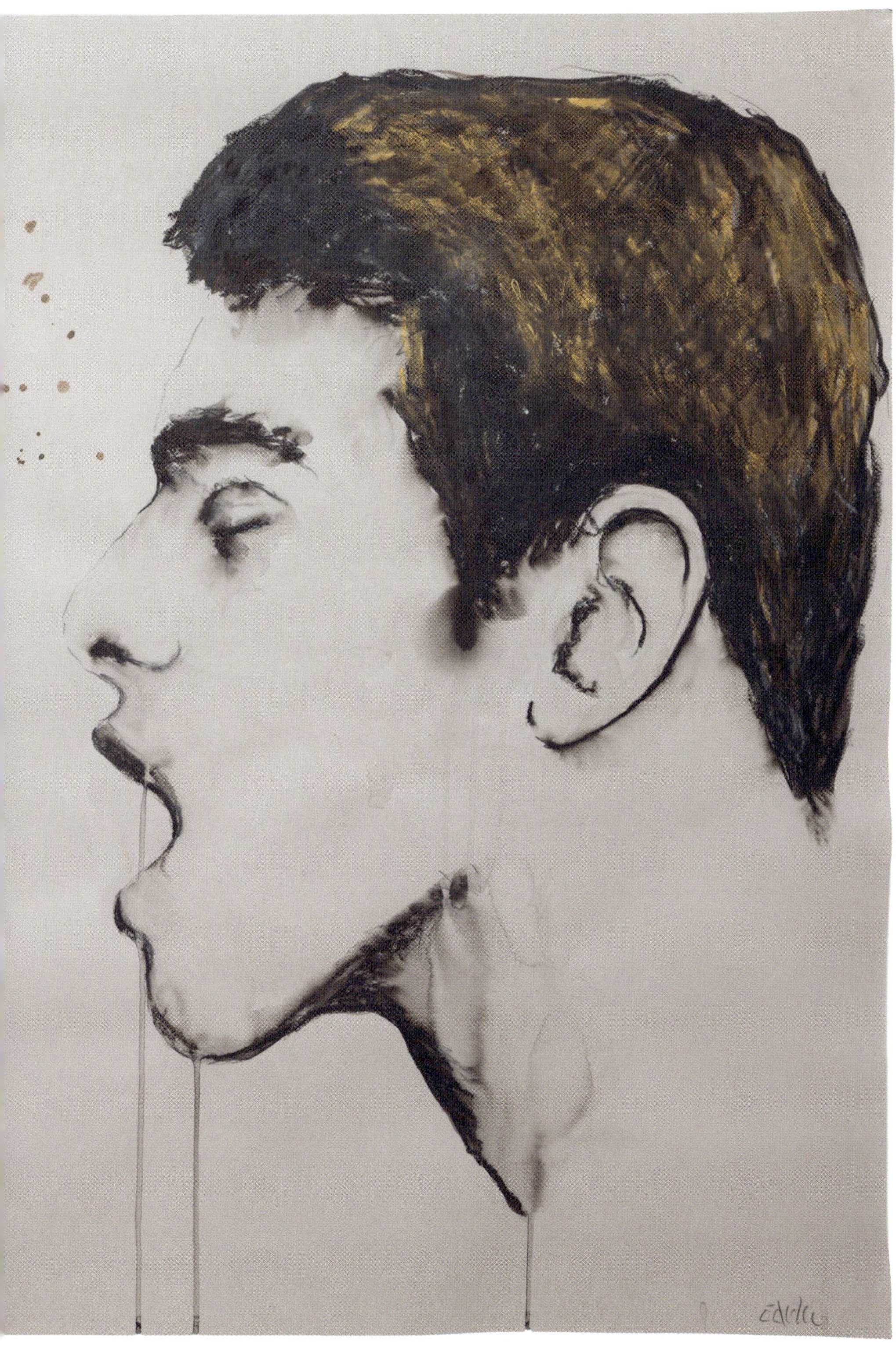

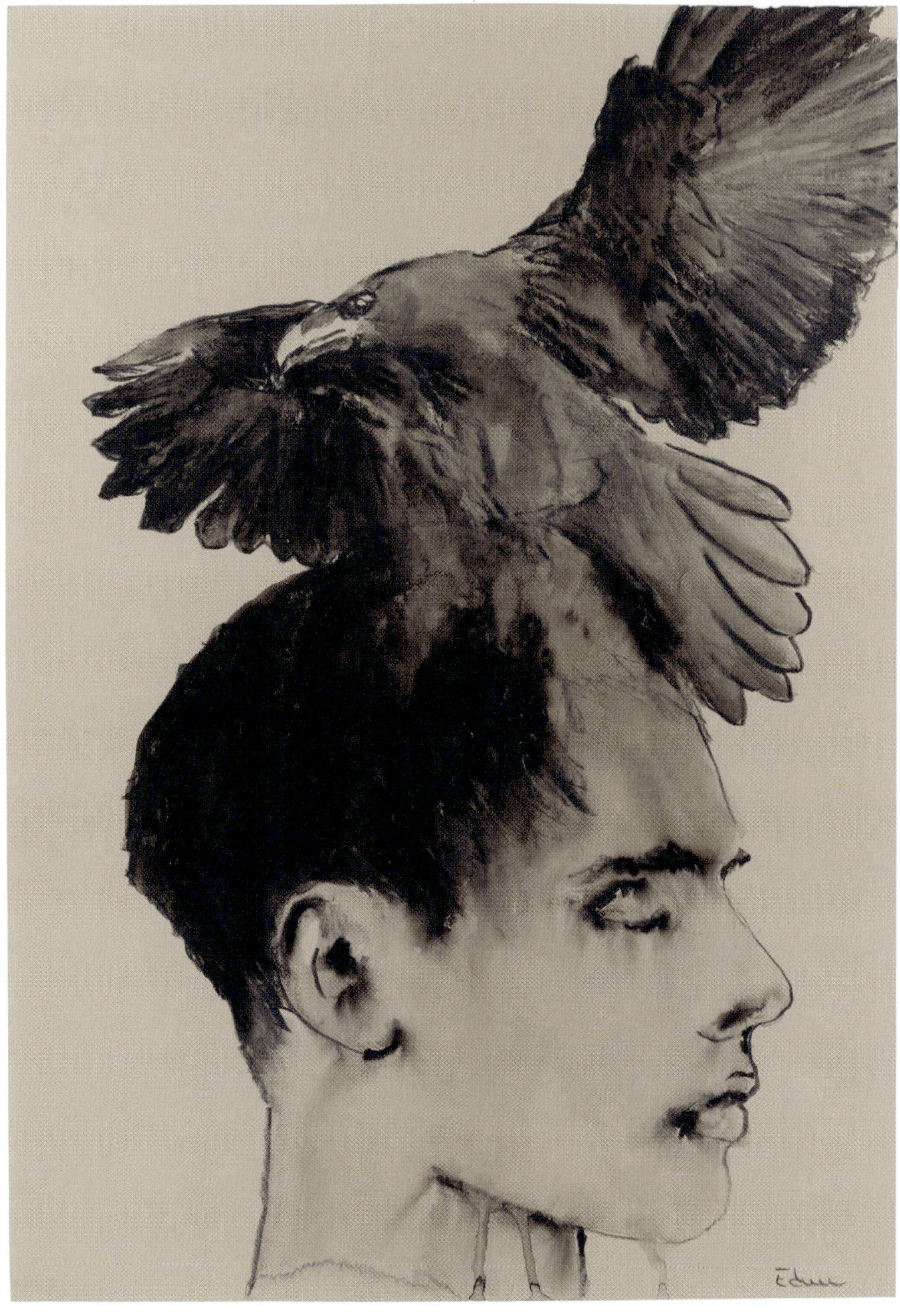

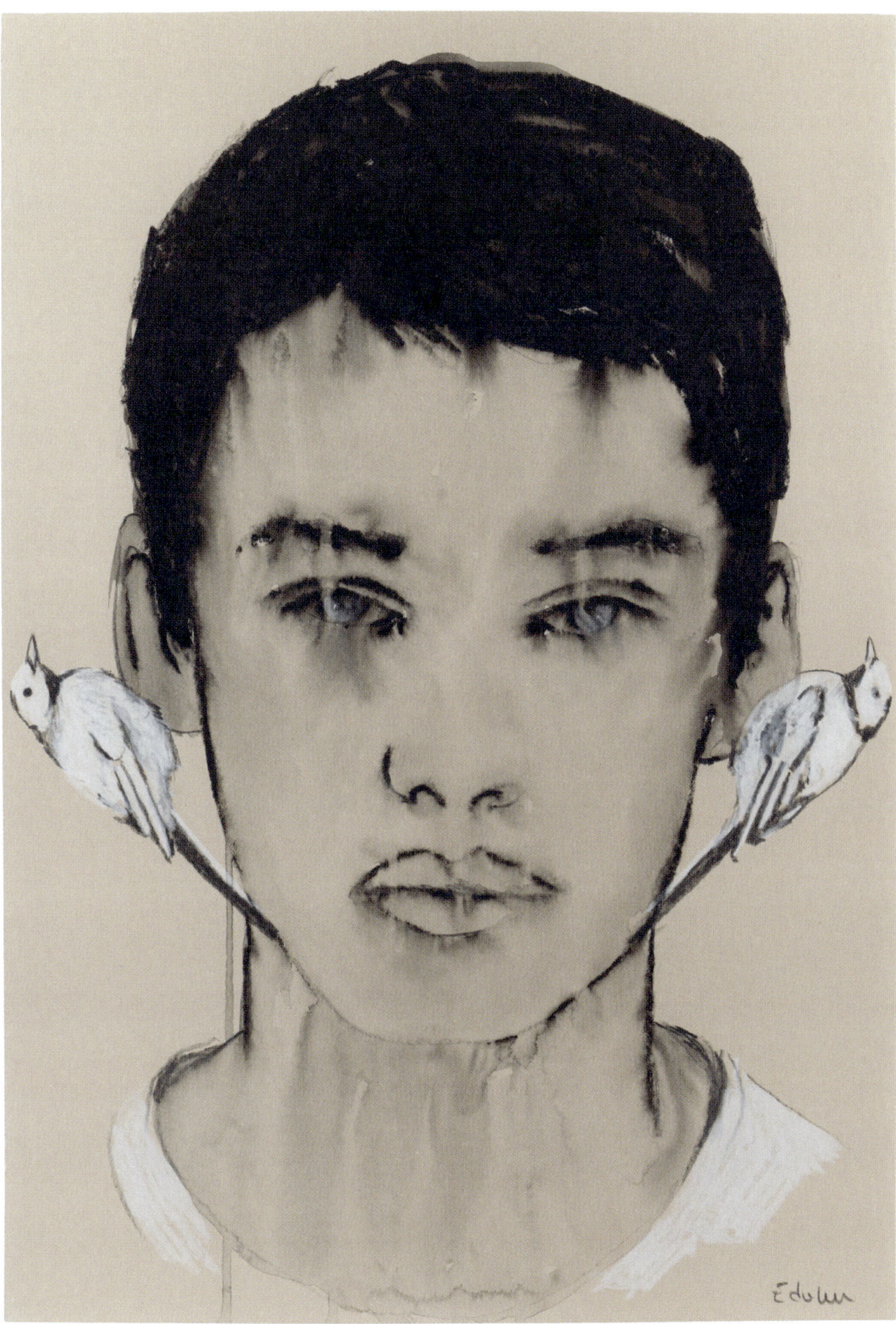

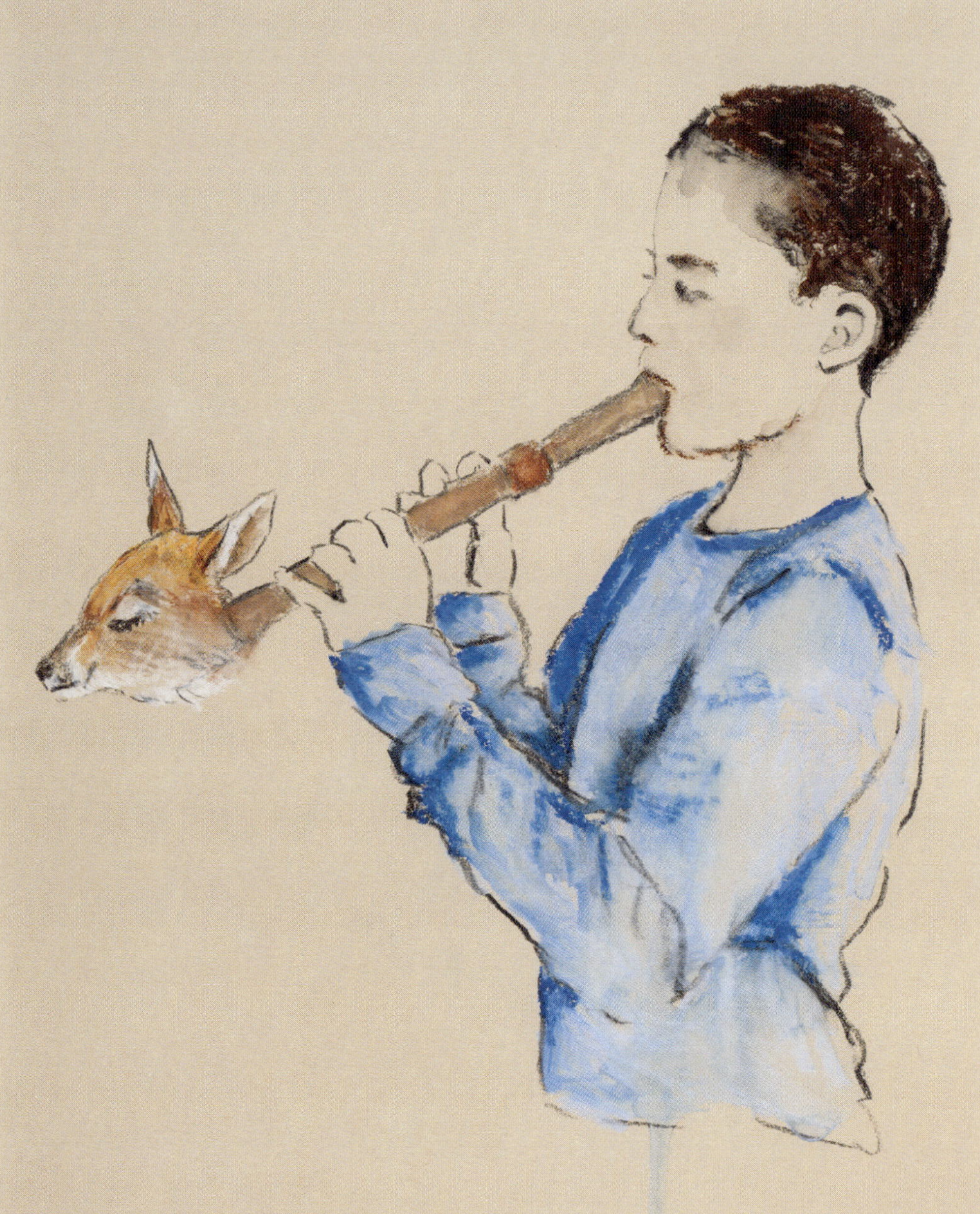

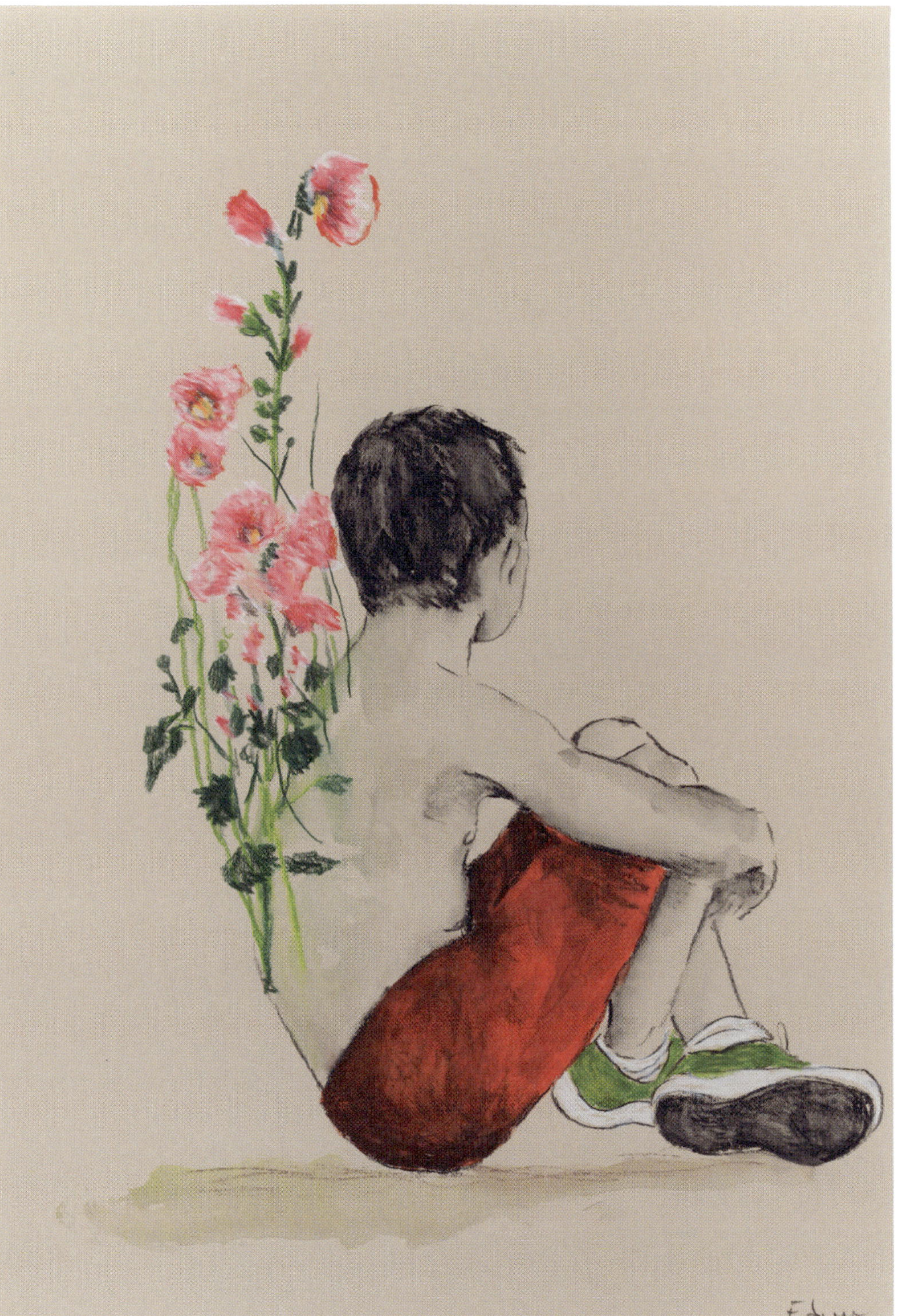

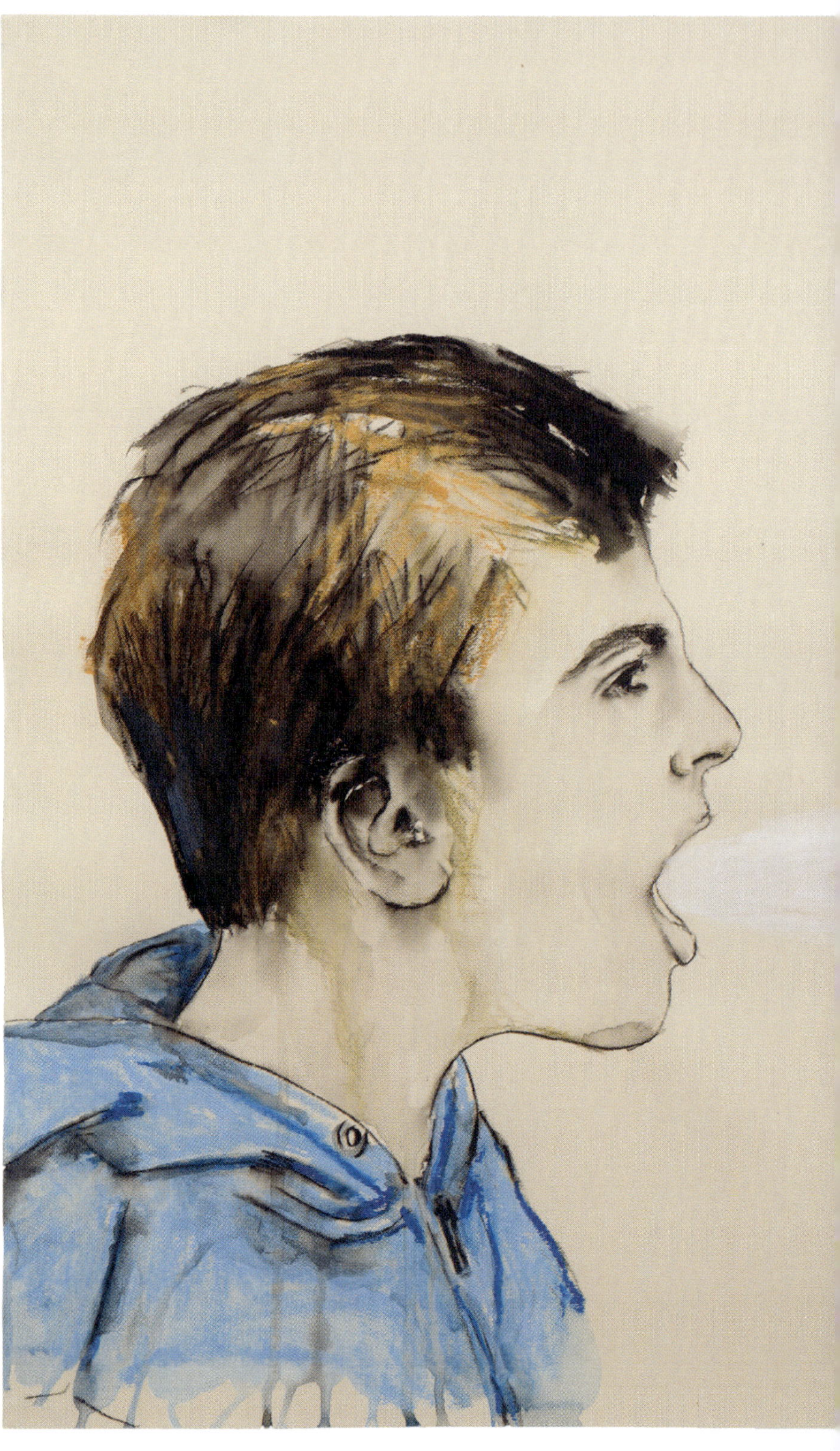

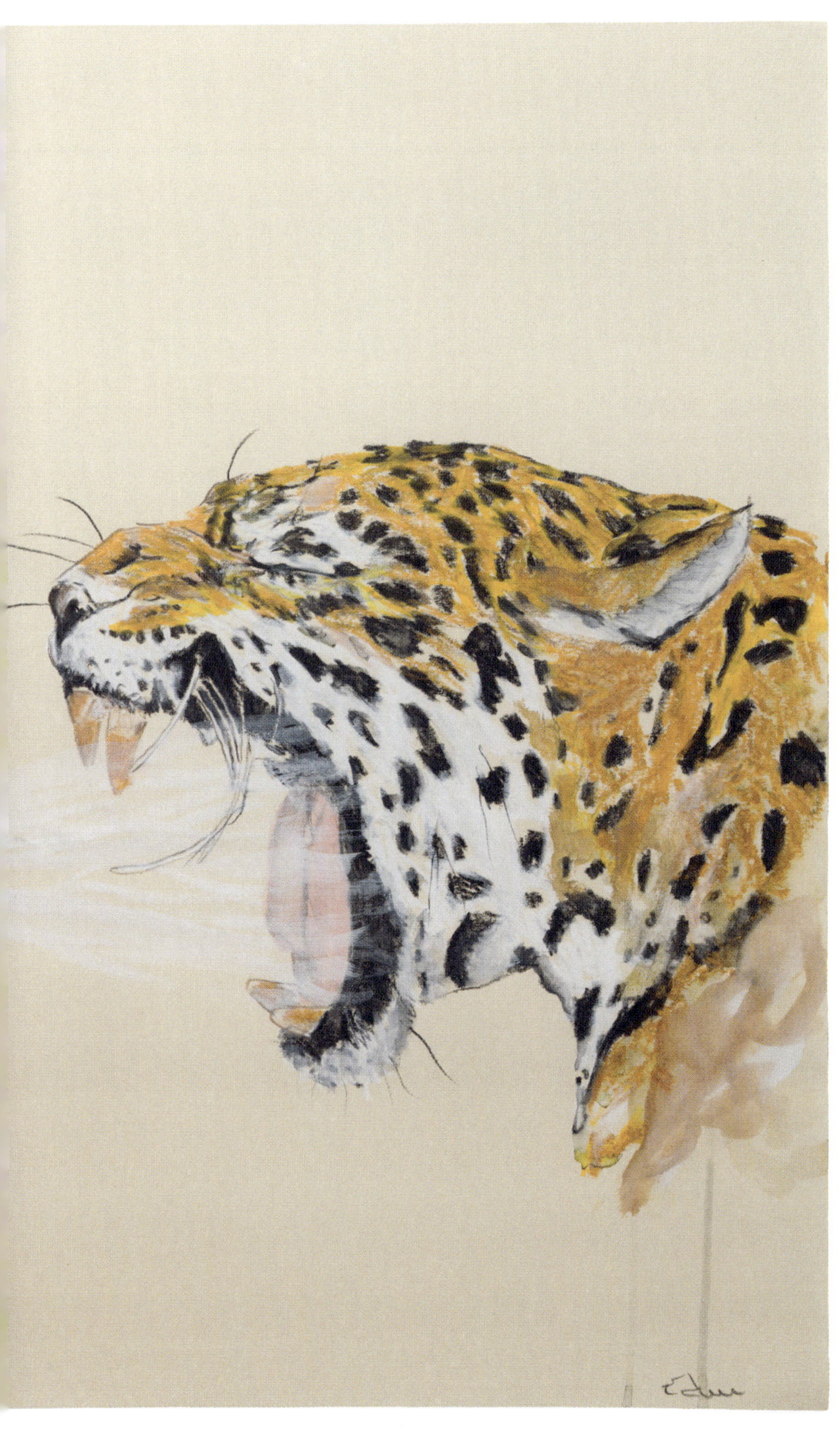

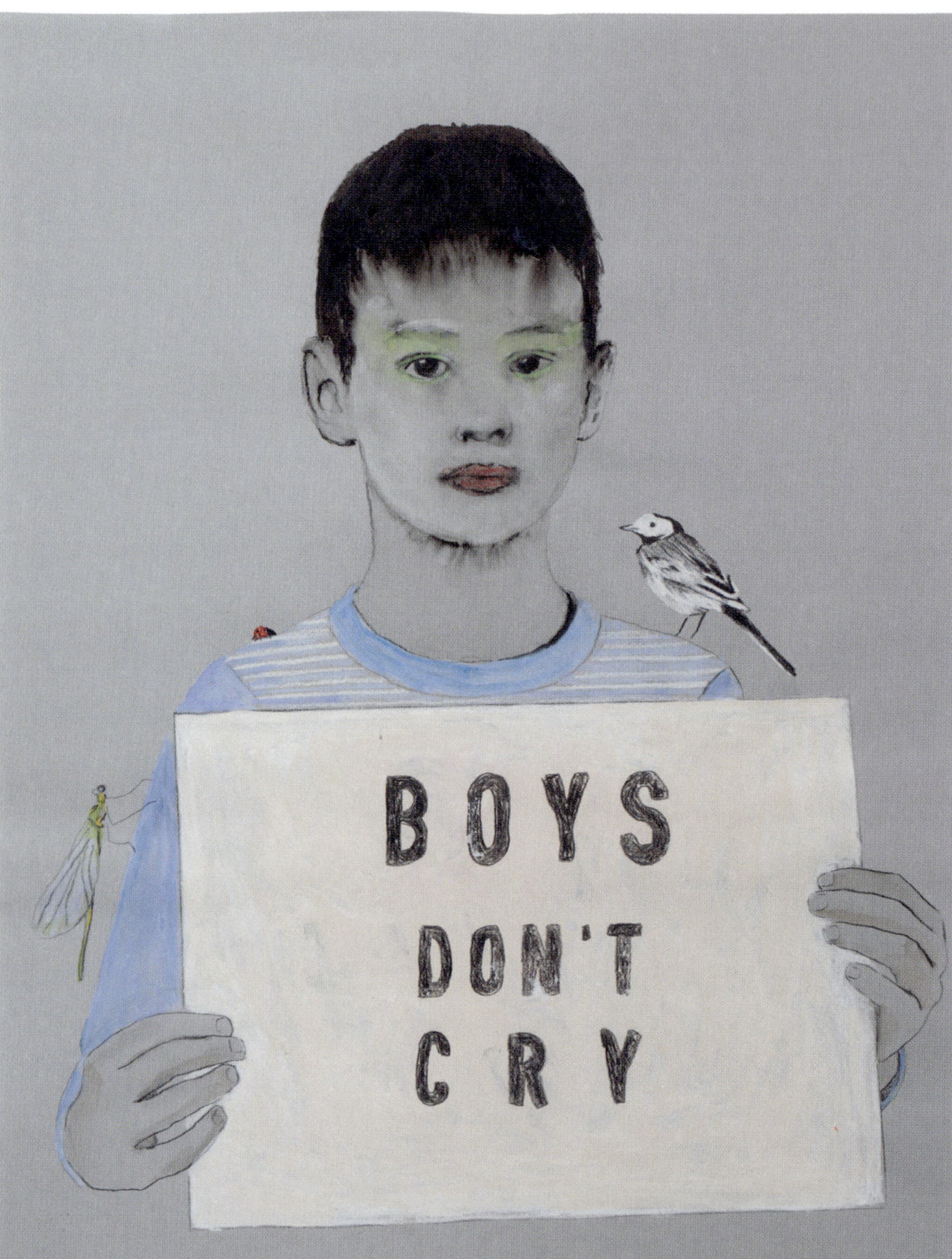
BOYS
DON'T
CRY

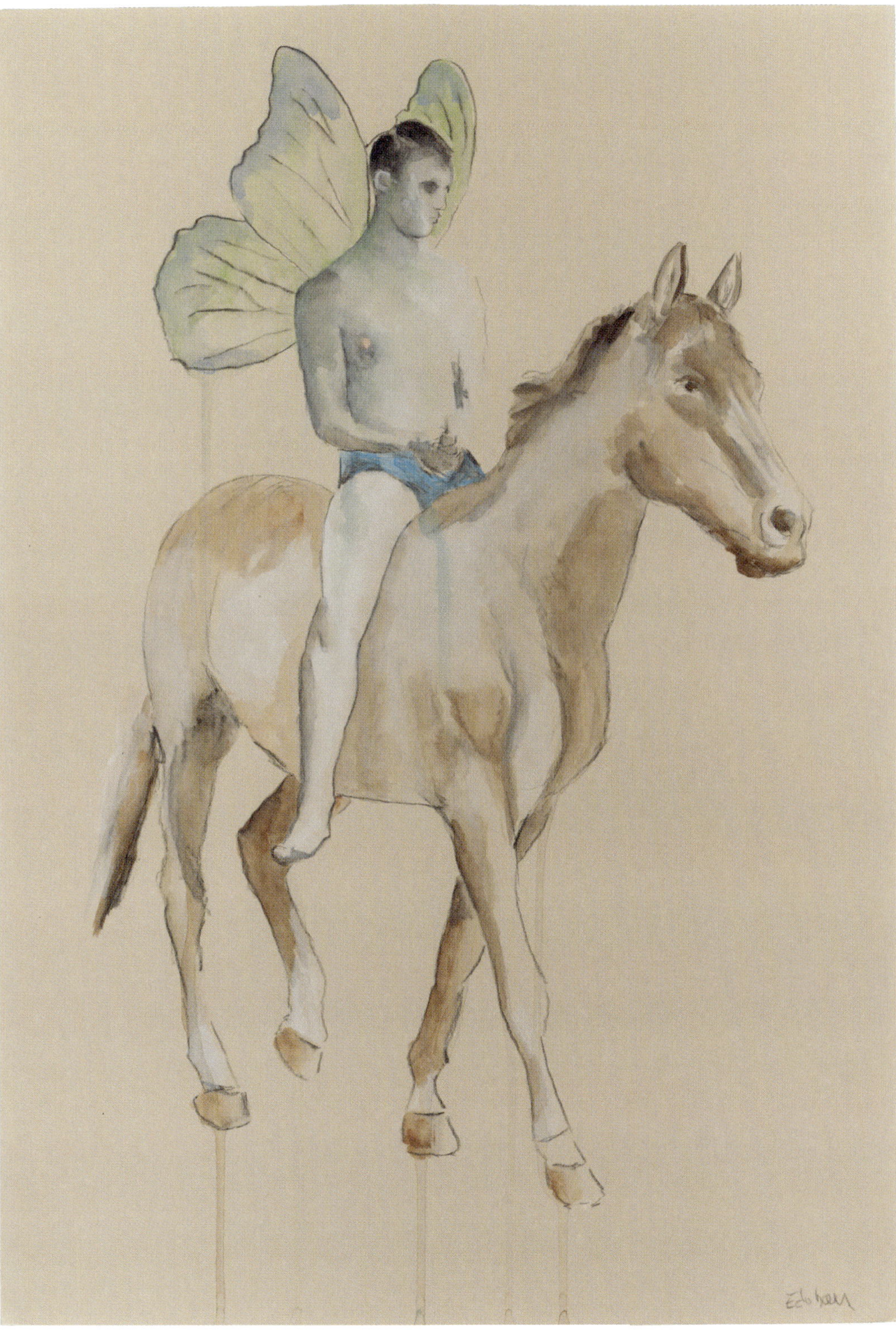

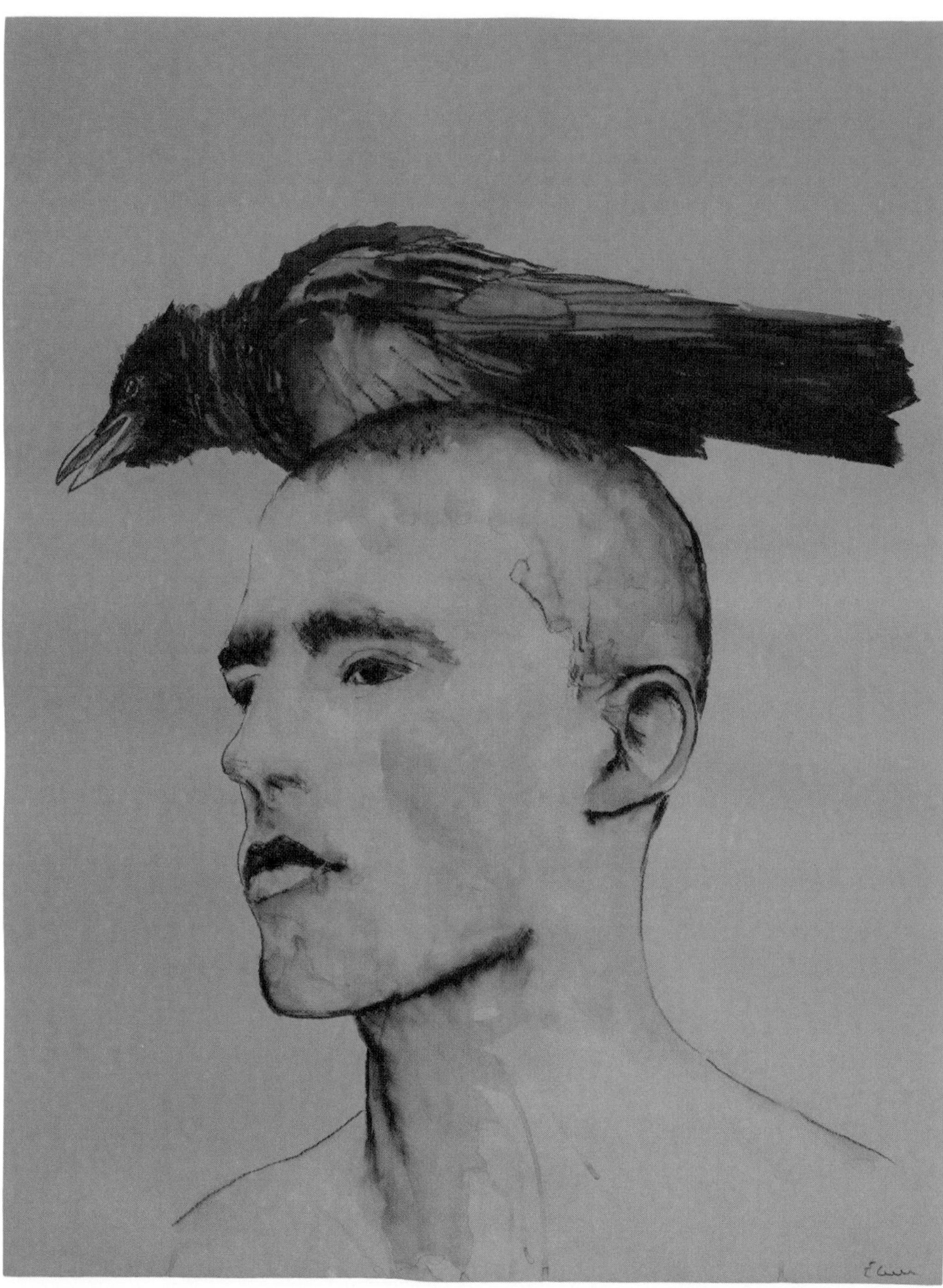

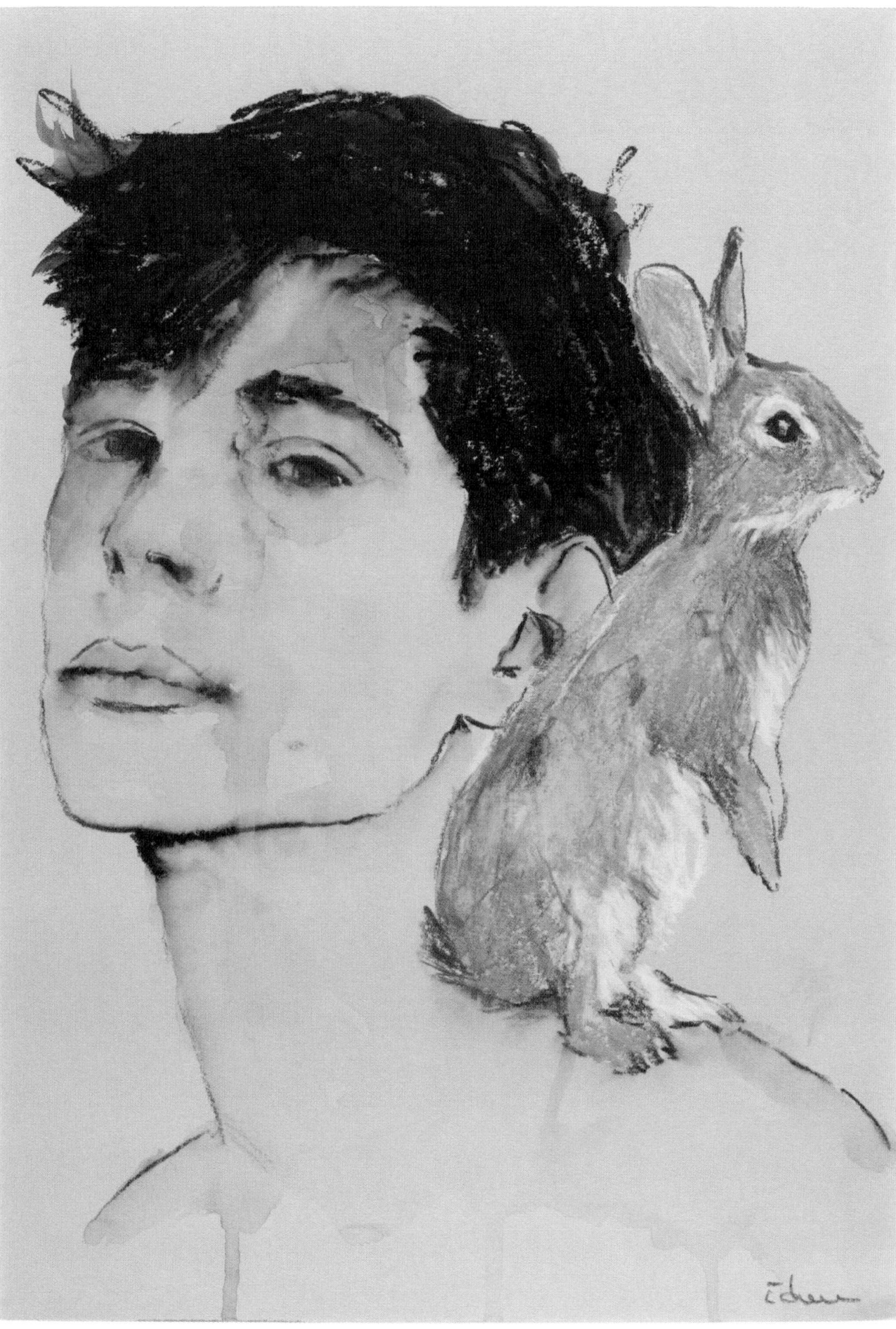

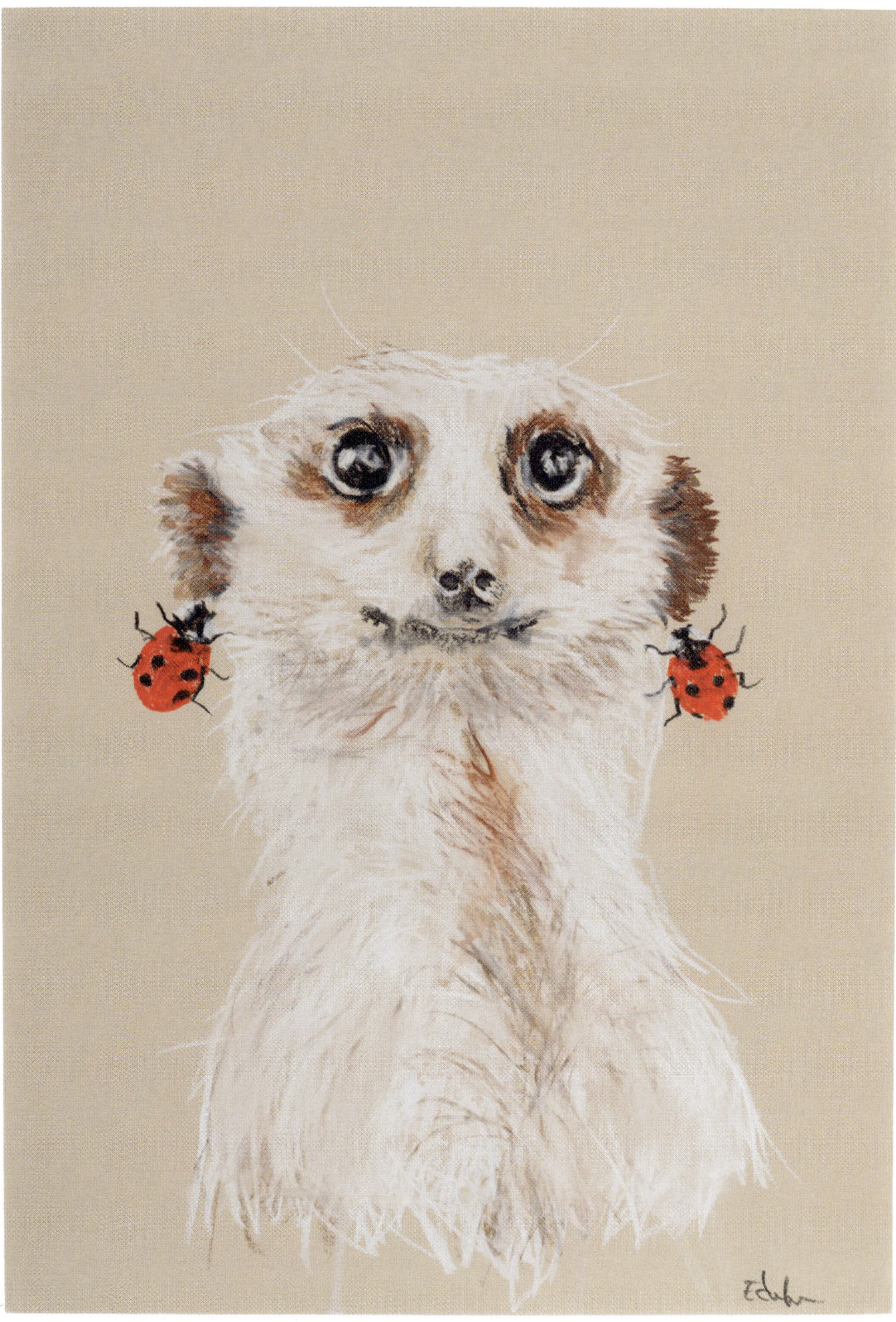

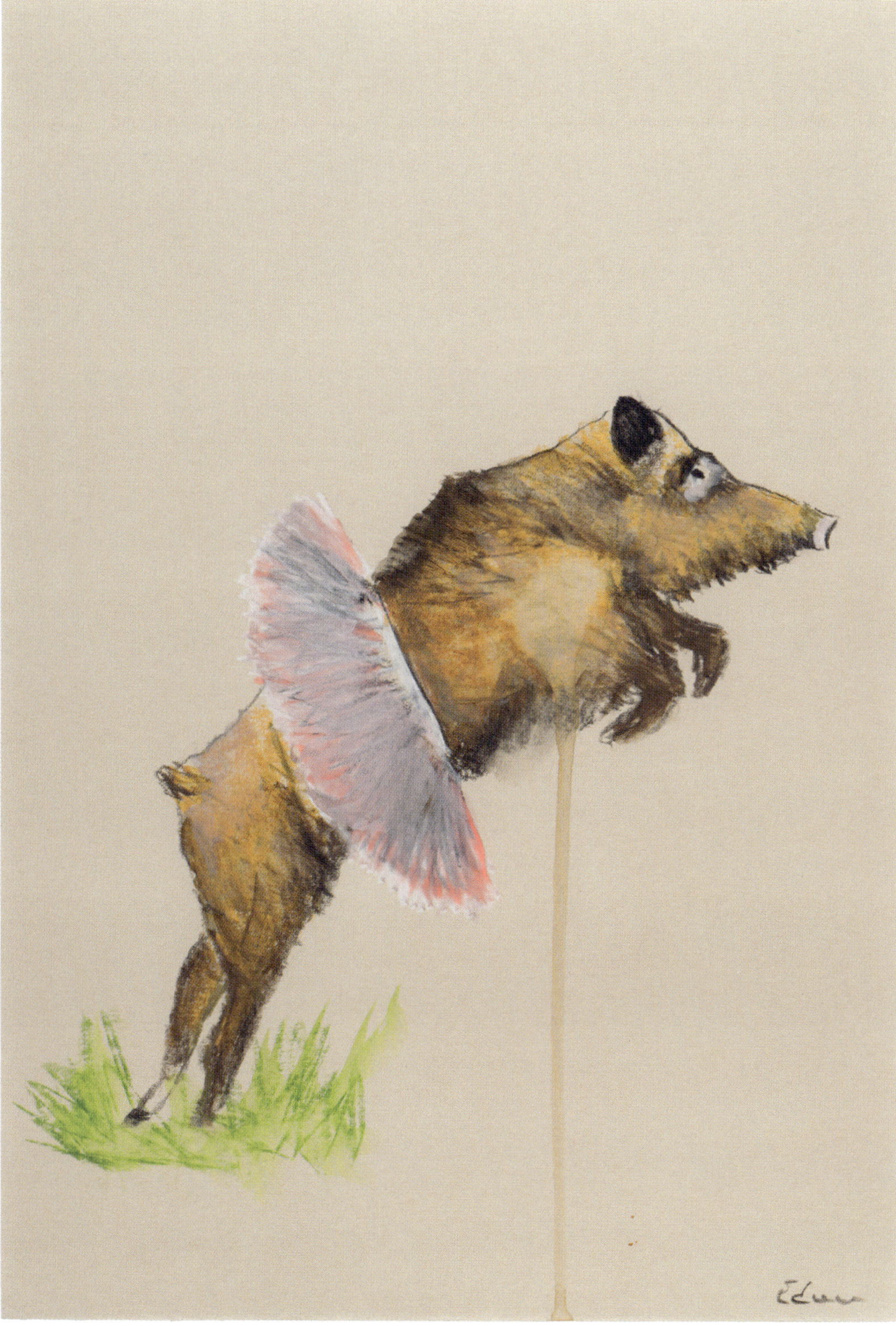

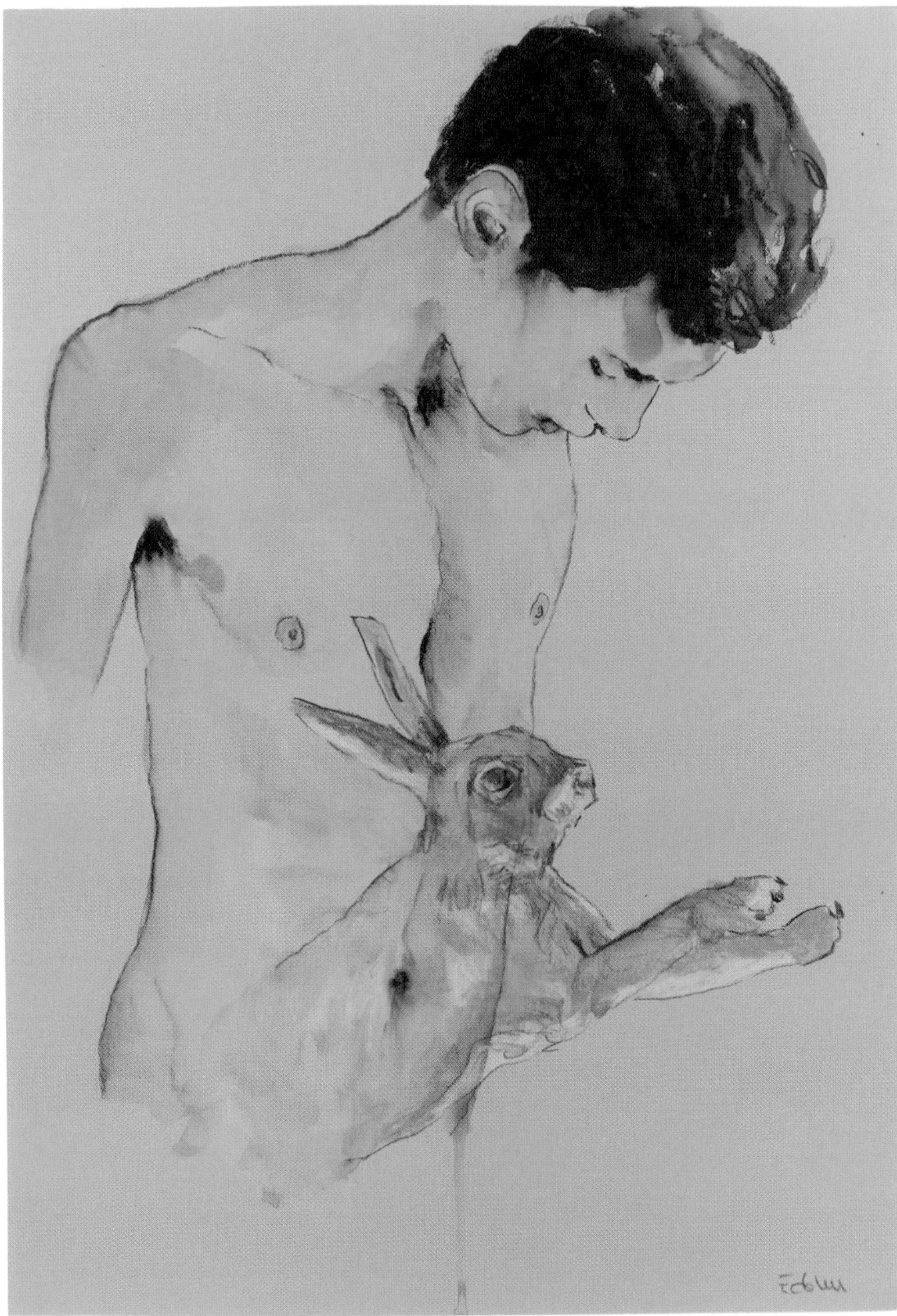

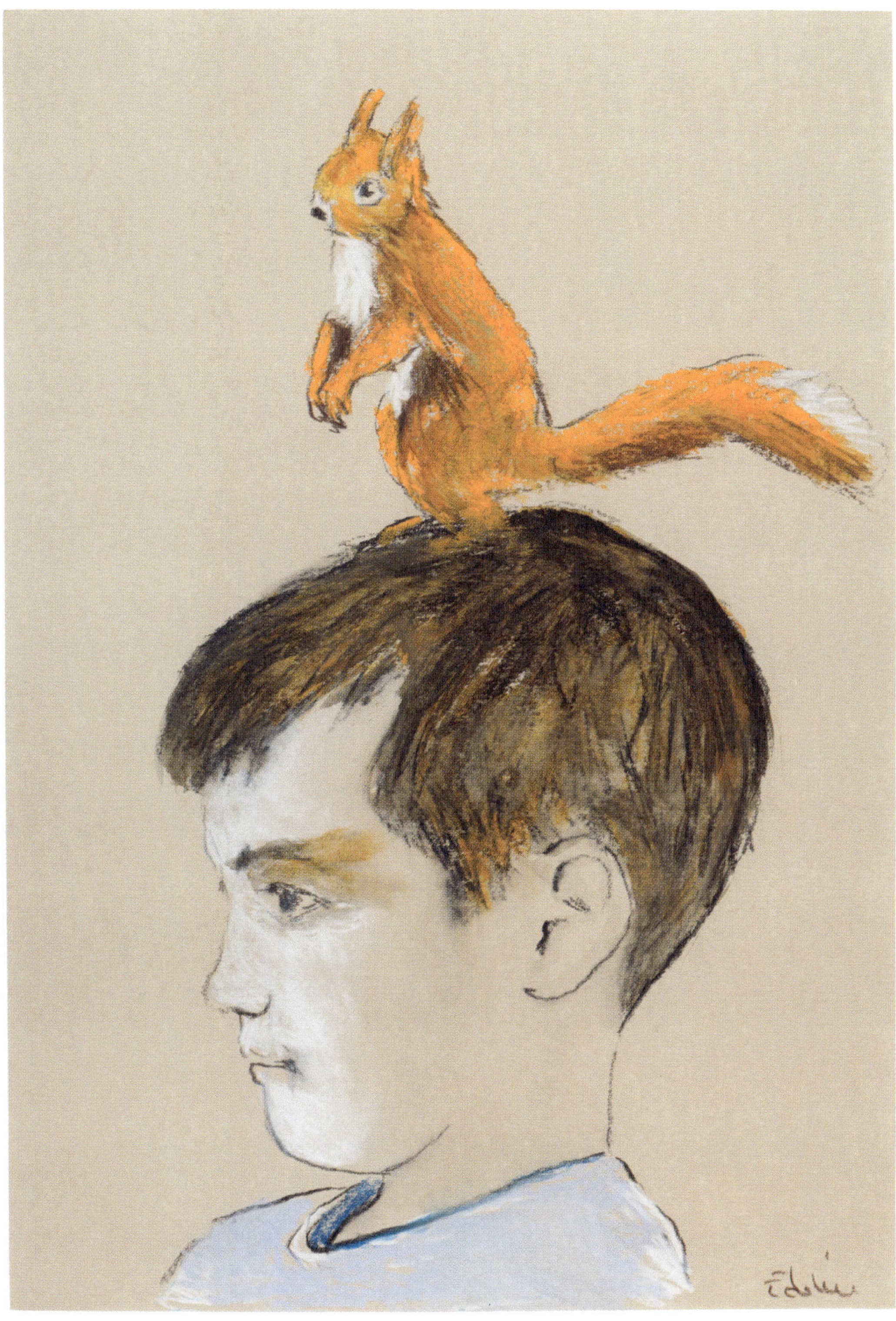

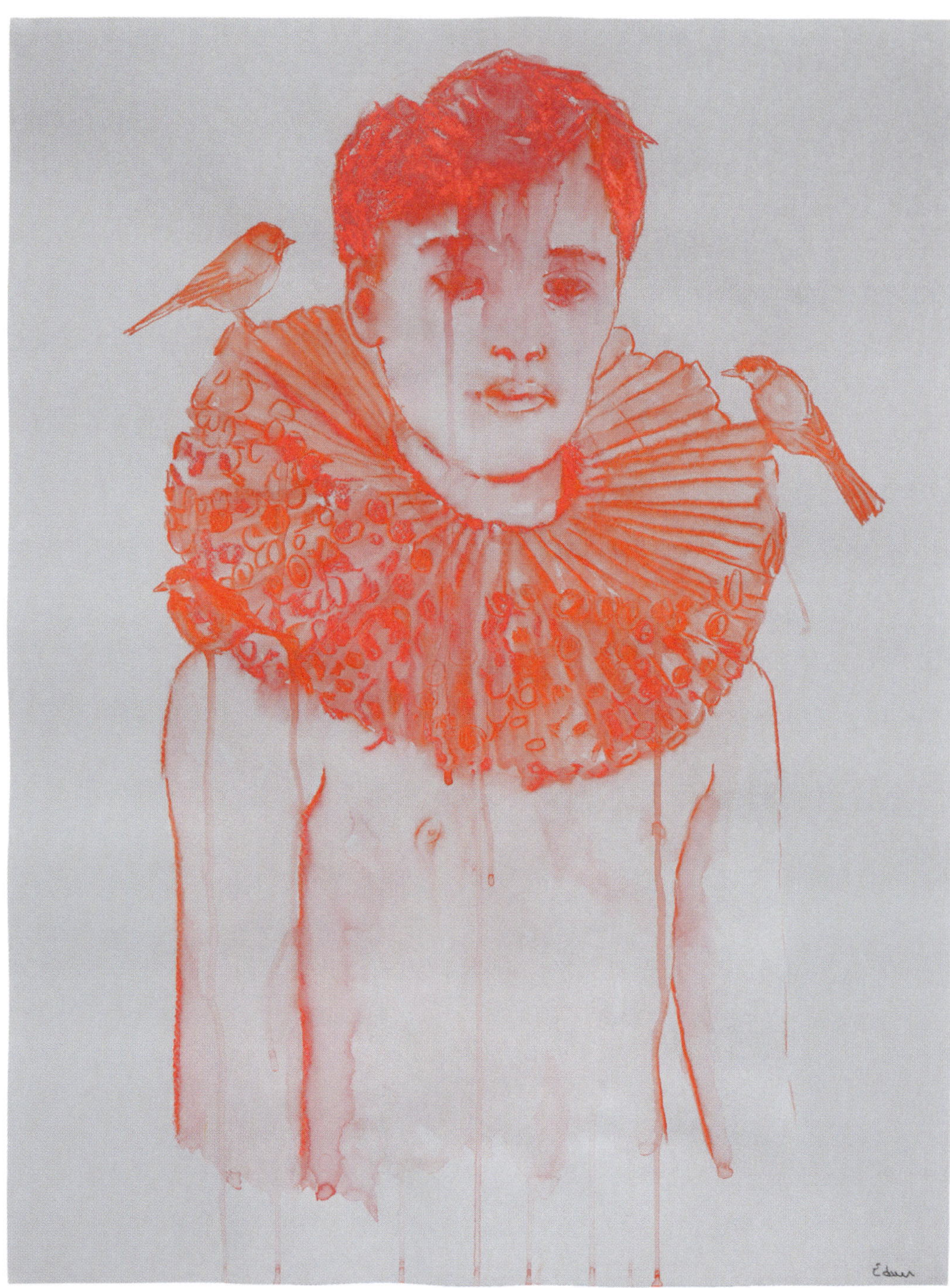

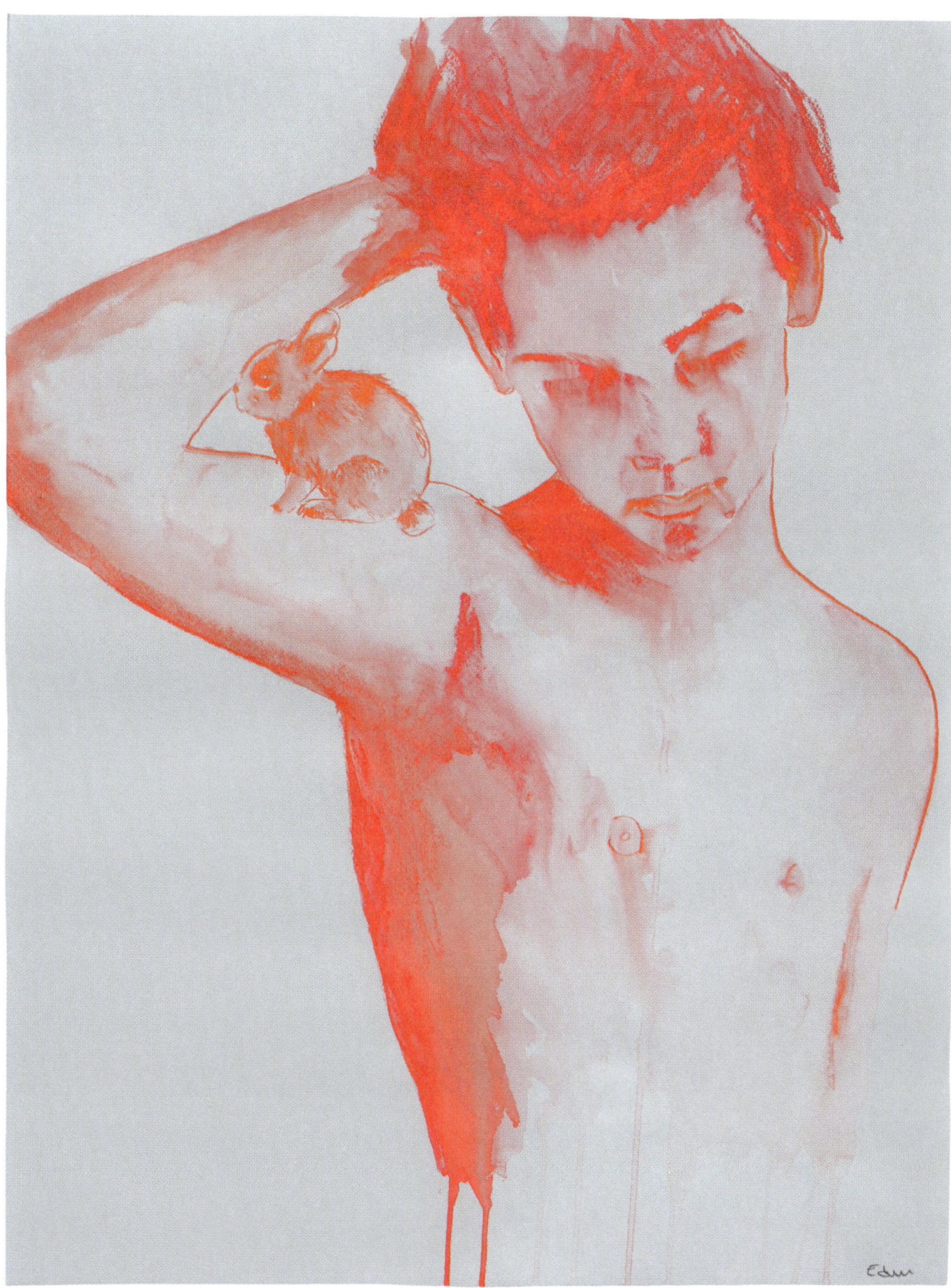

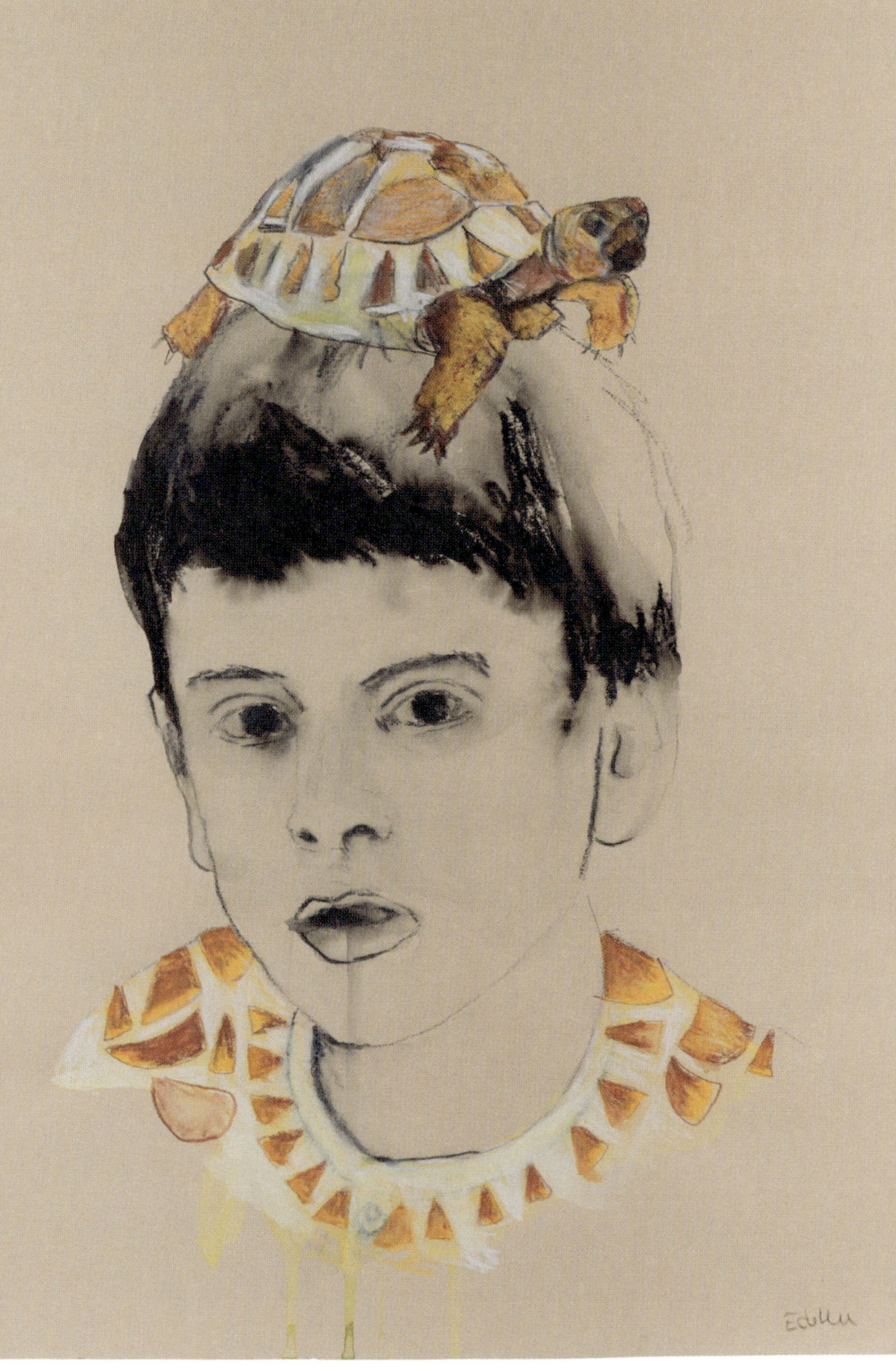

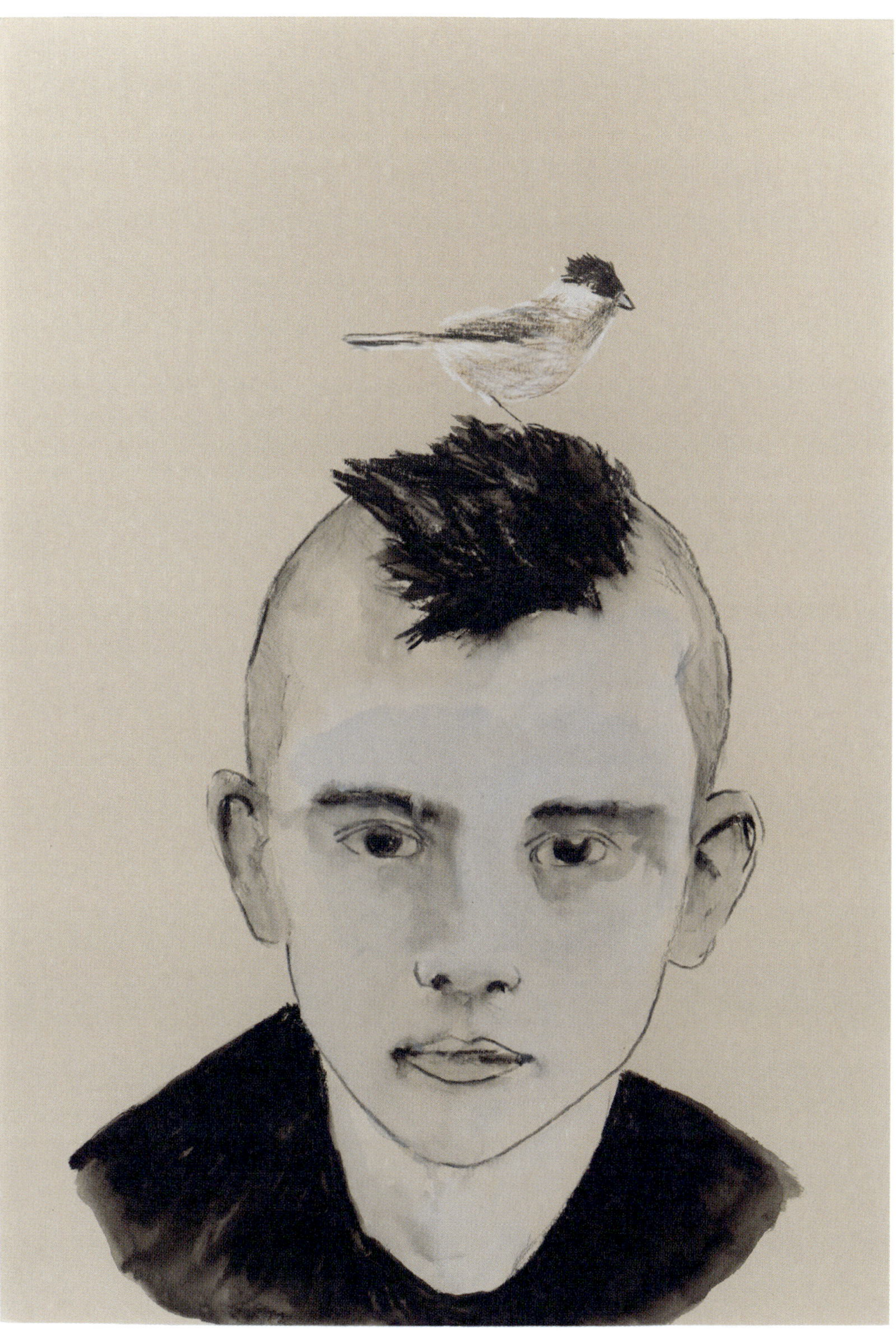

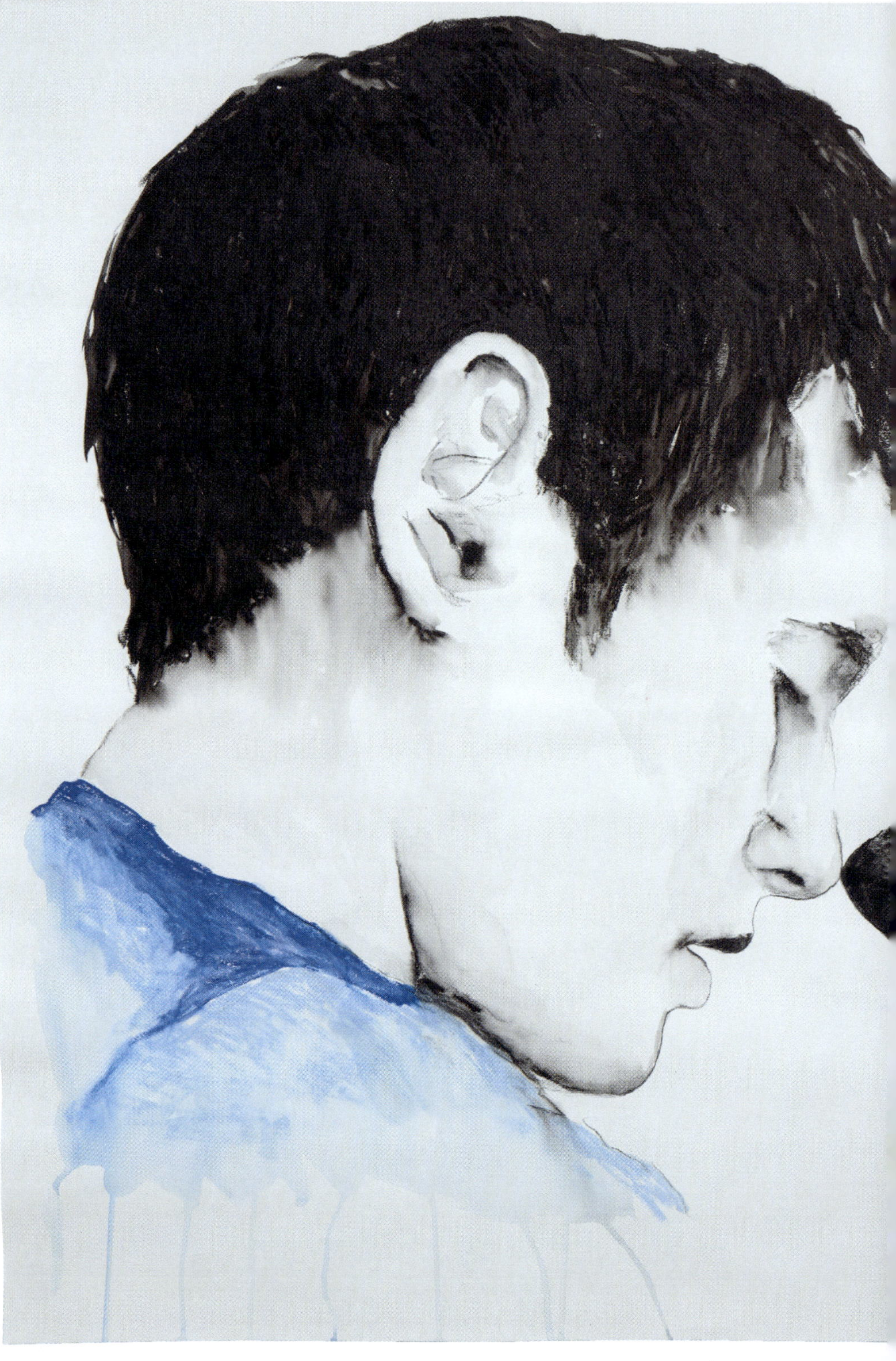

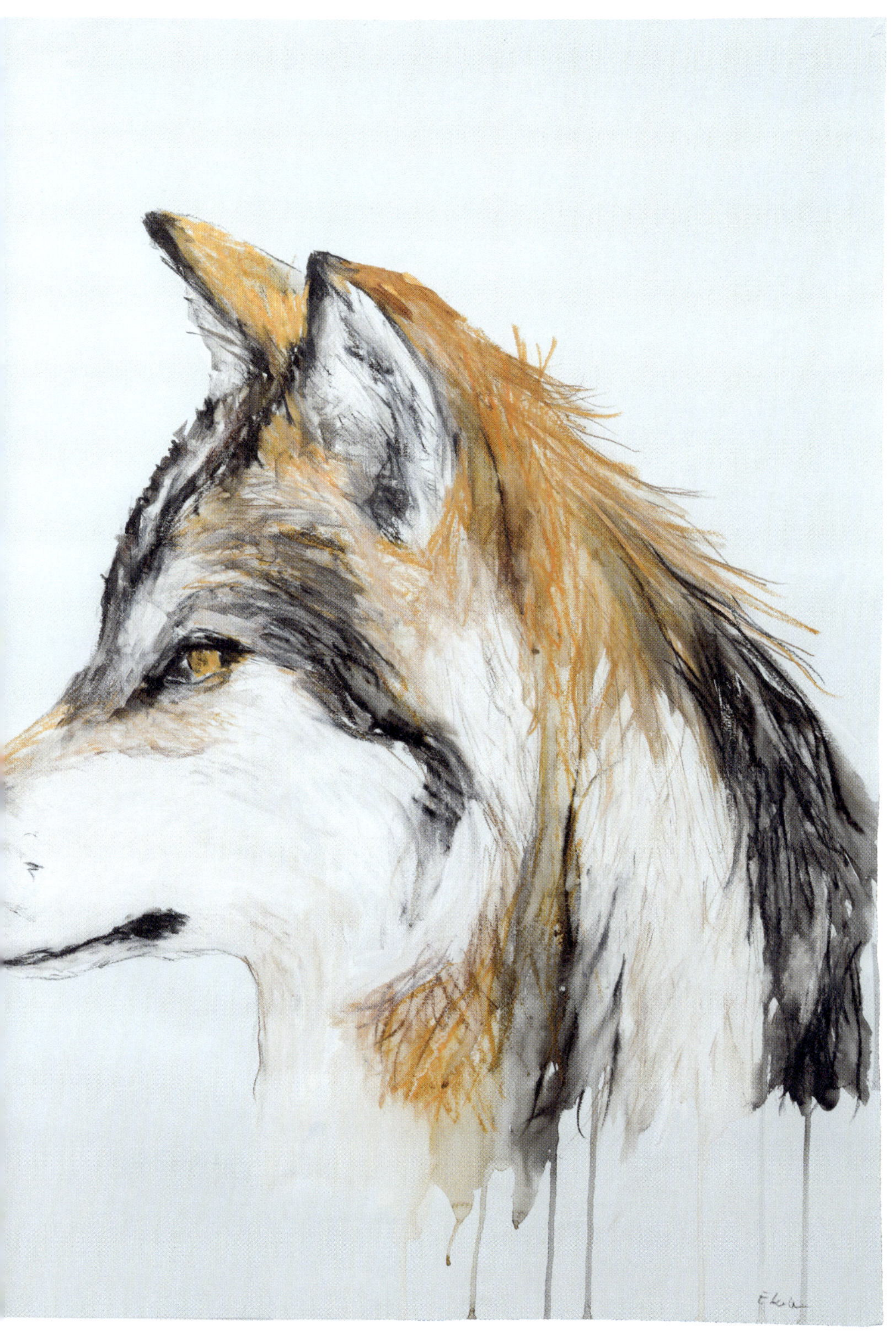

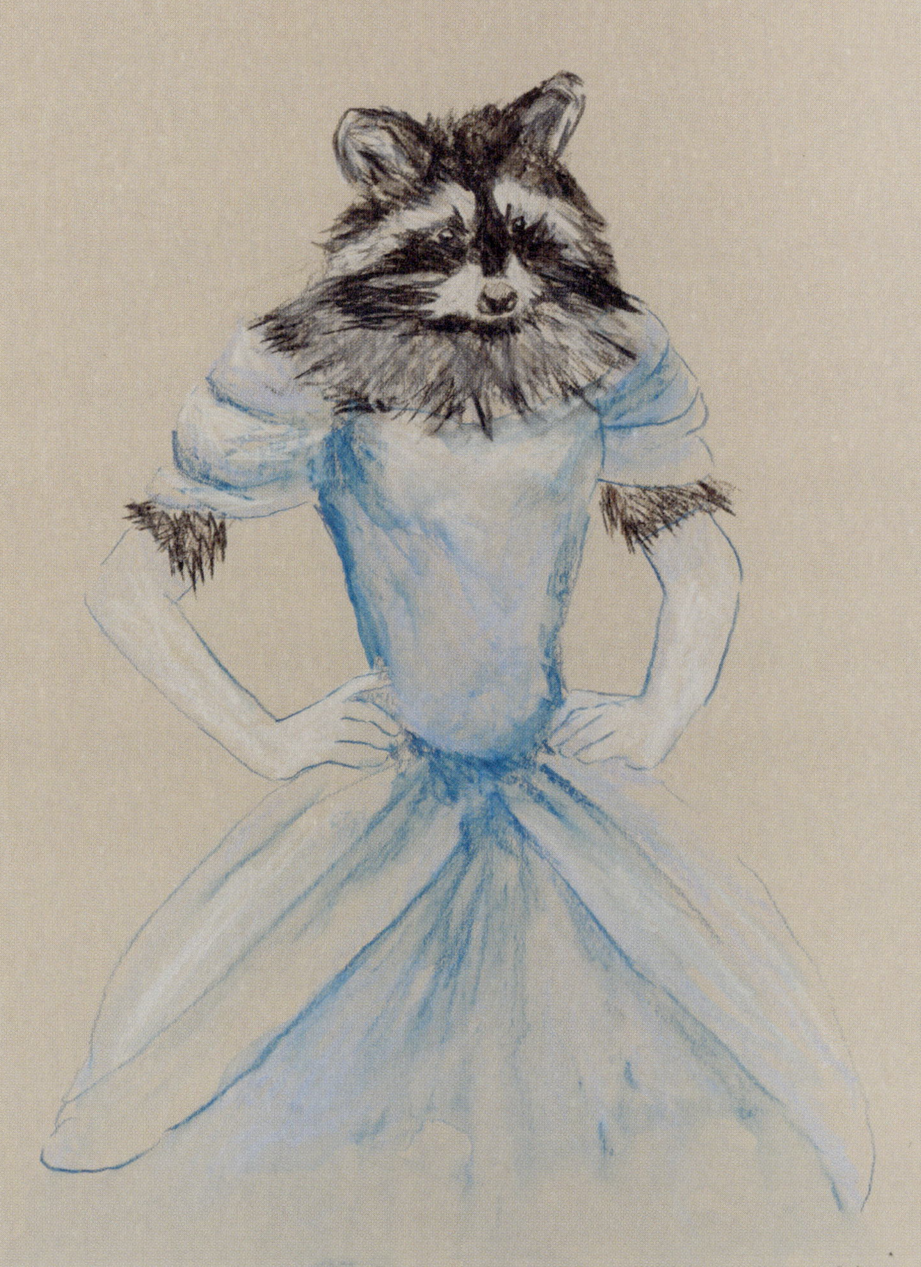

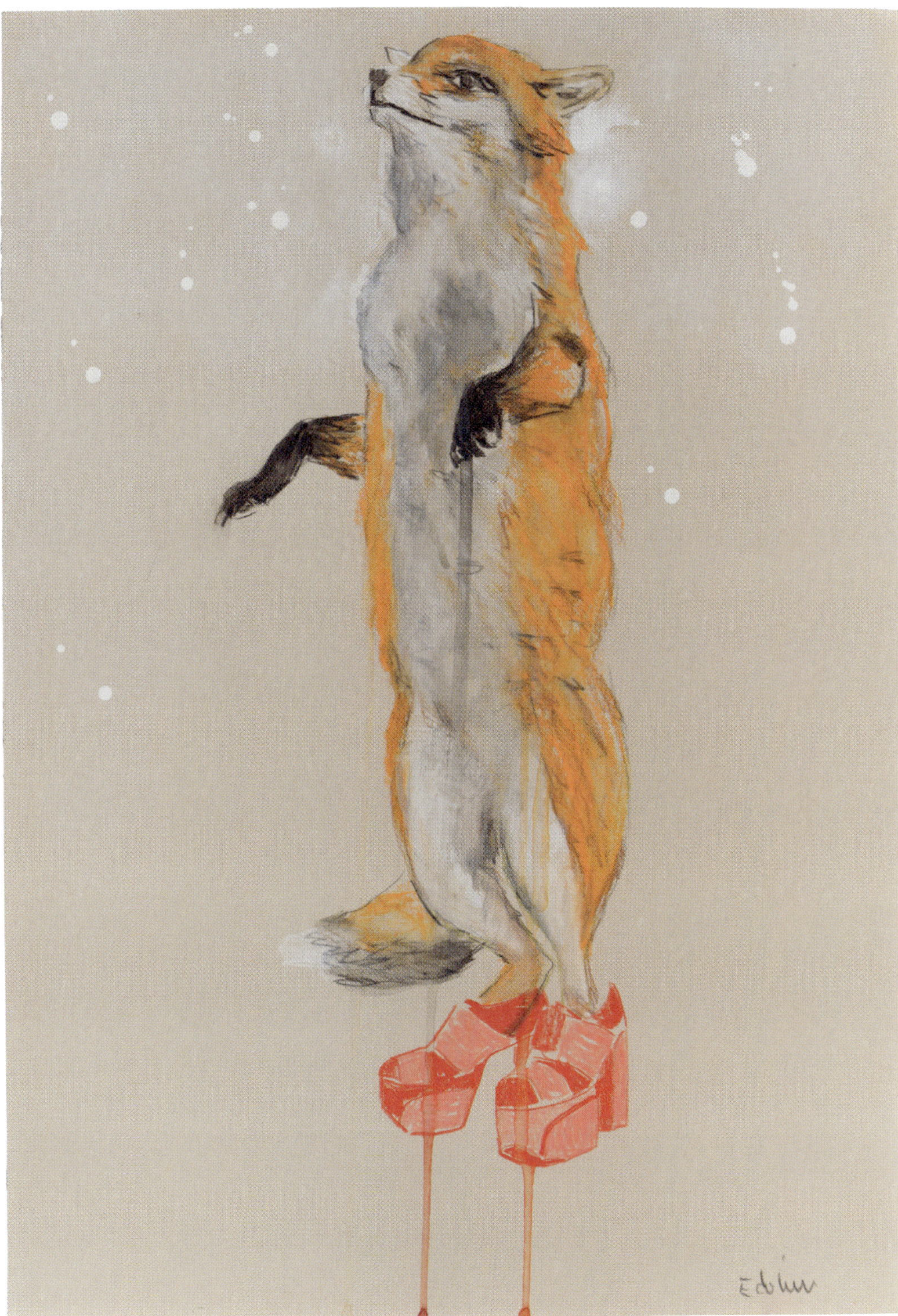
Edlin

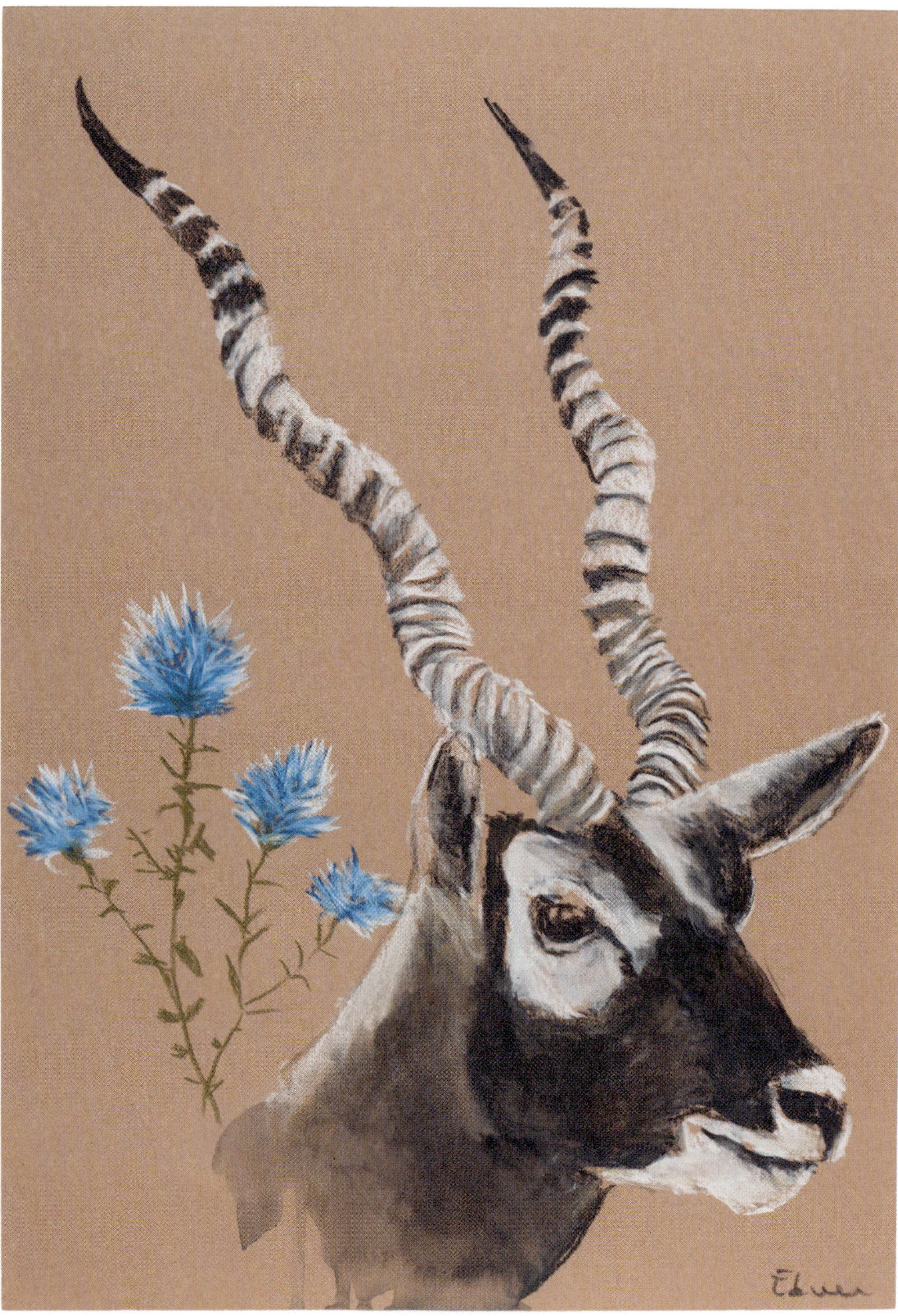

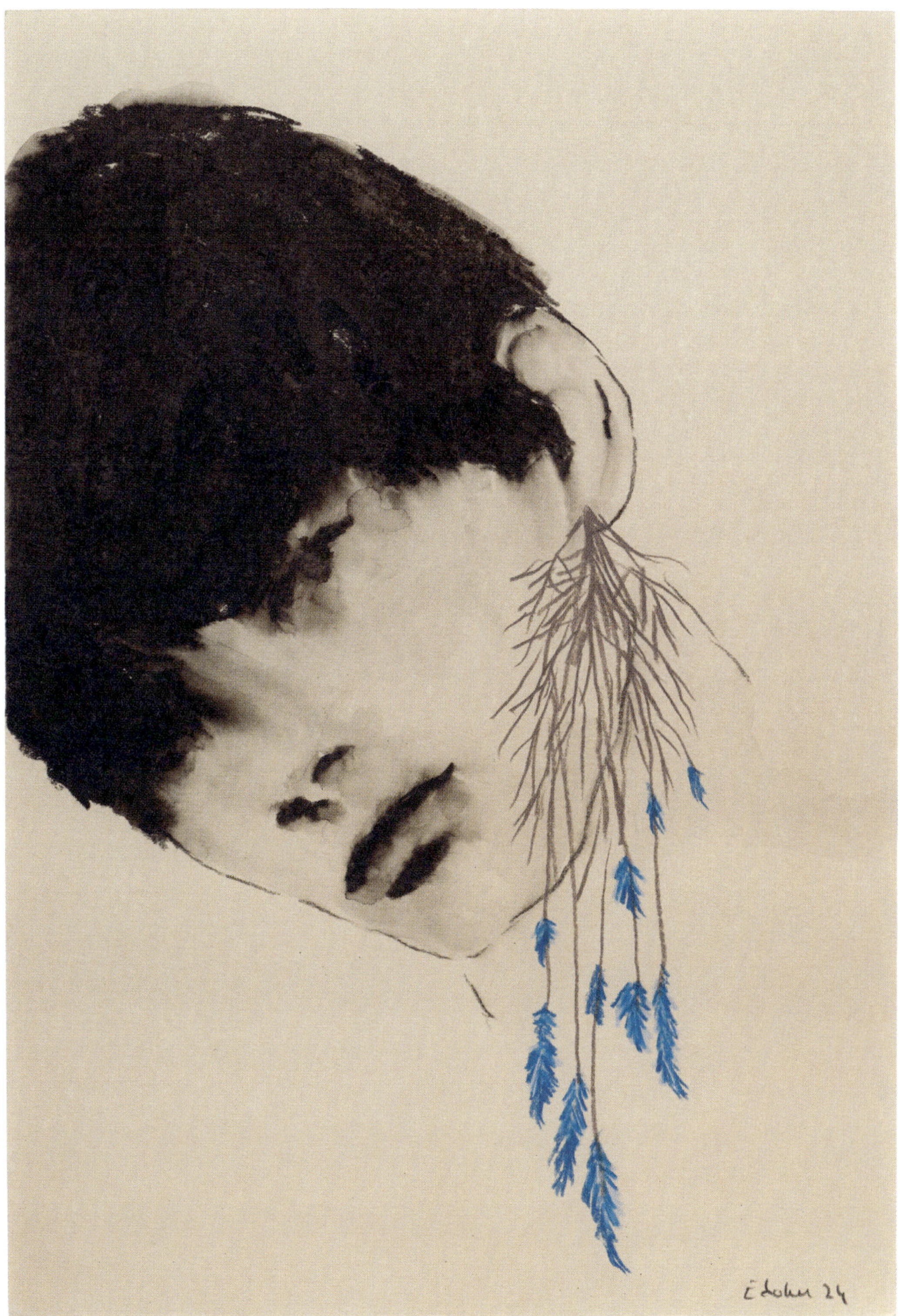

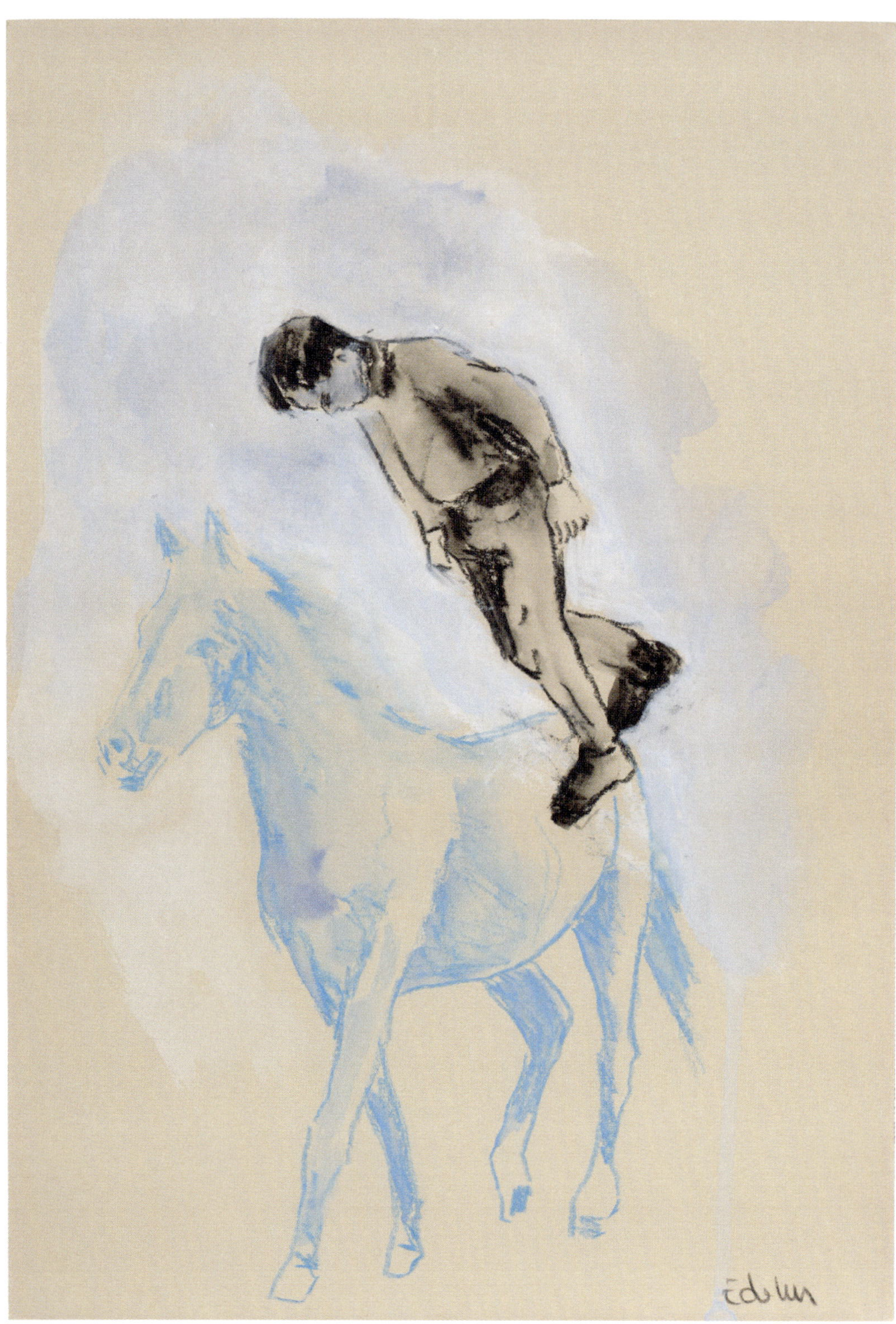

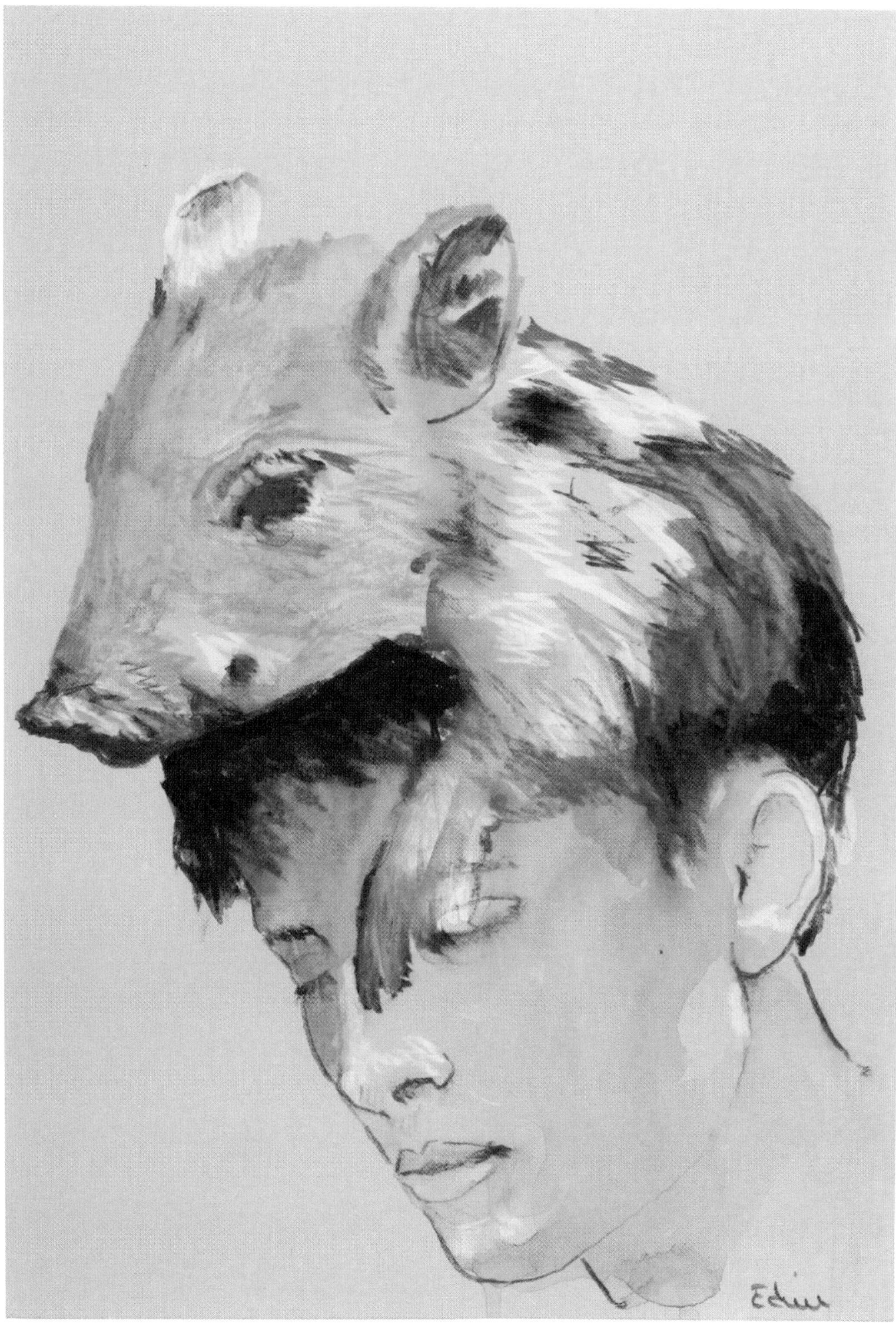

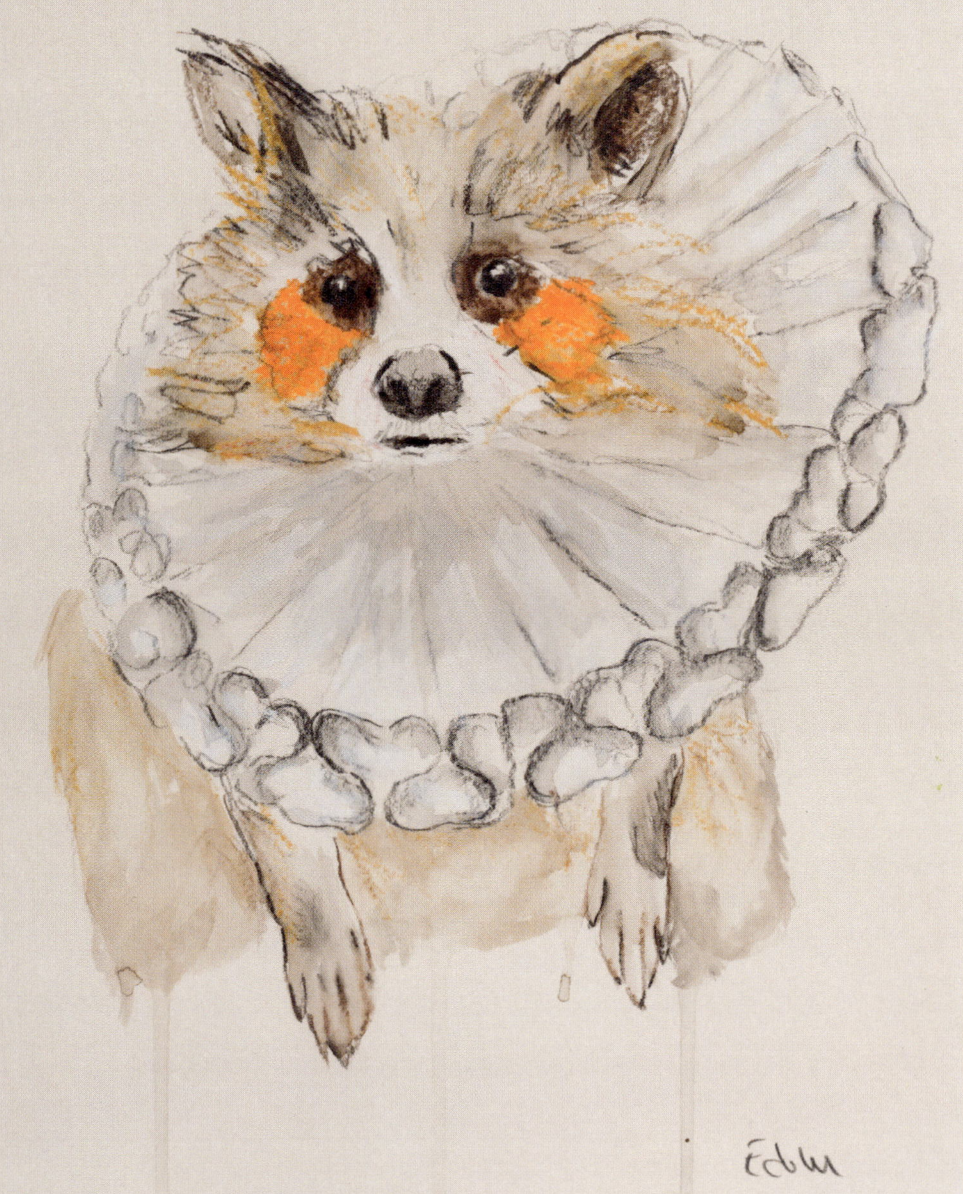

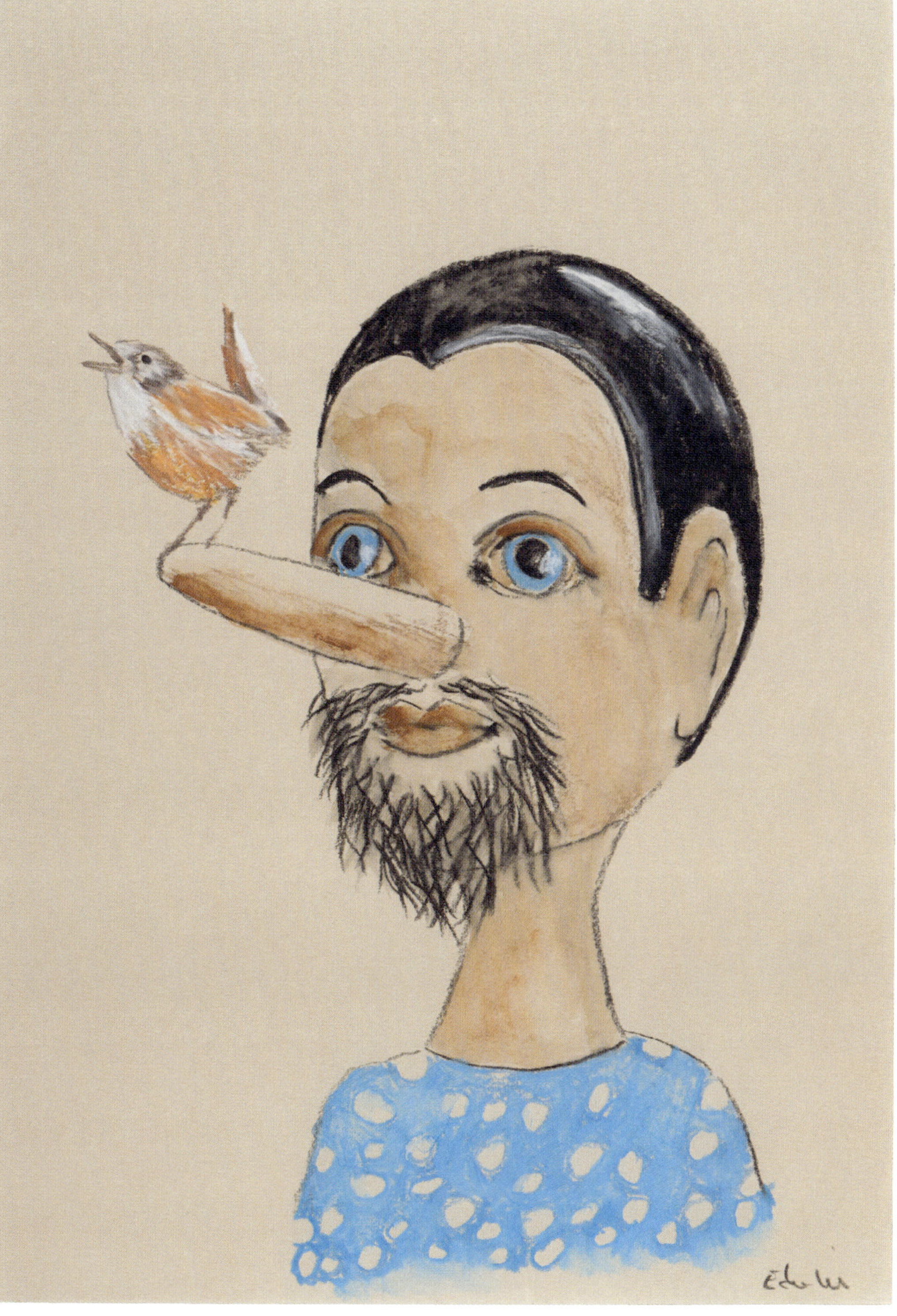

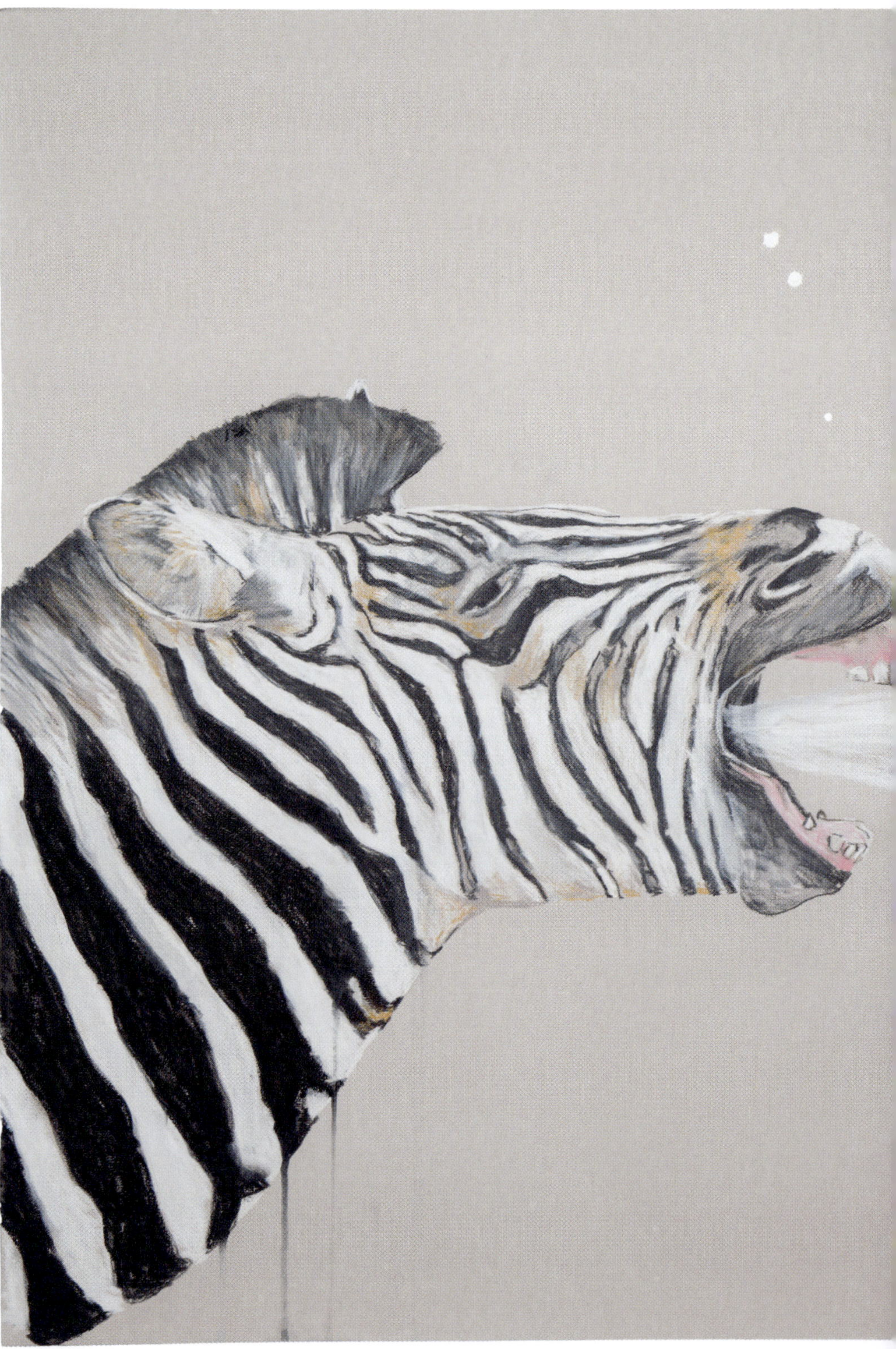

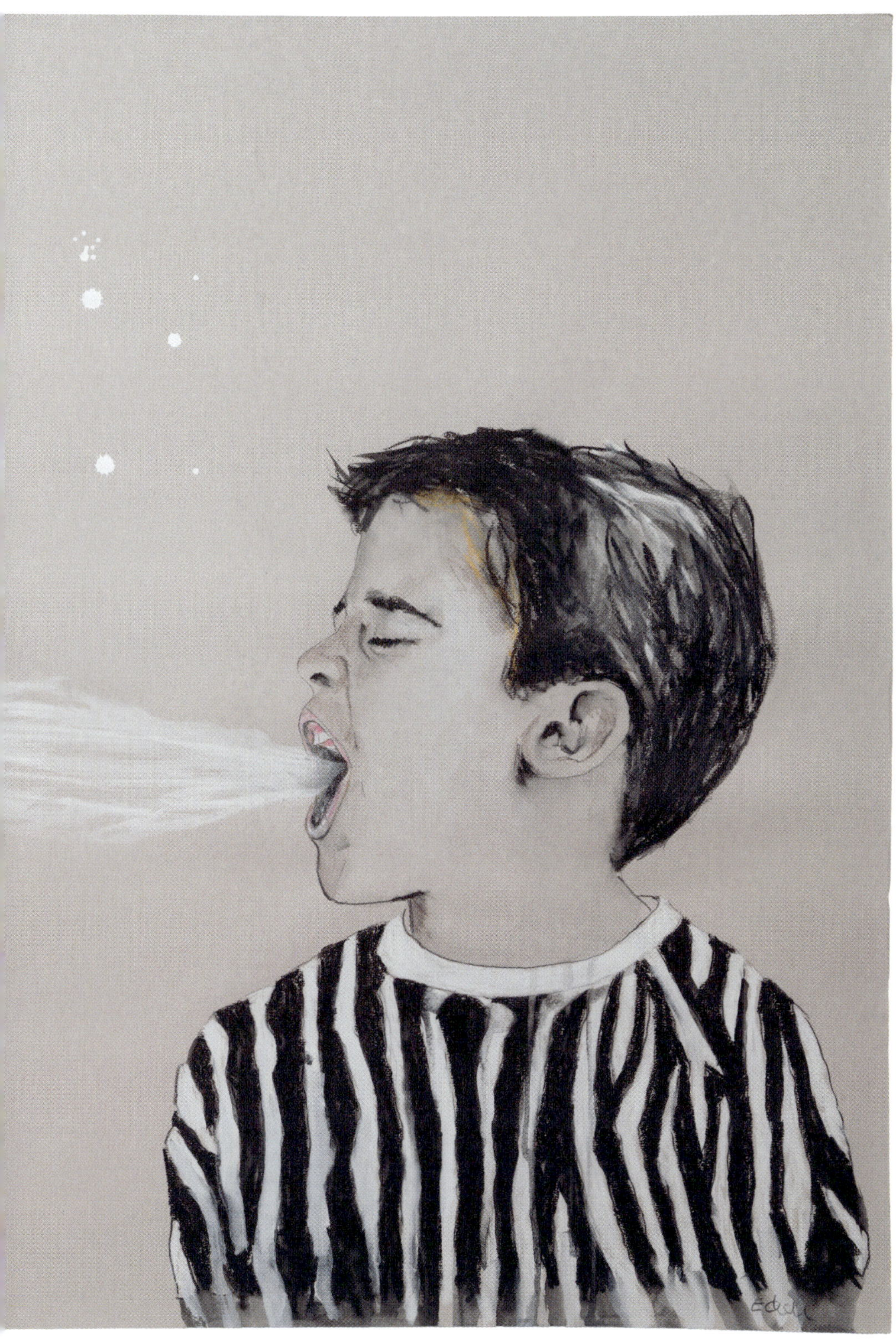

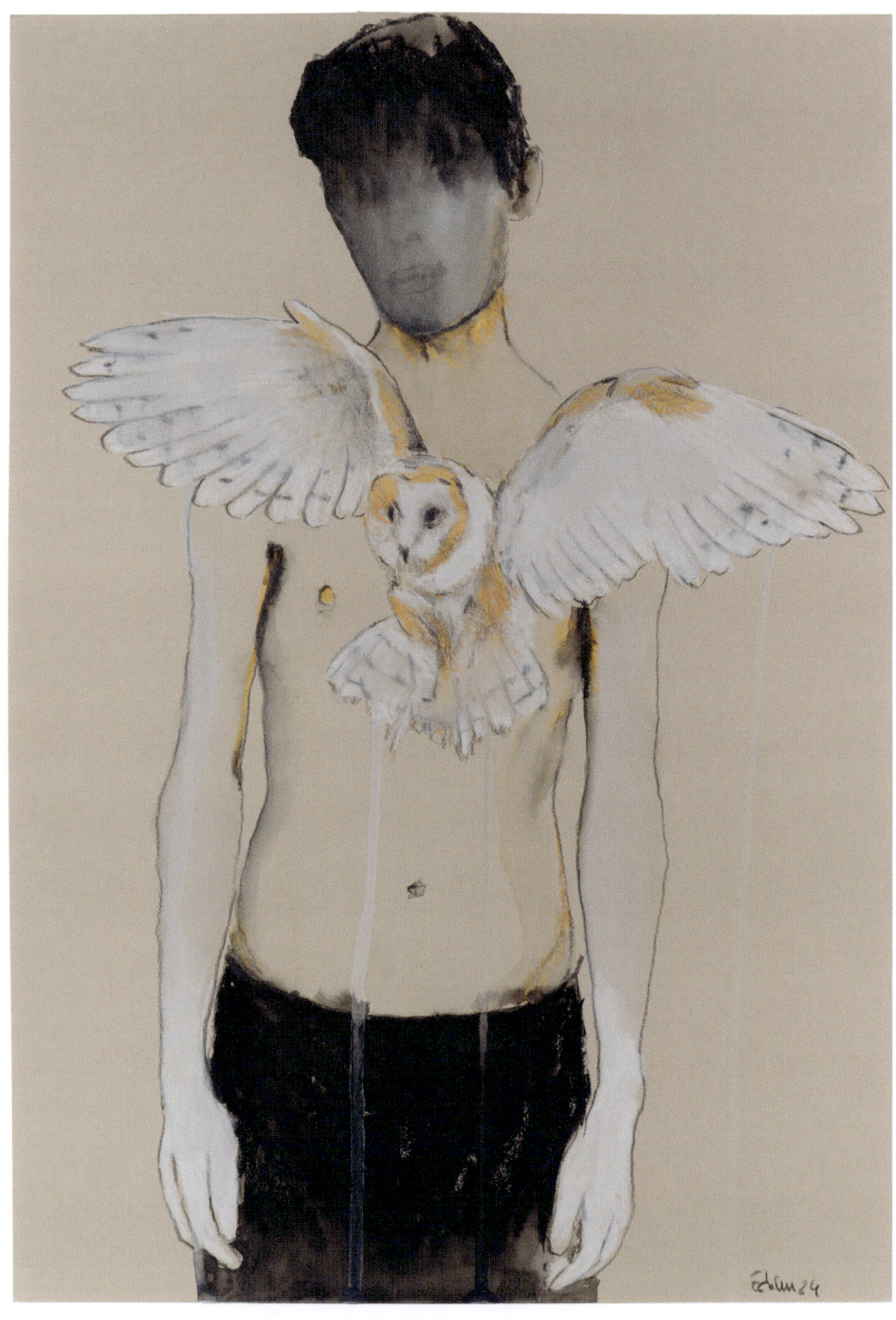

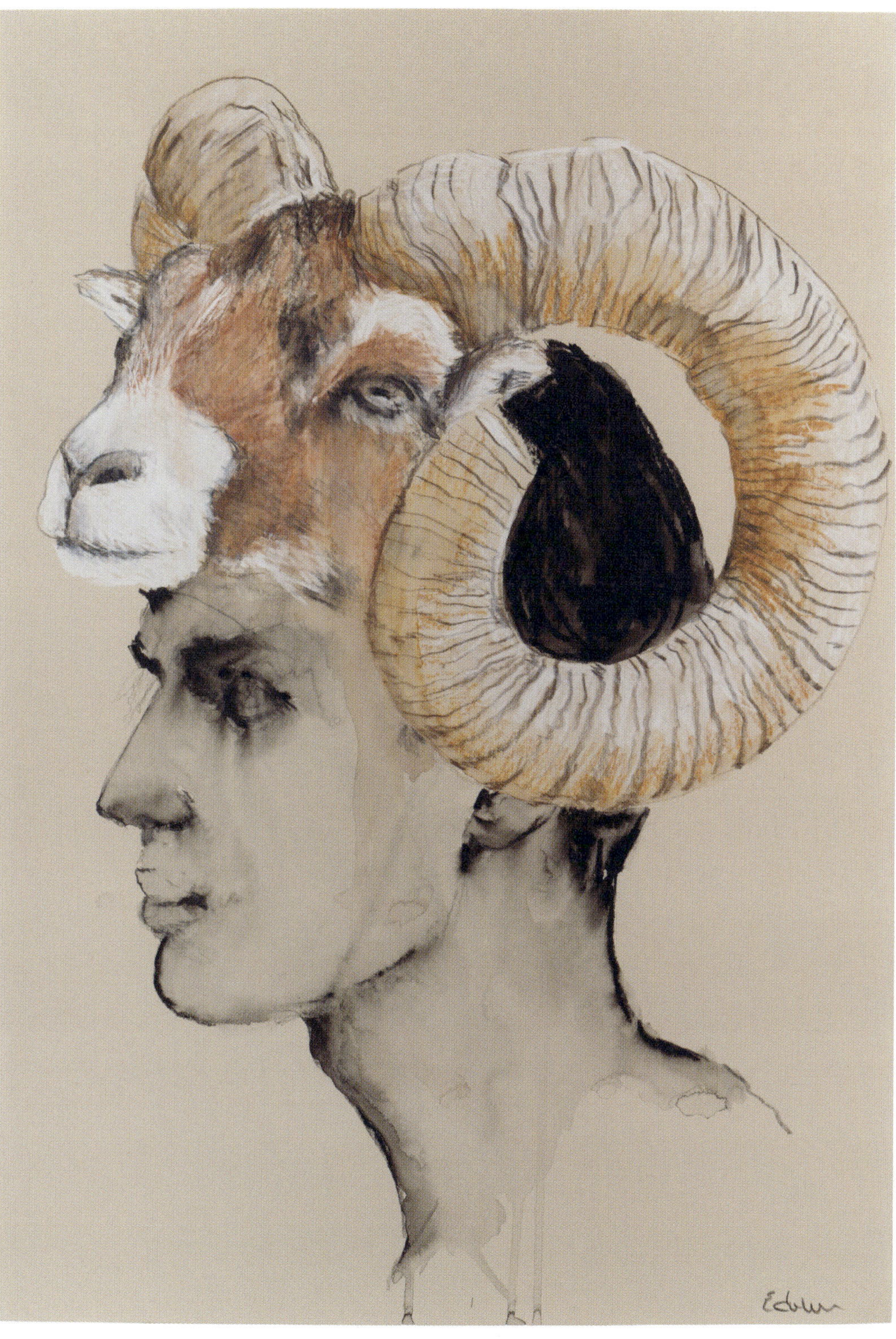

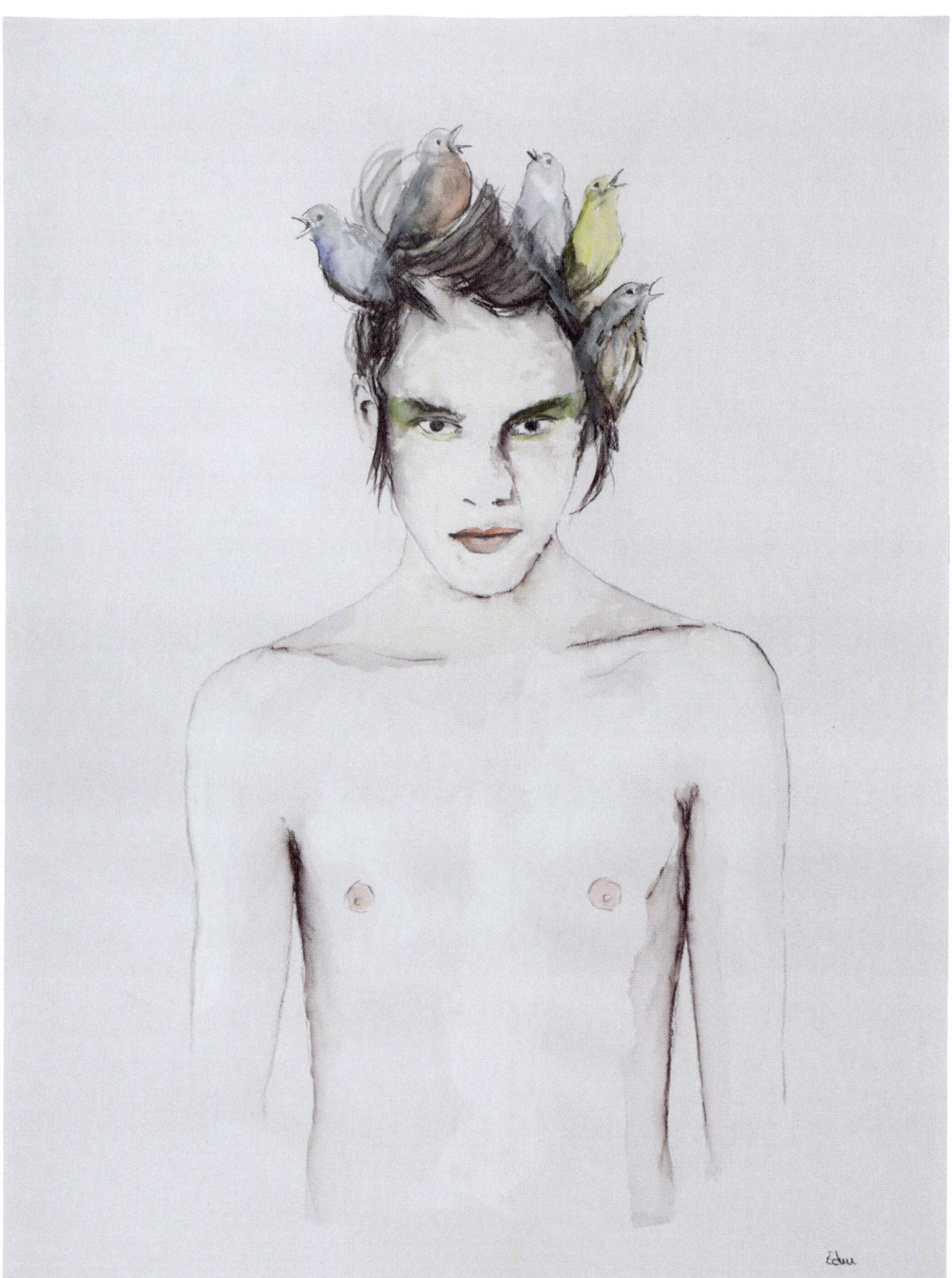

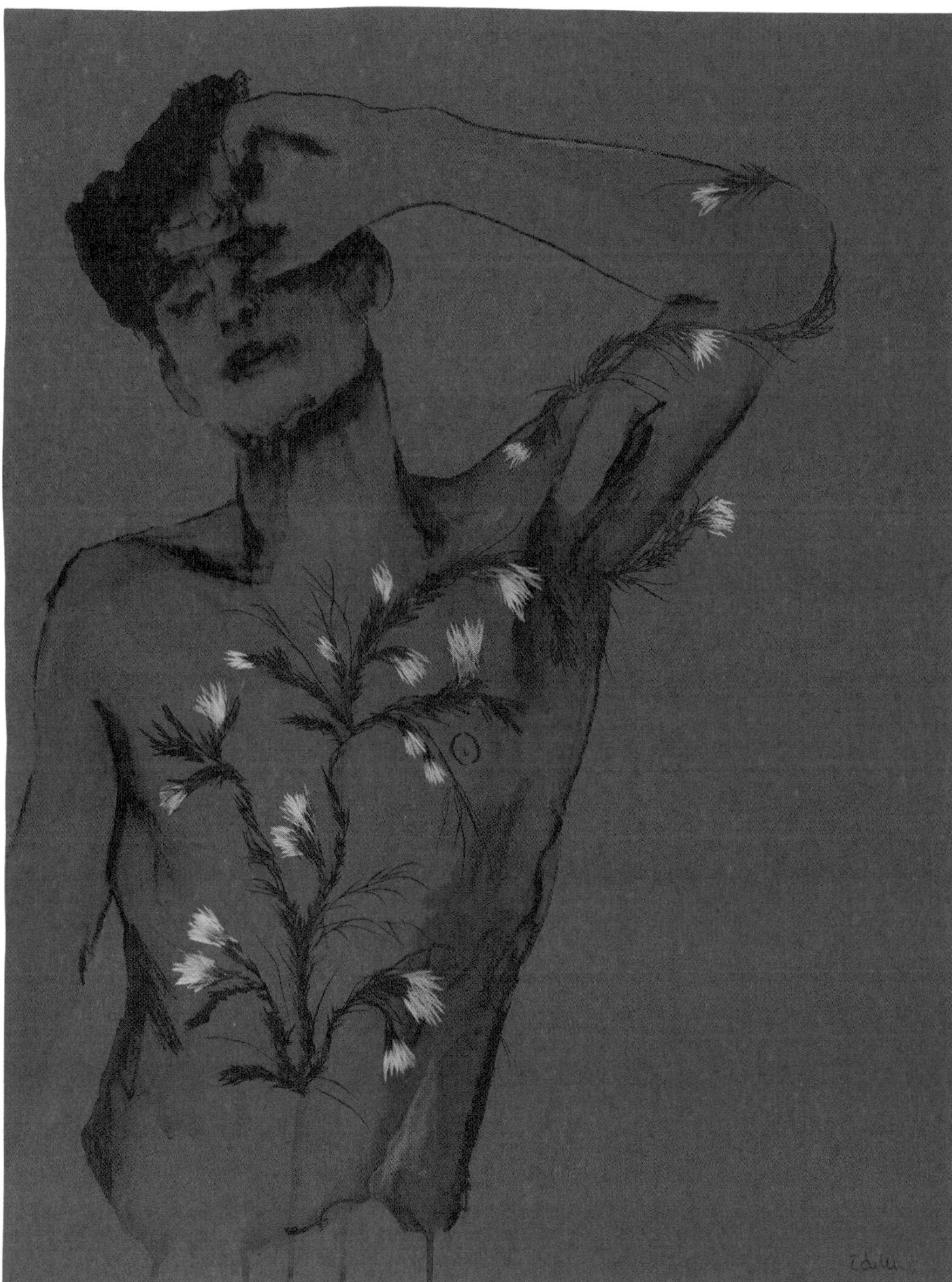

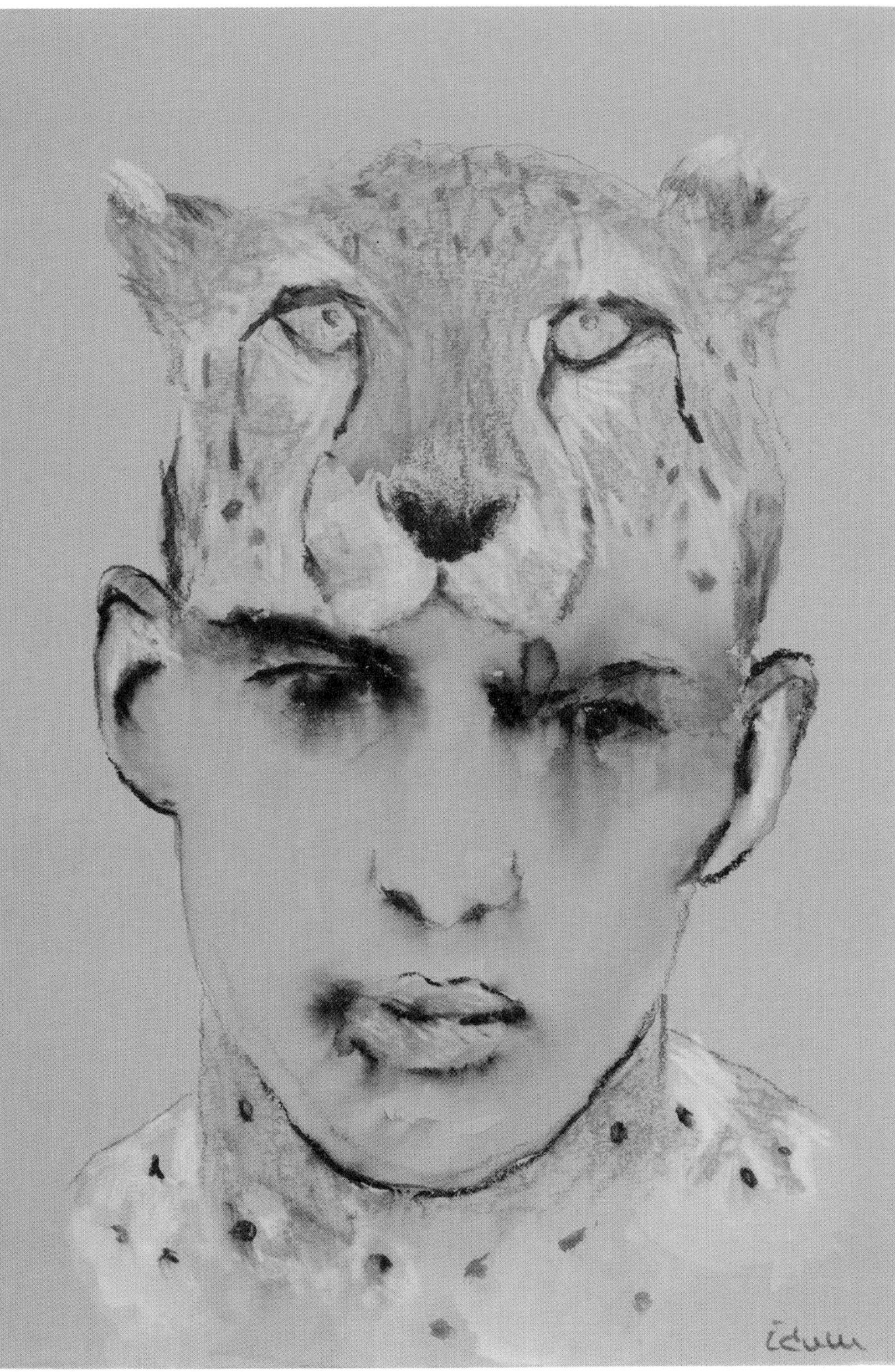

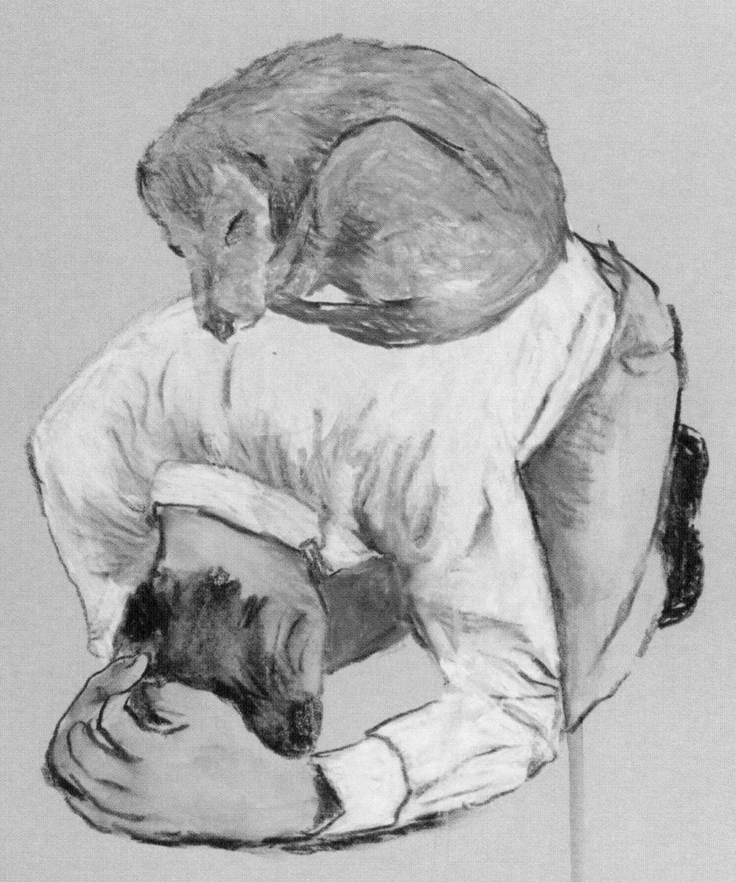

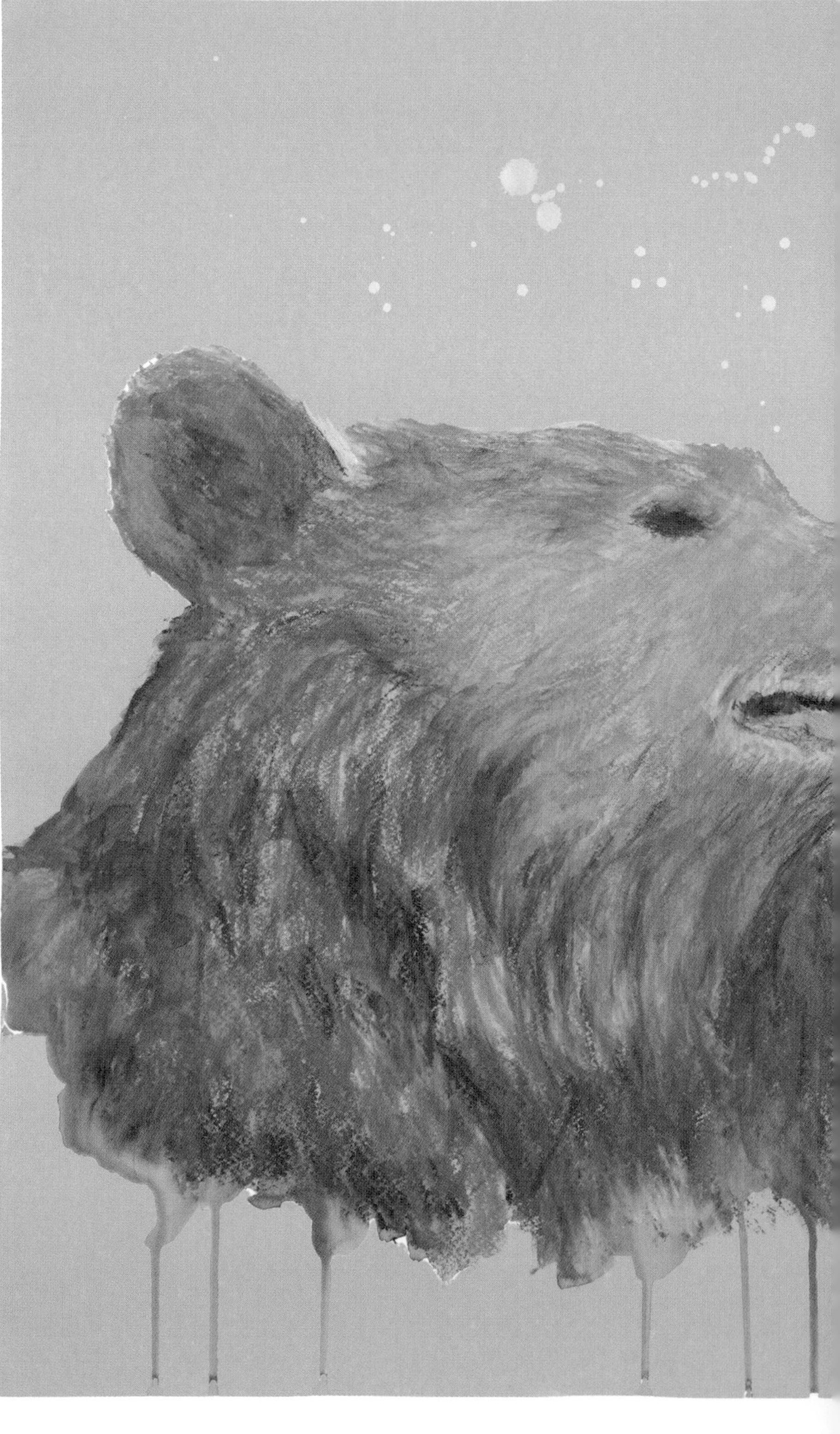

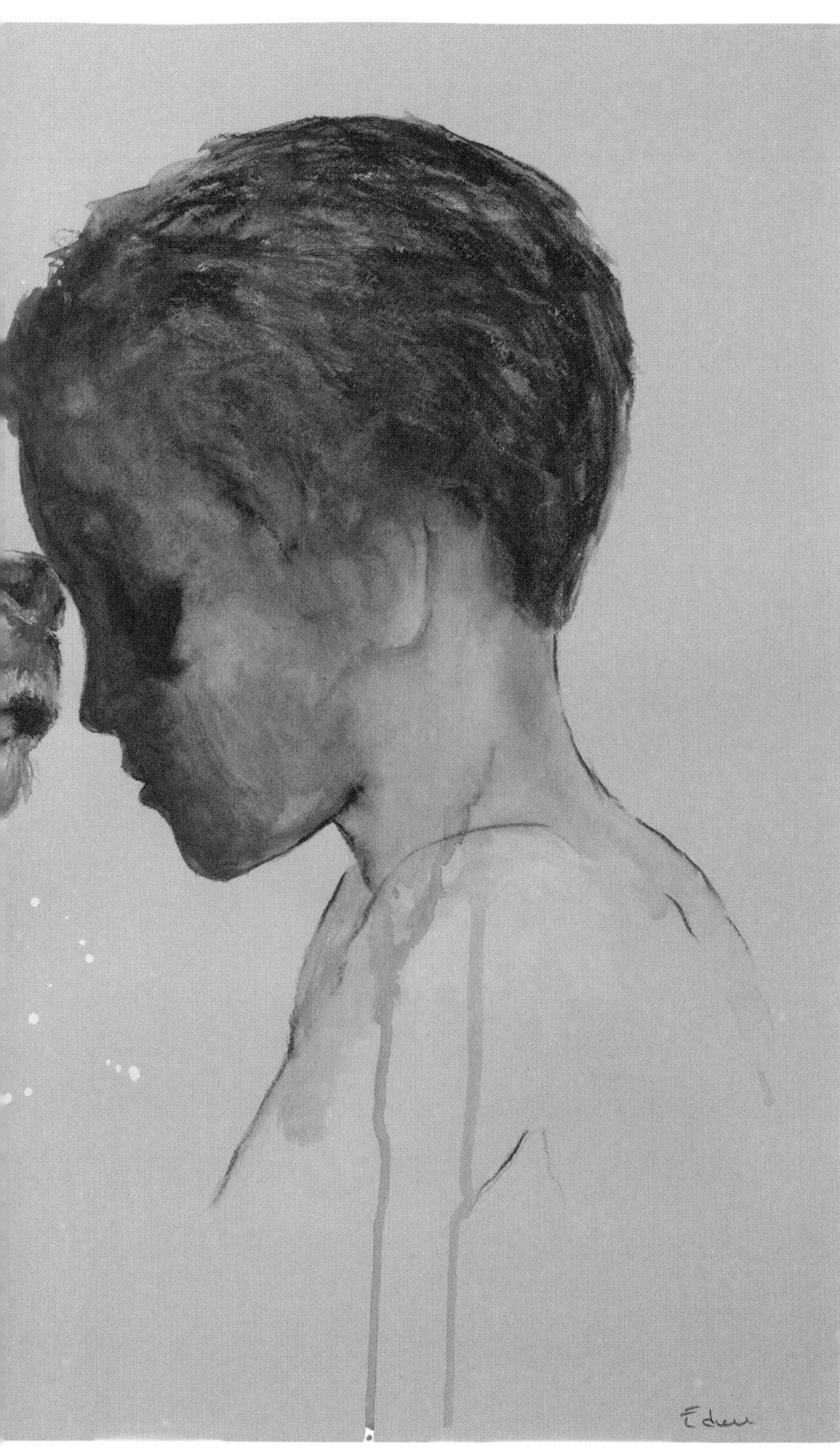

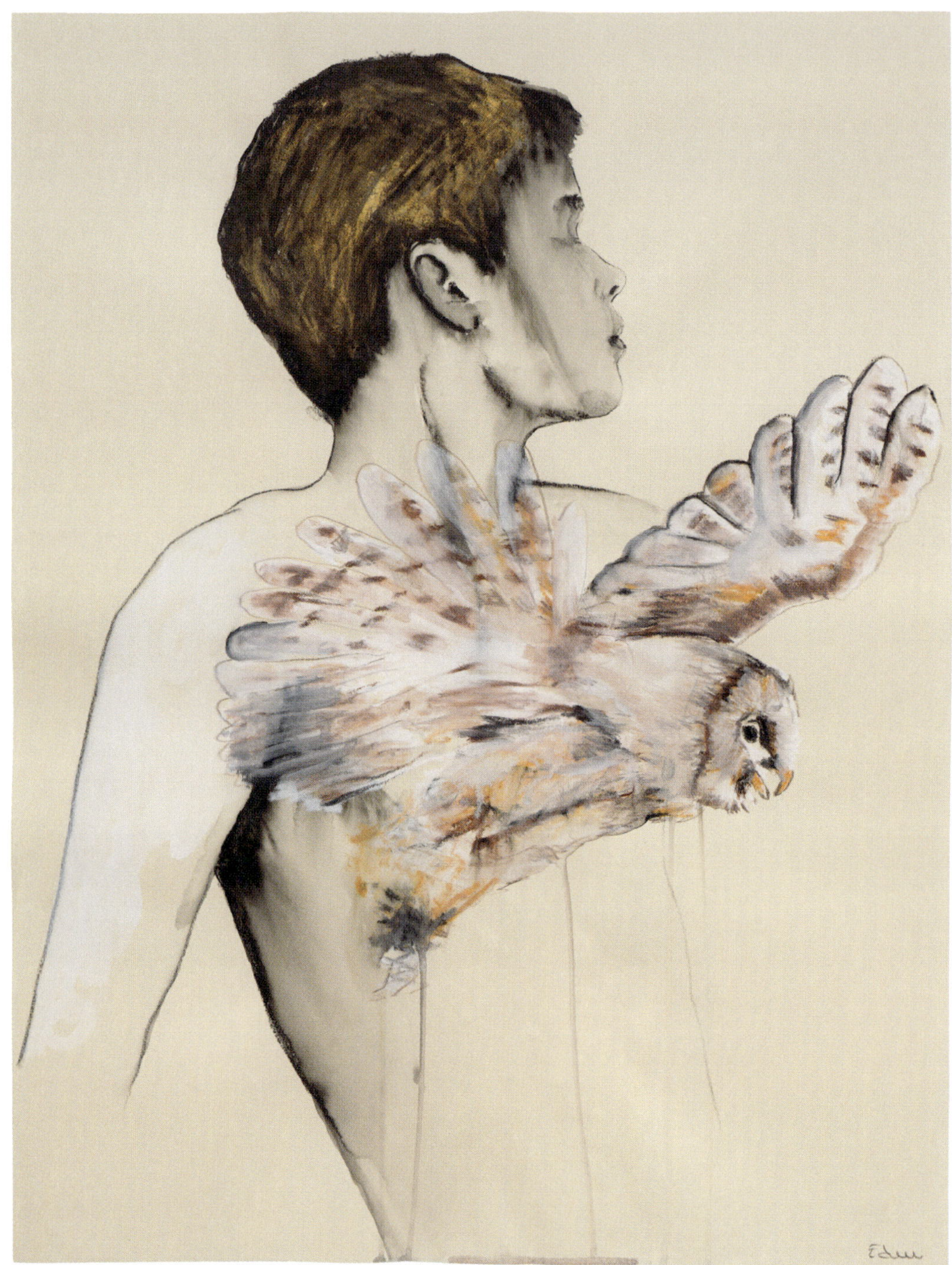

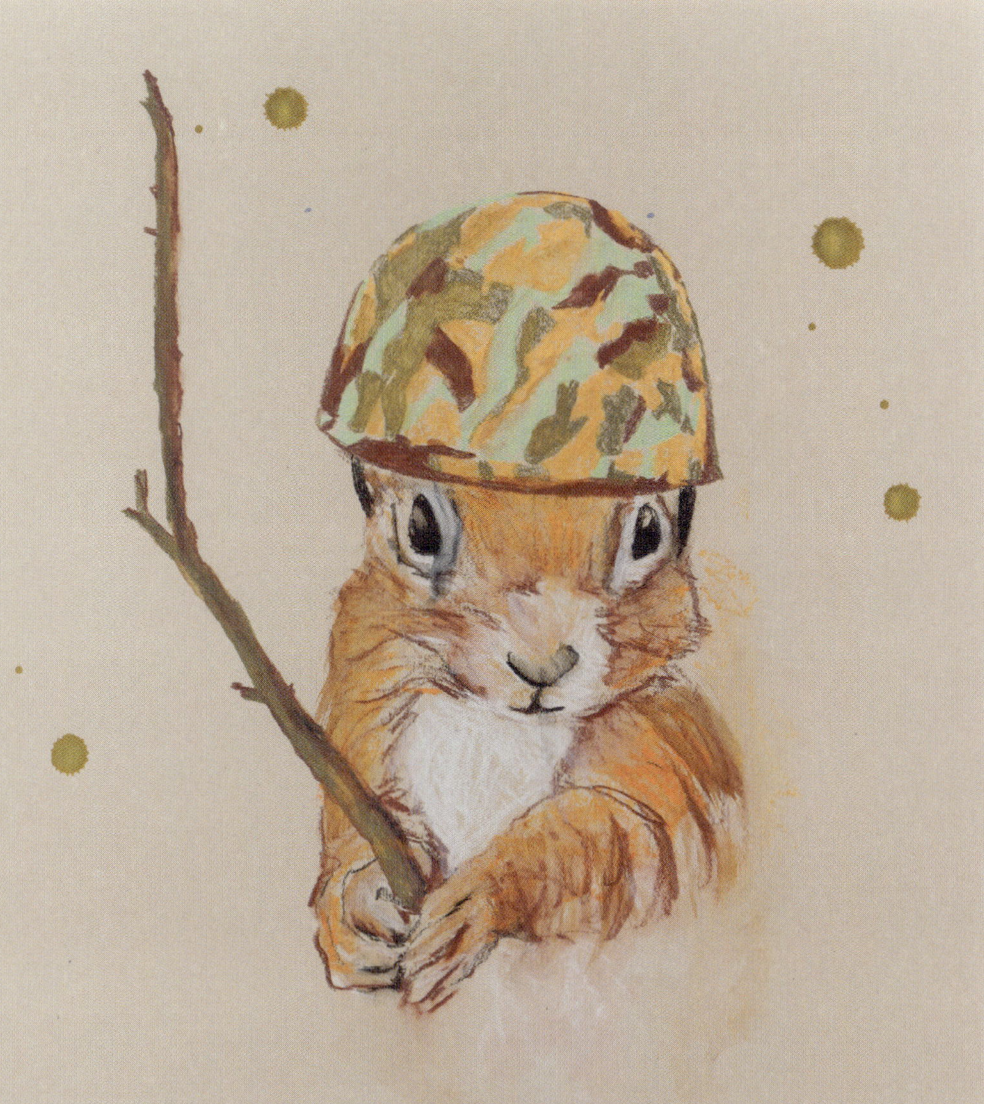

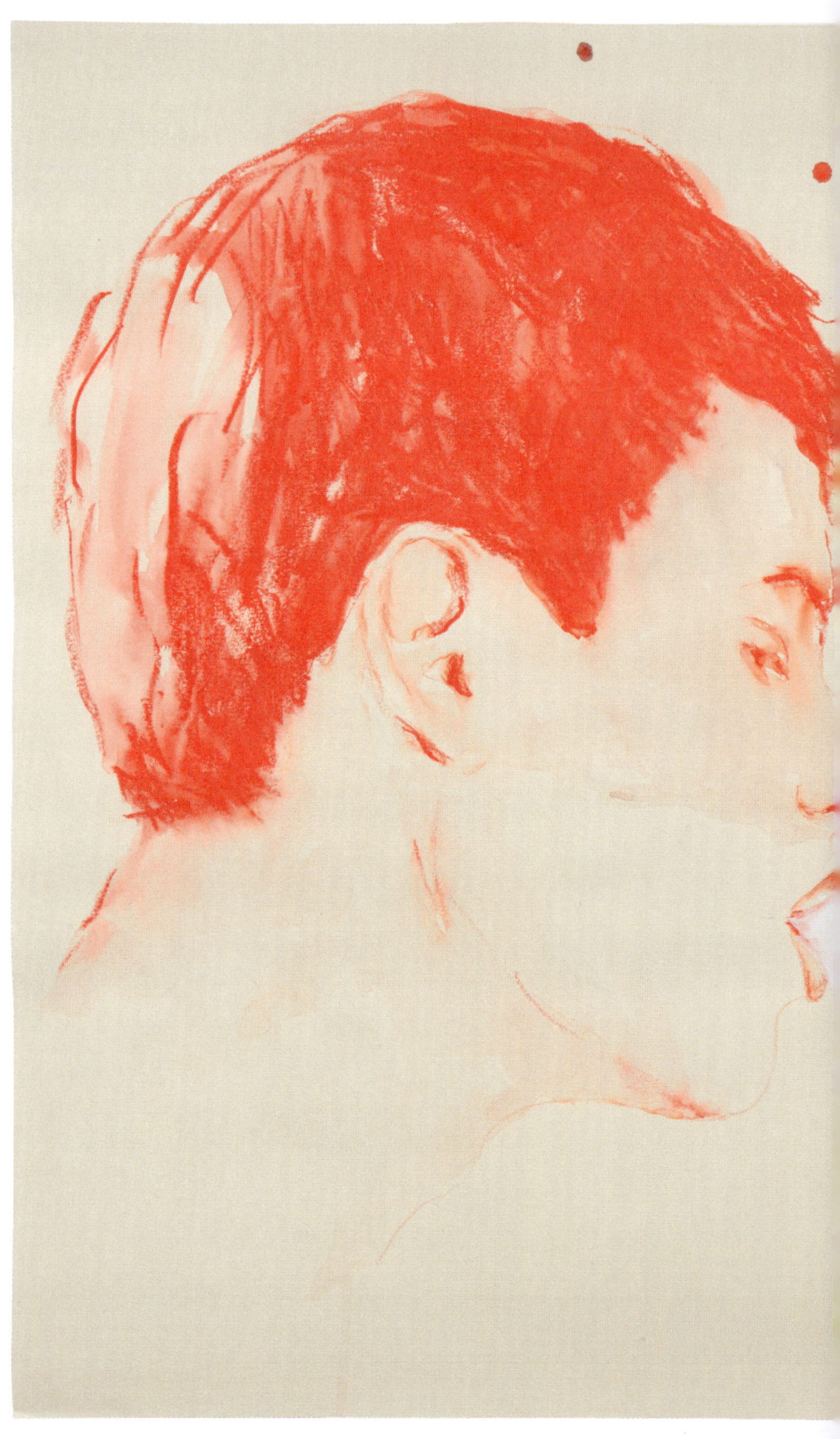

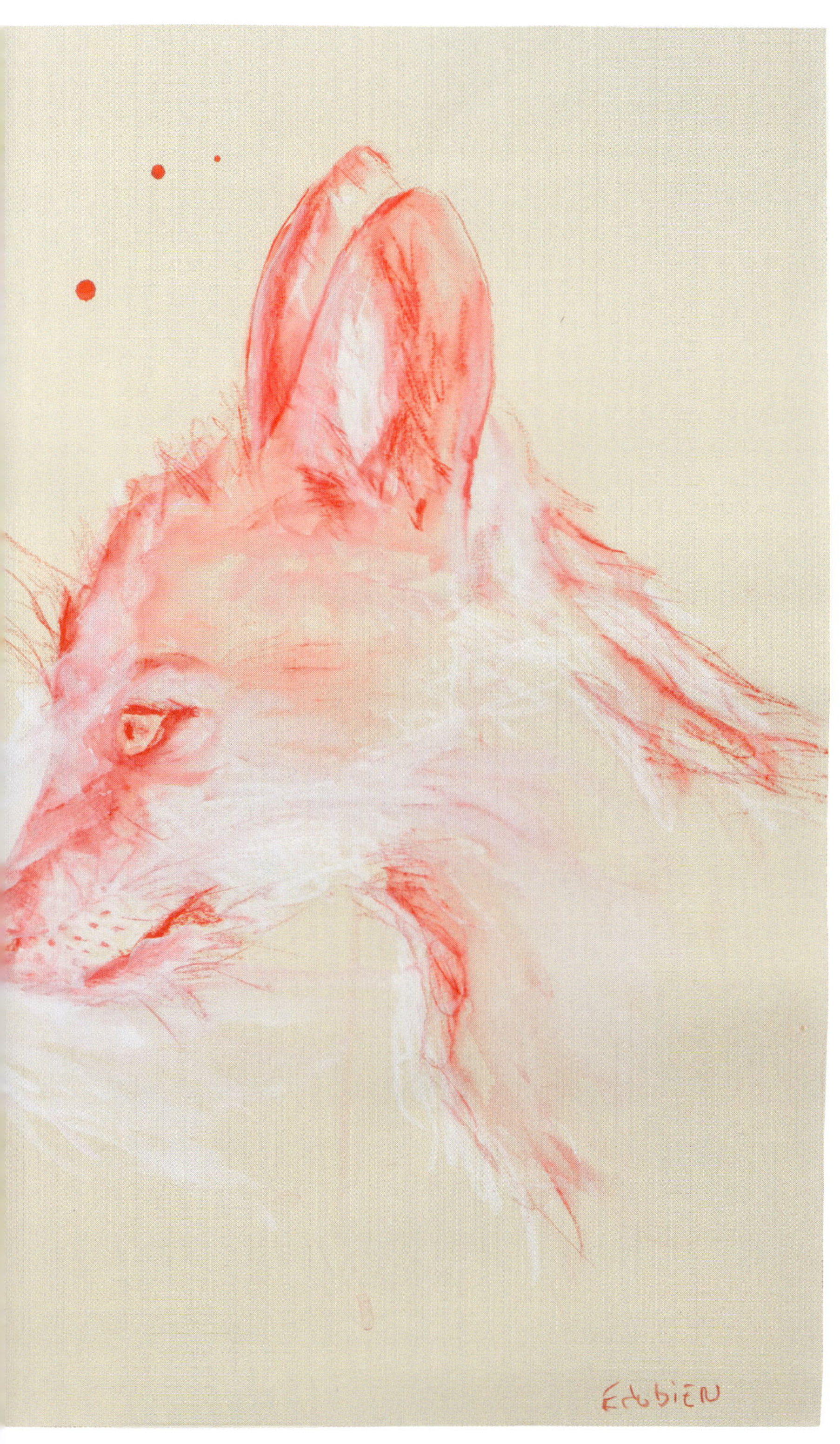

EtuBien

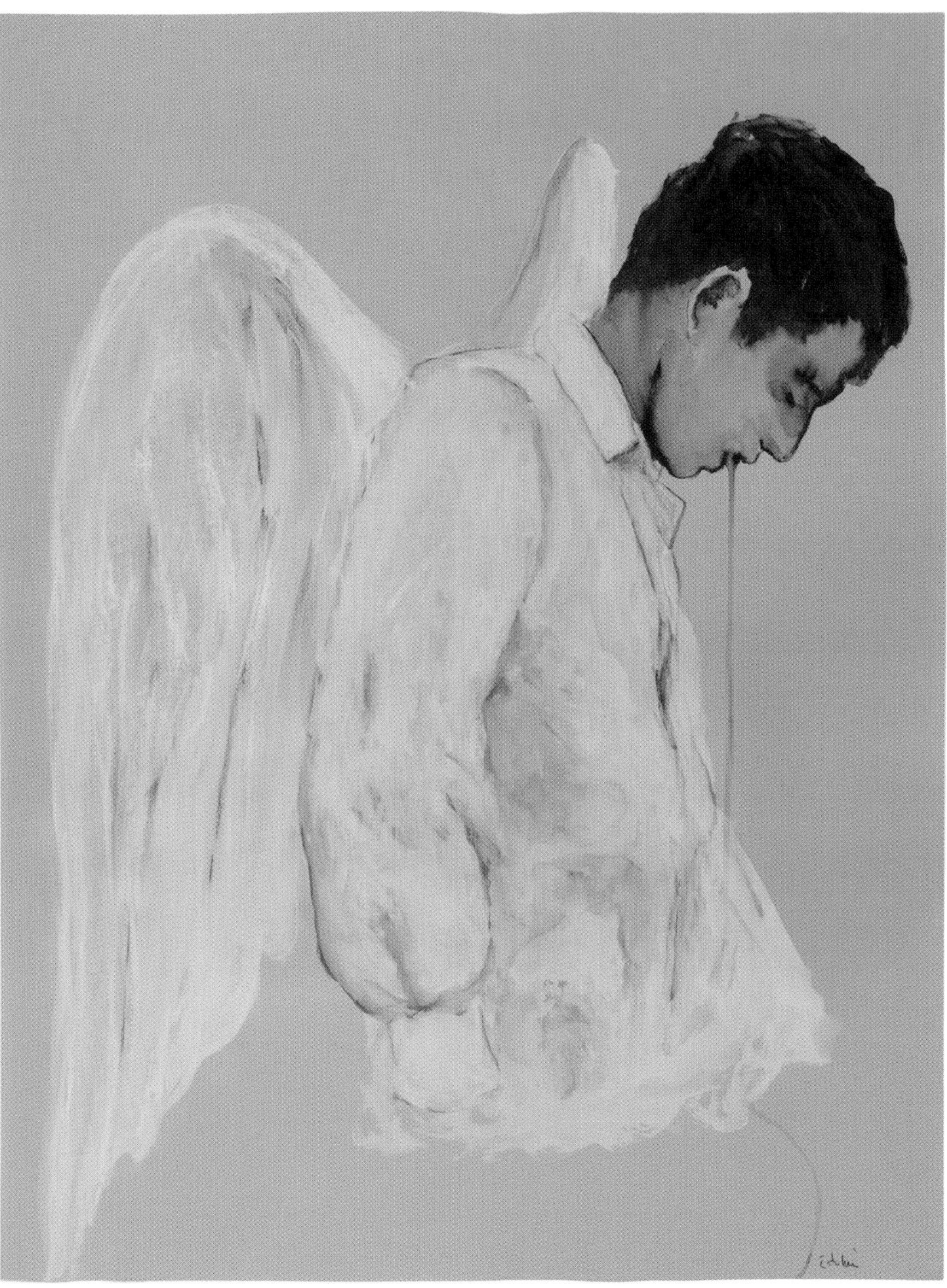

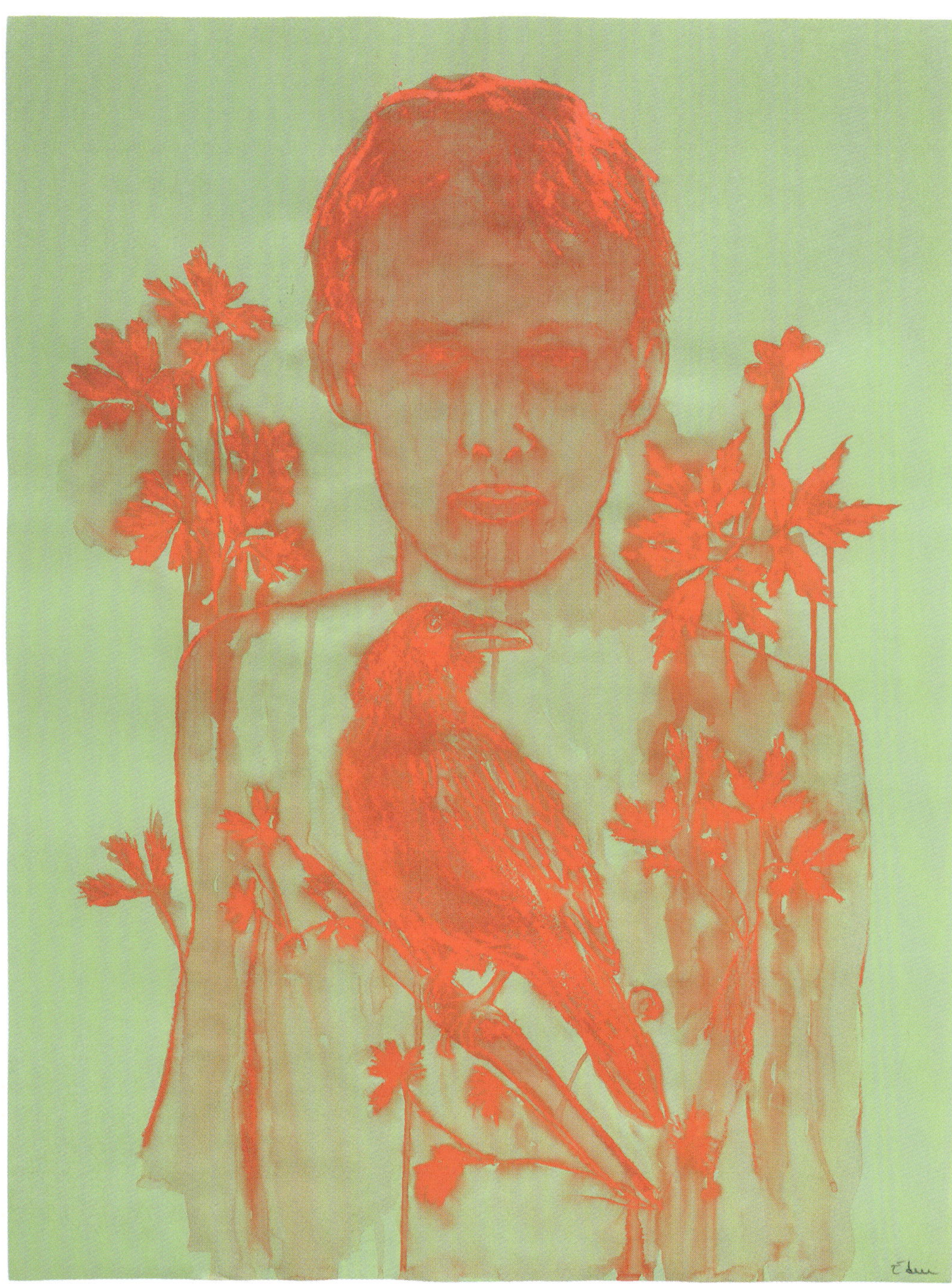

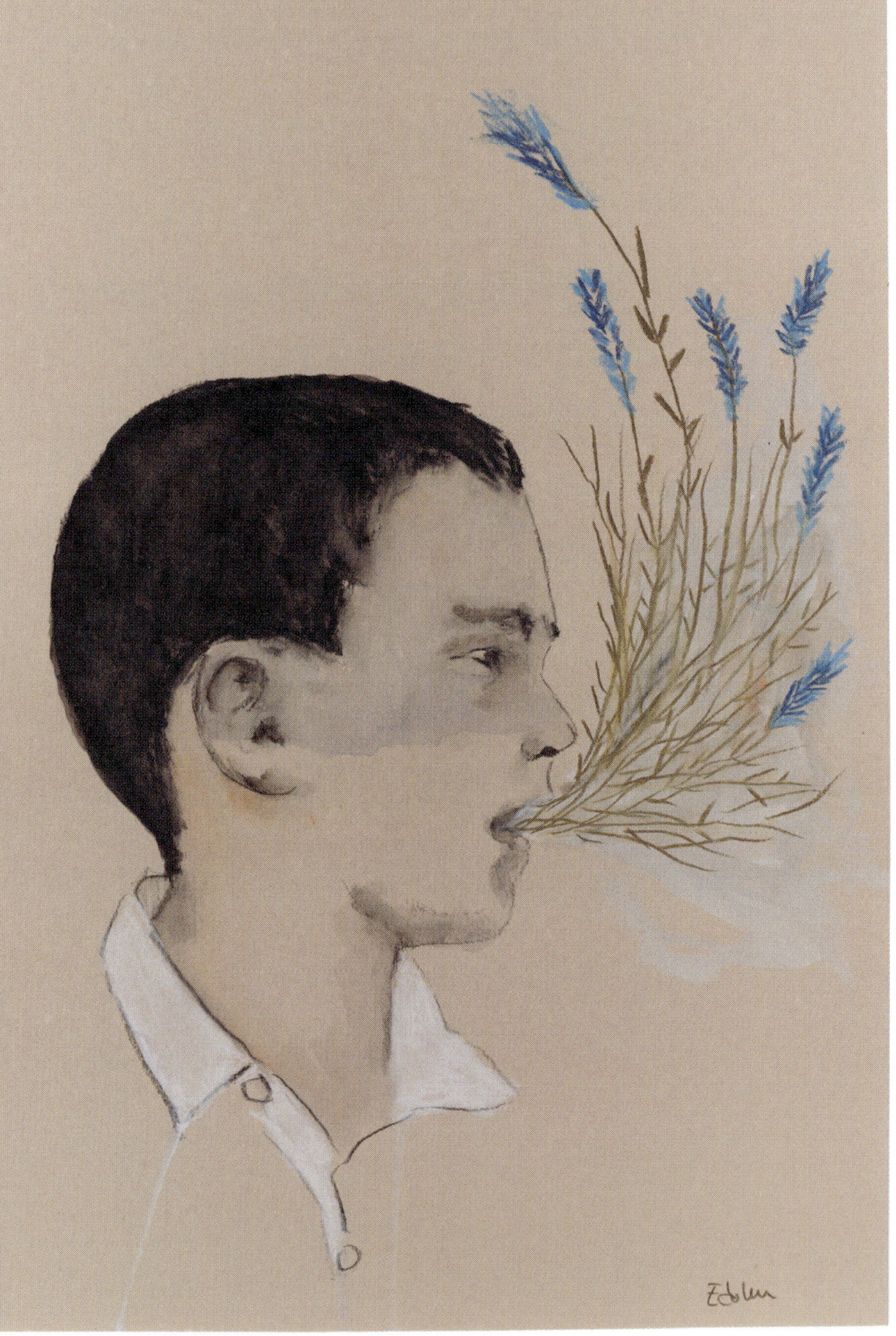

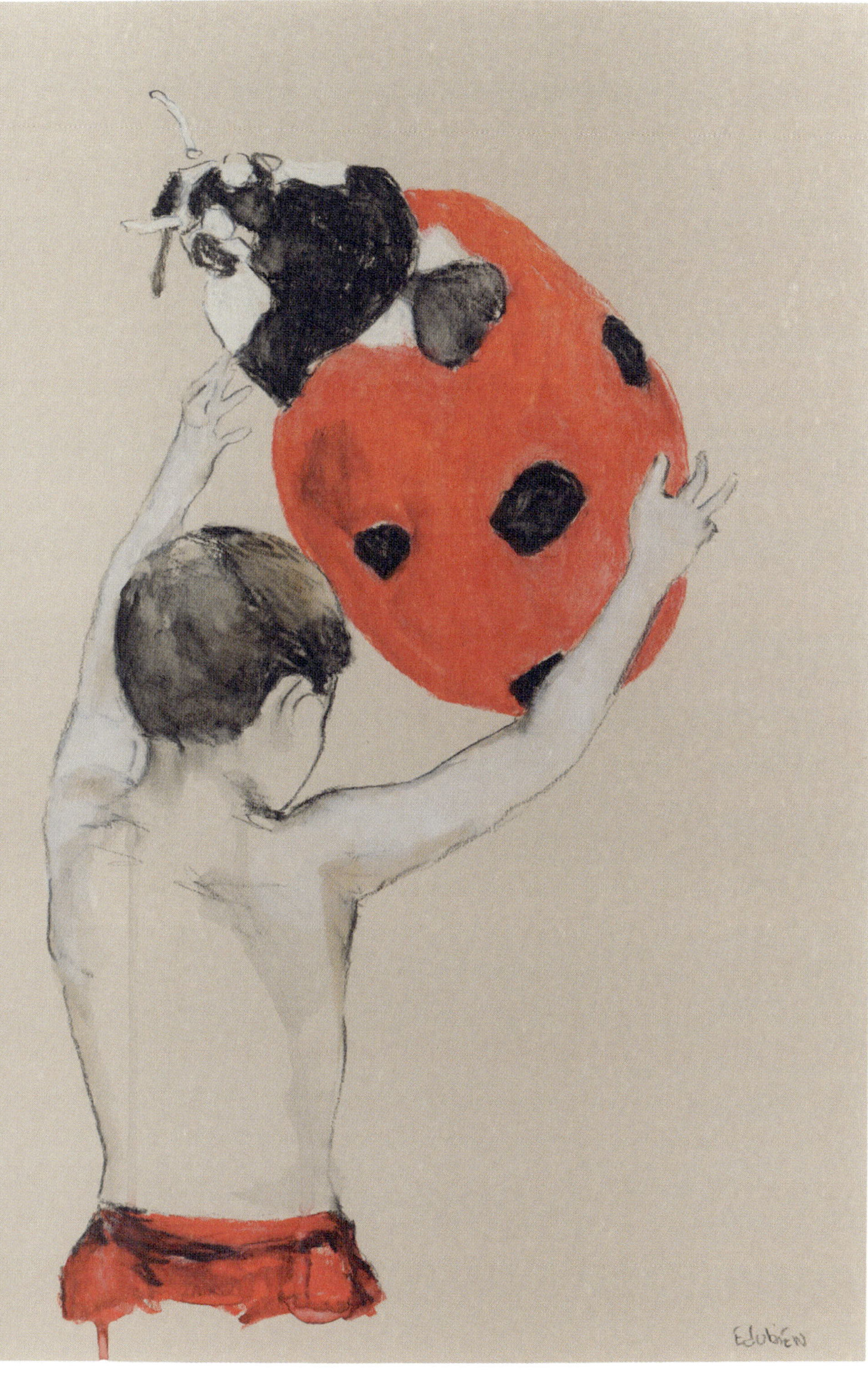

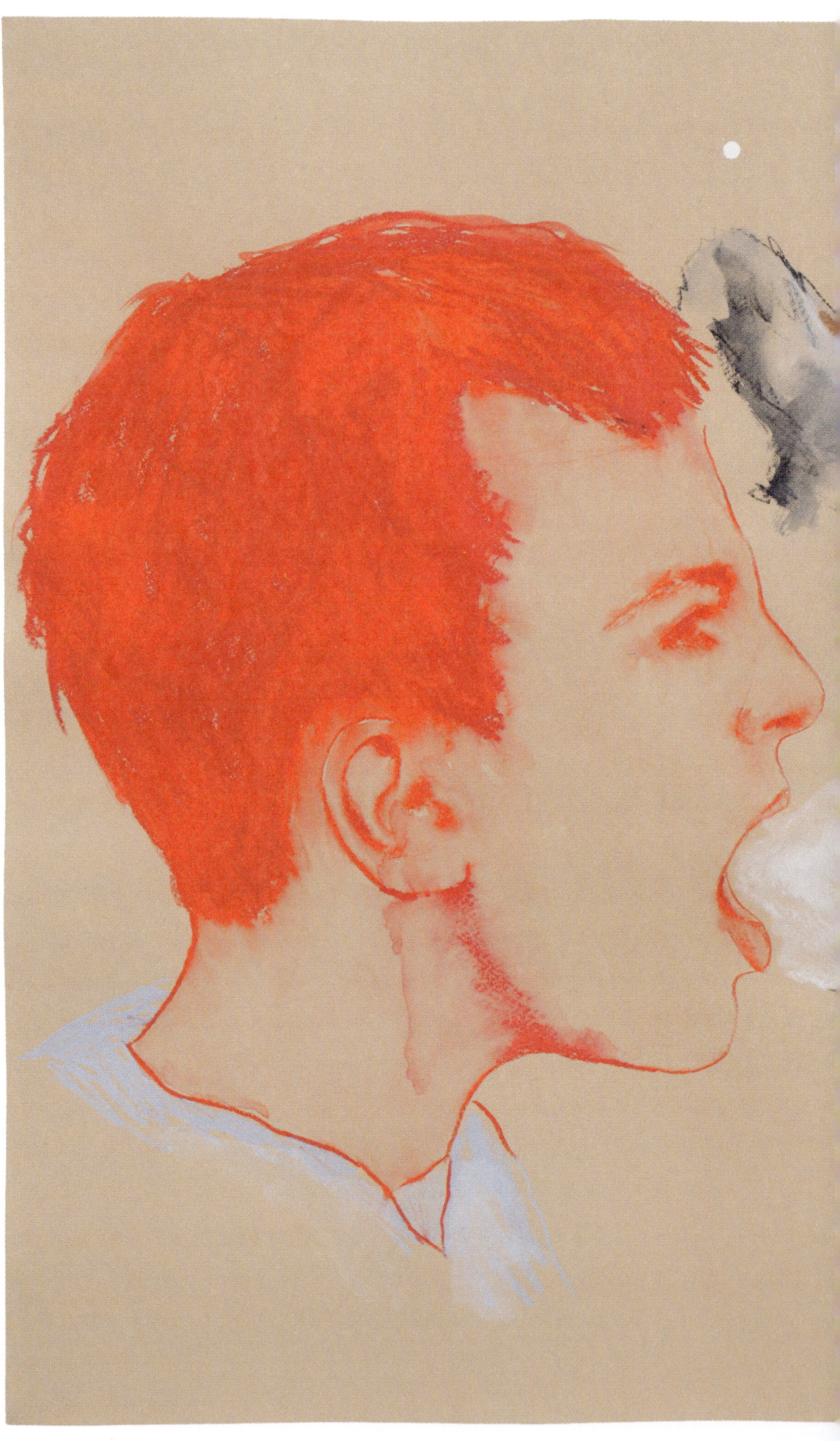

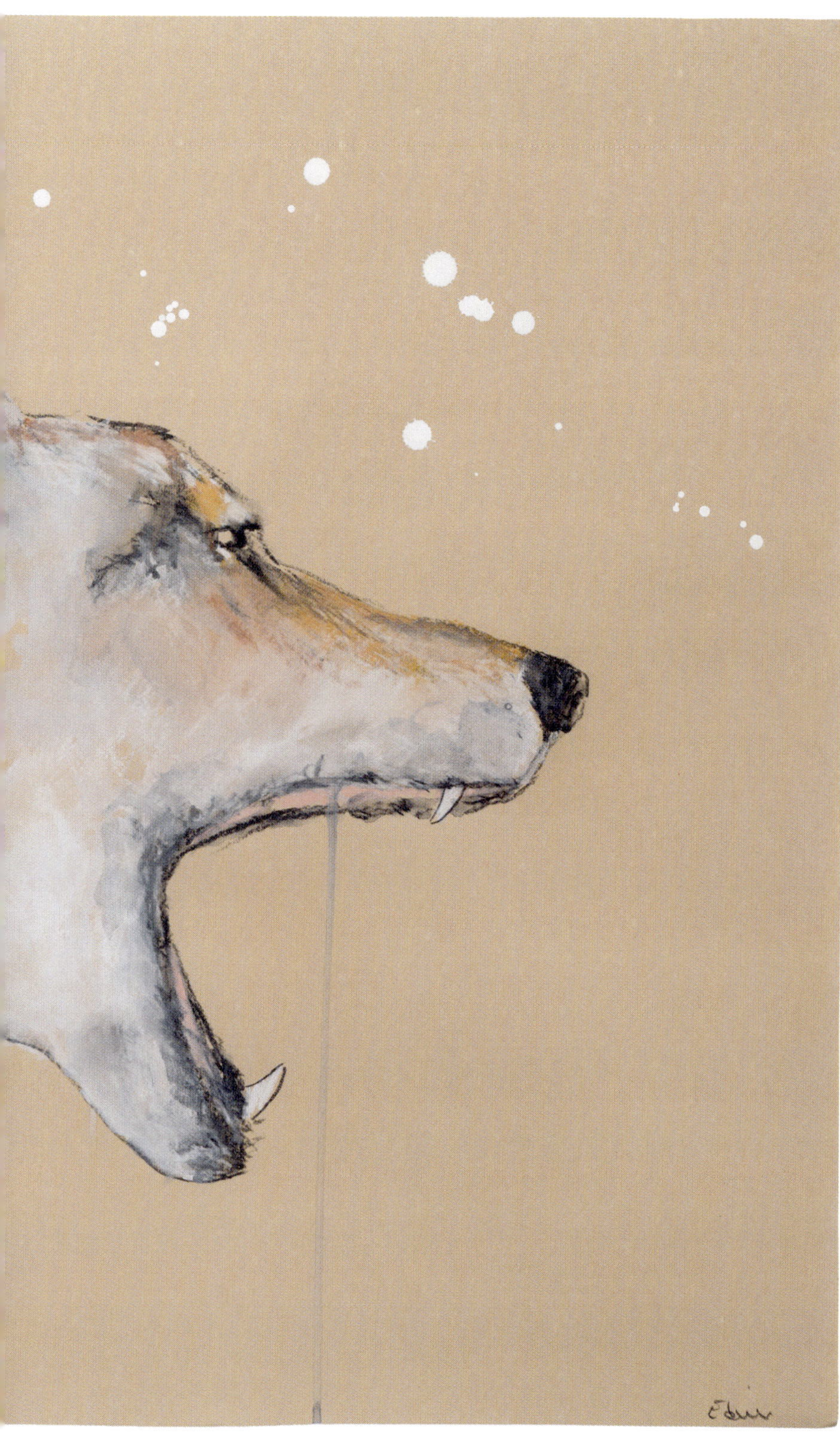

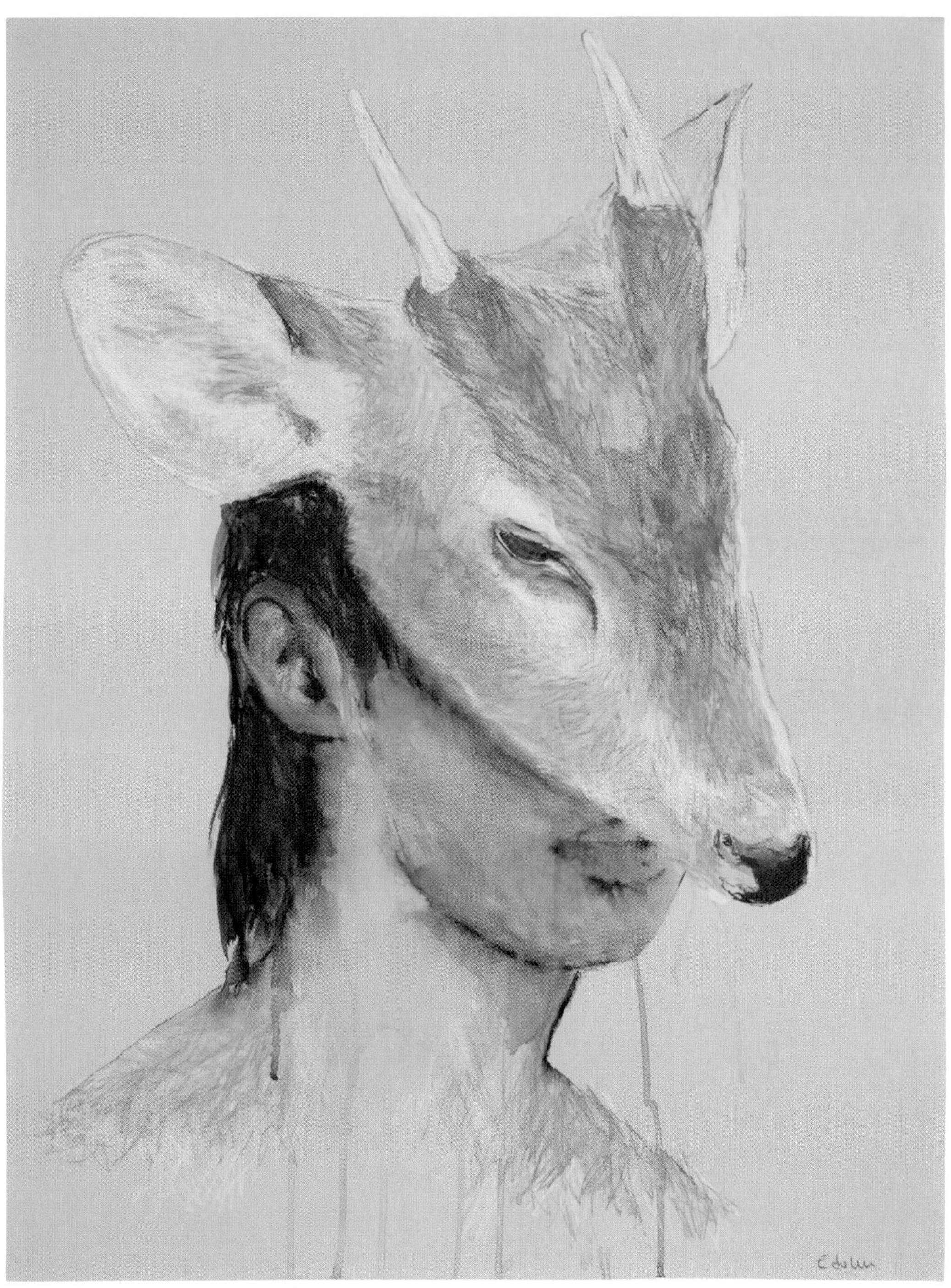

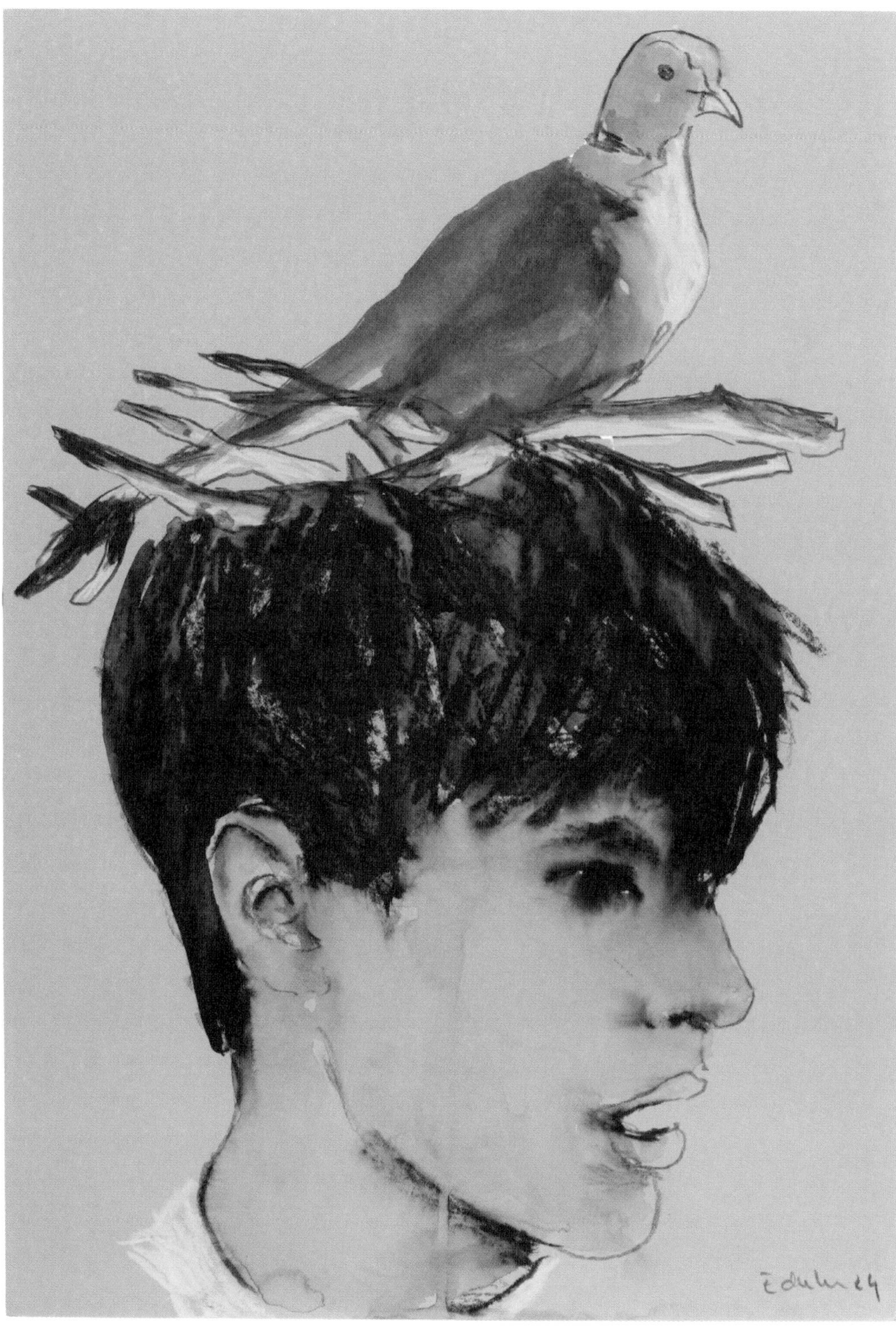

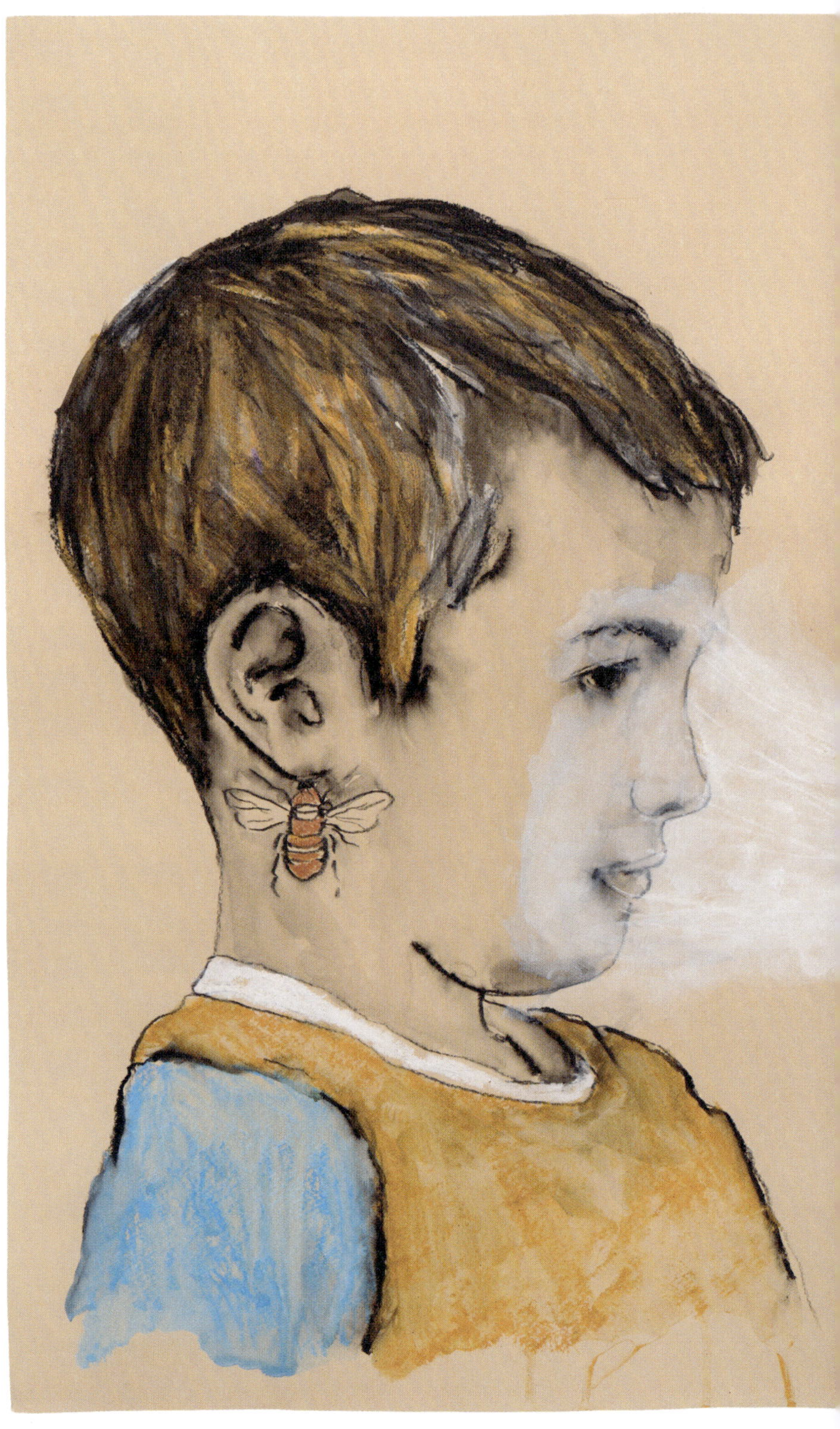

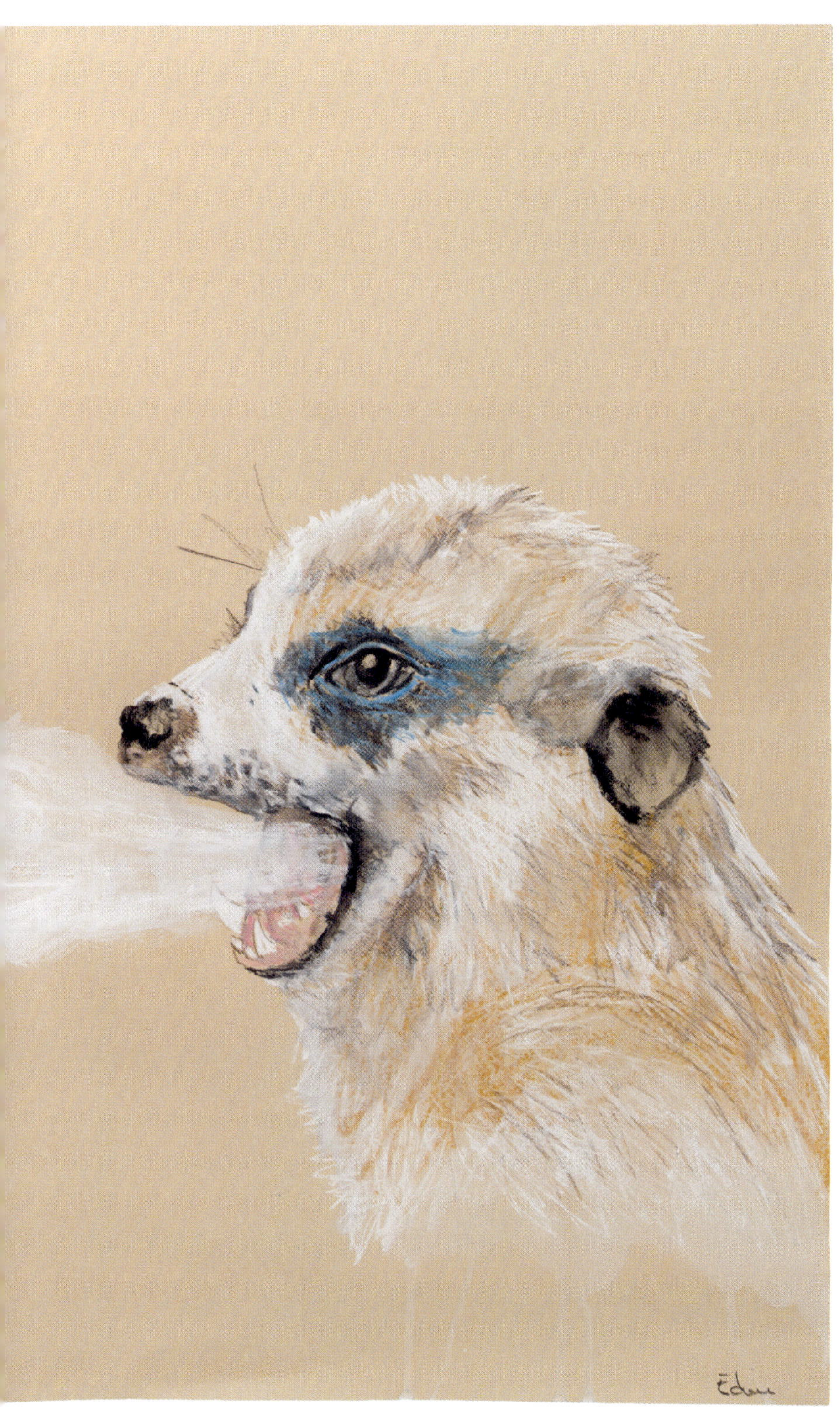

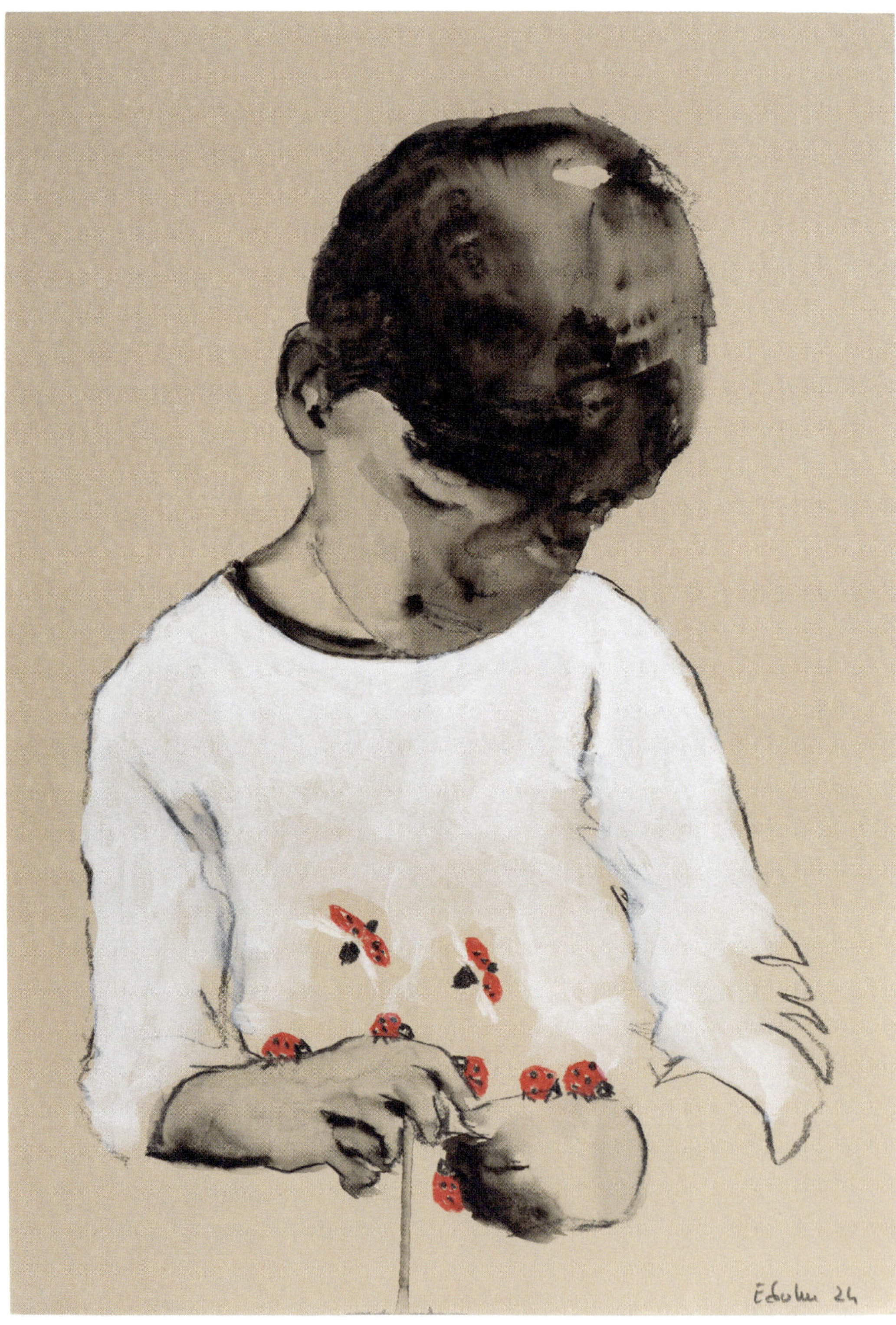

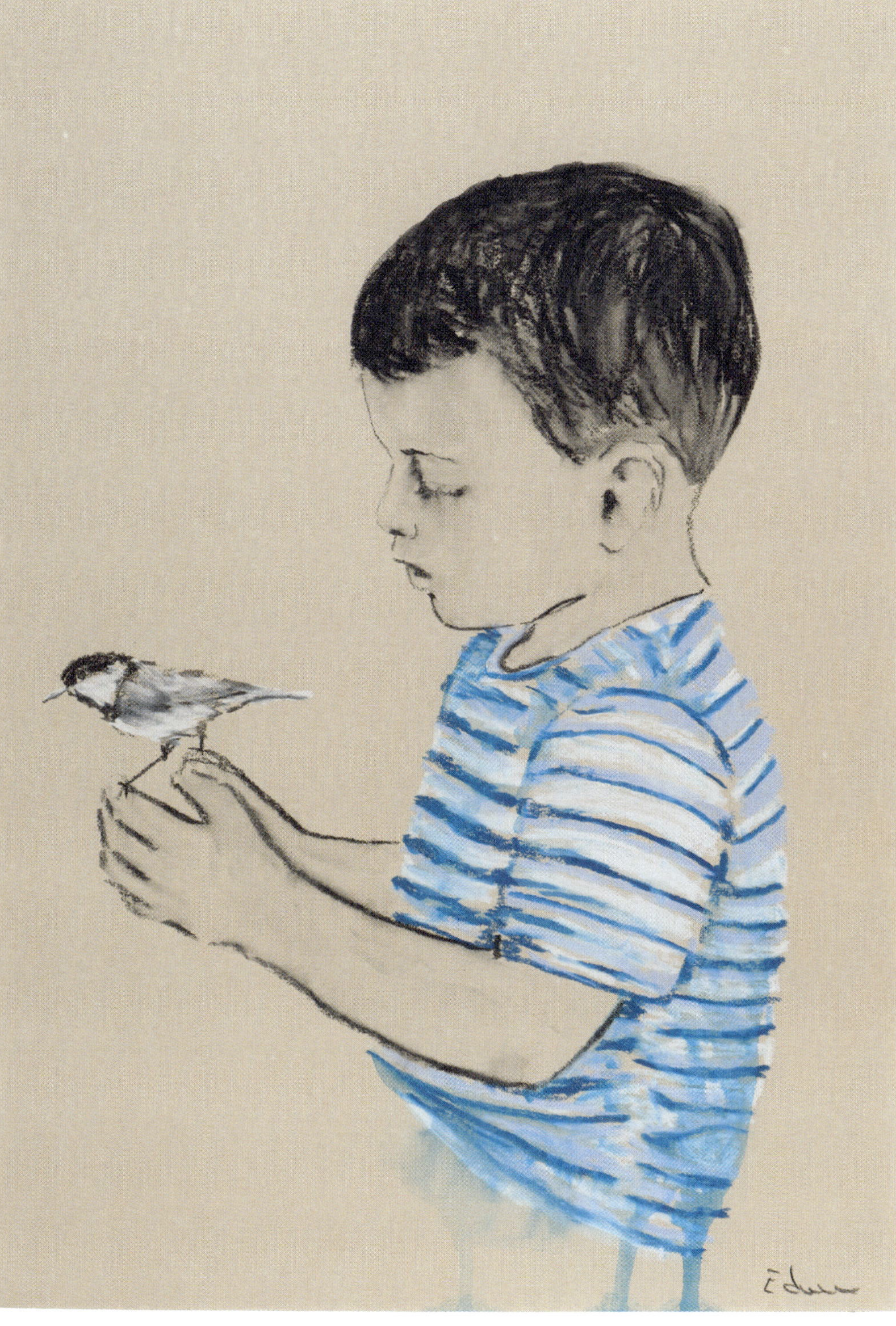

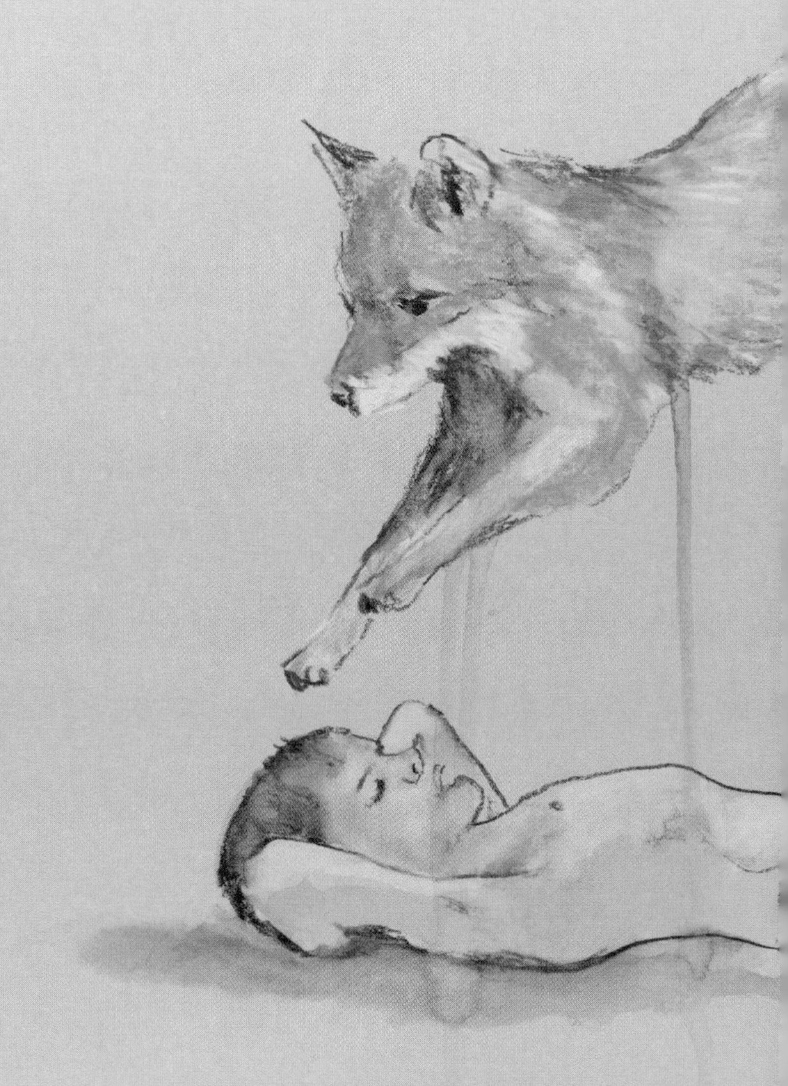

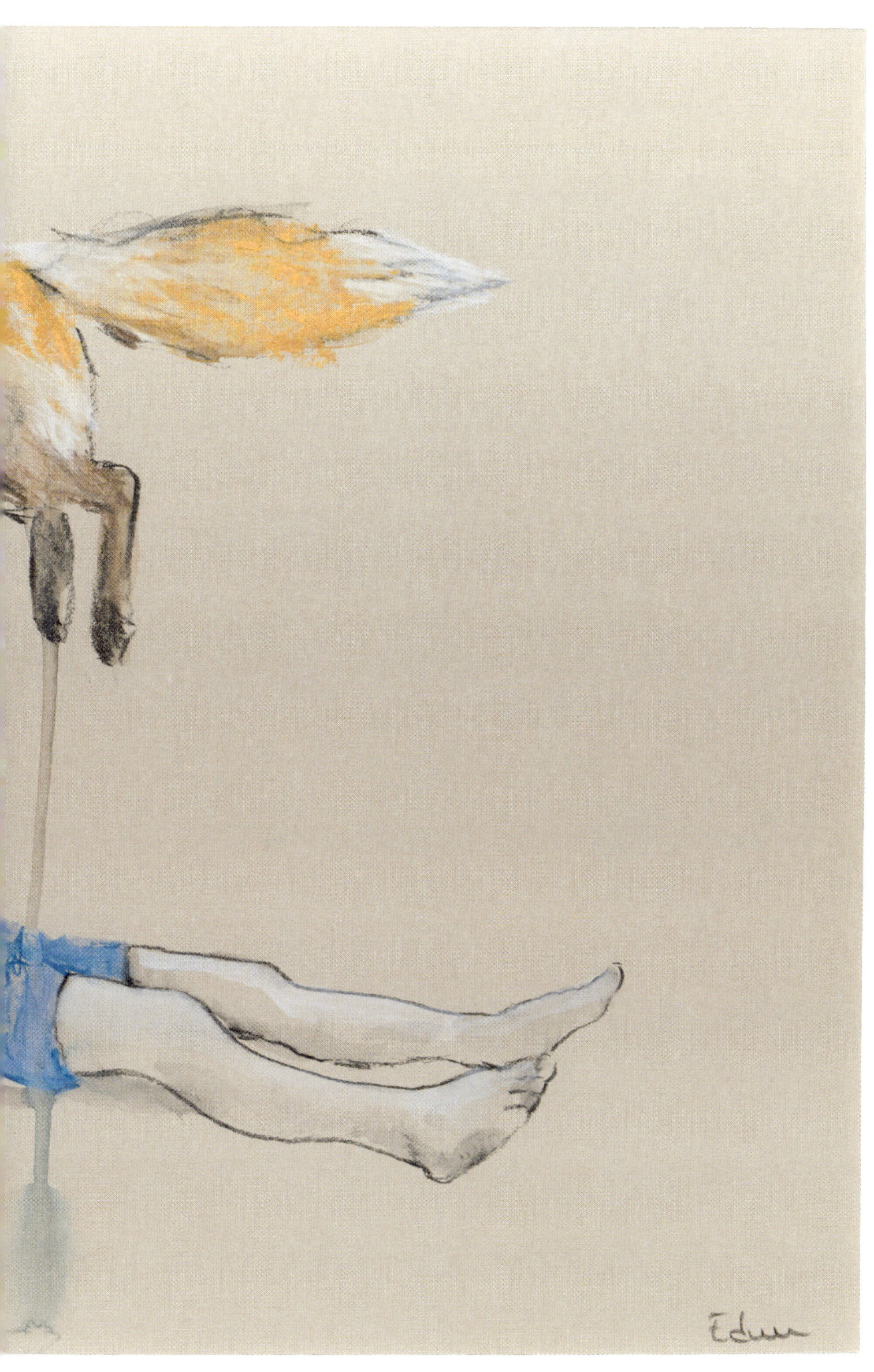

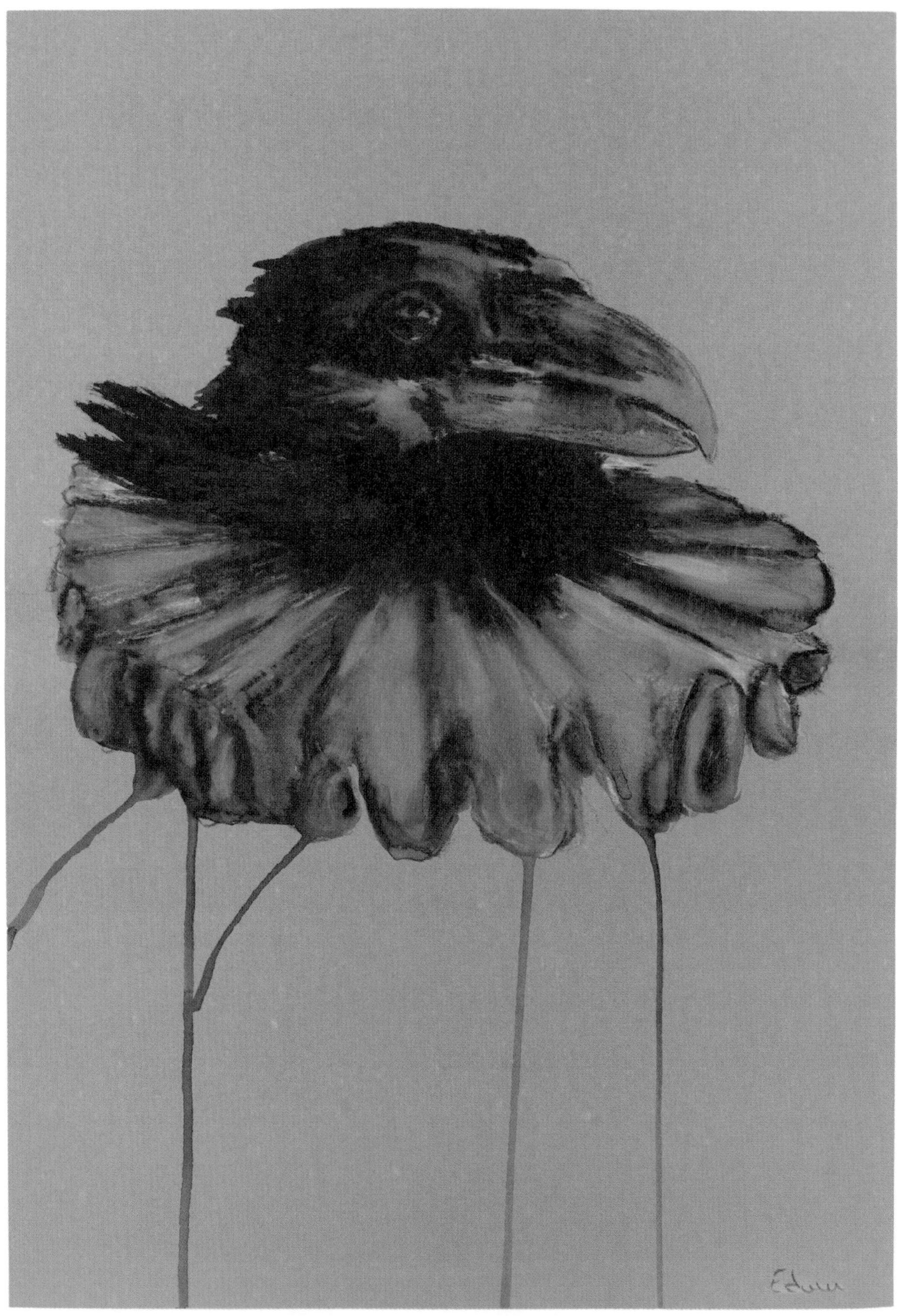

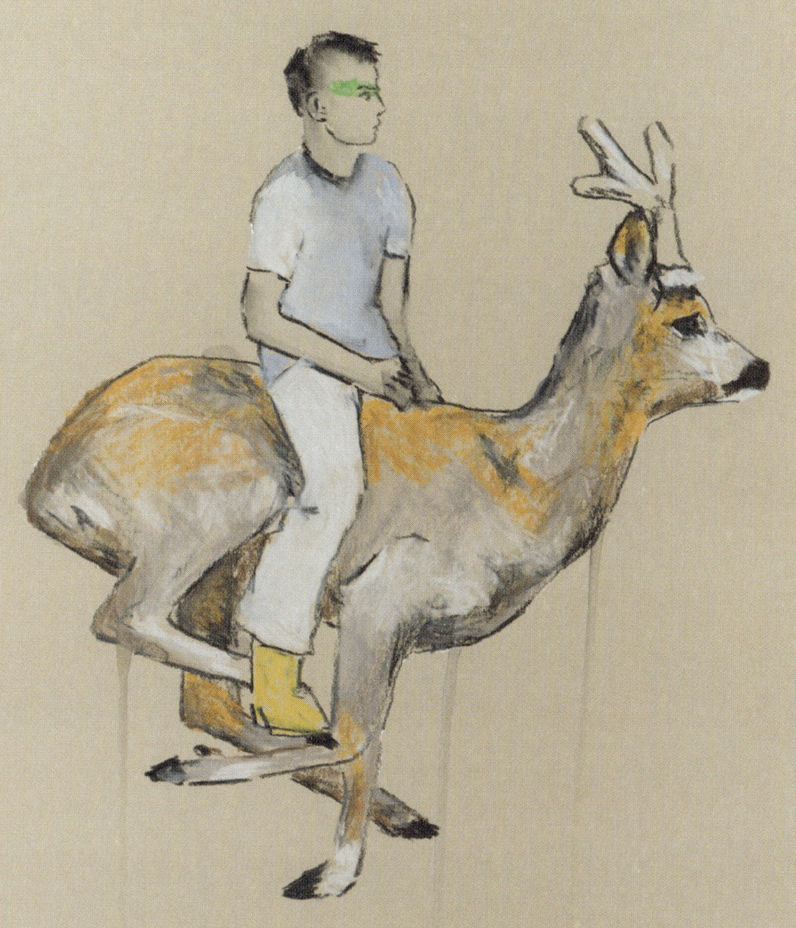

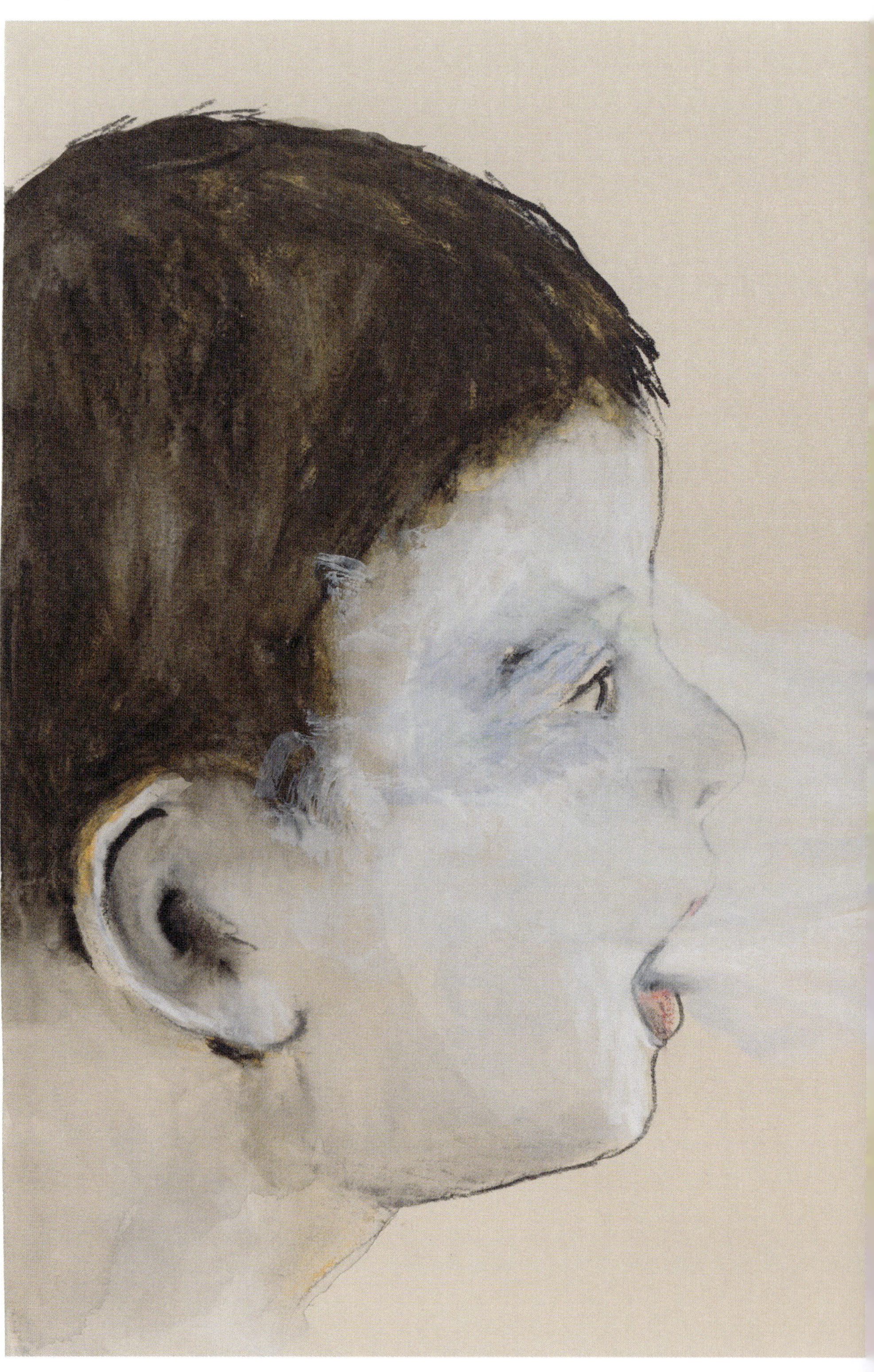

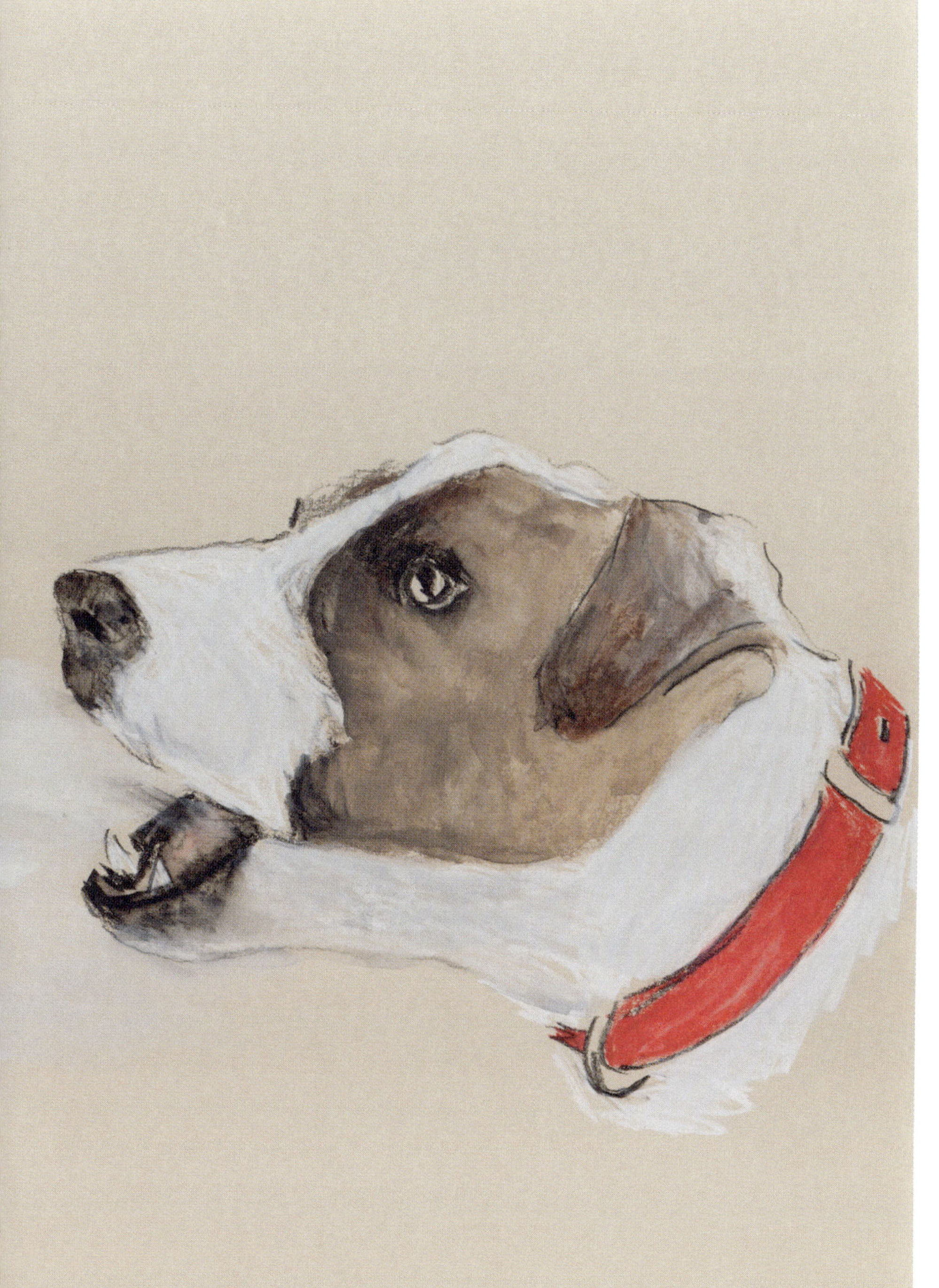
Edeler 21

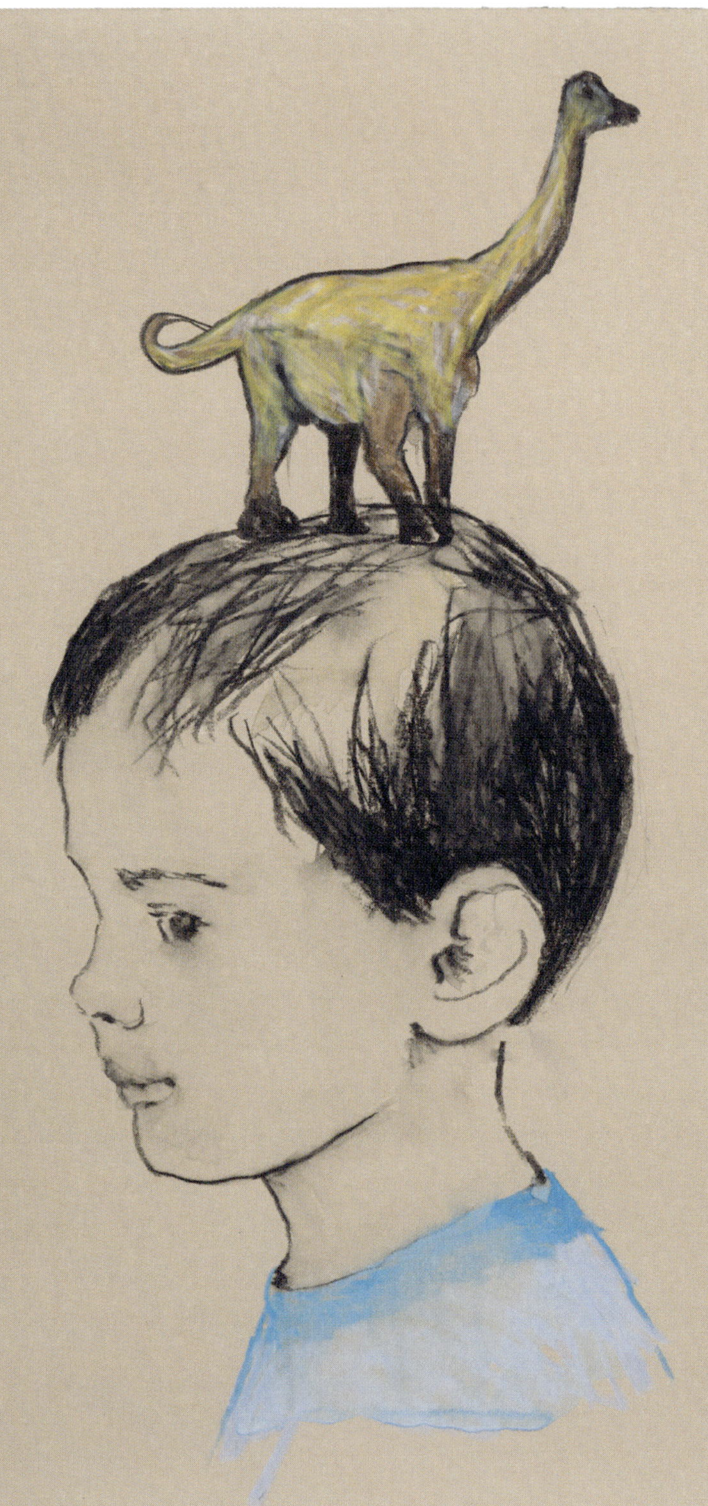

The Endless
Glimmer

For all the Garances in the world

Exhibition at the Musée de la Chasse et de la
Nature from December 10, 2024 to May 4, 2025

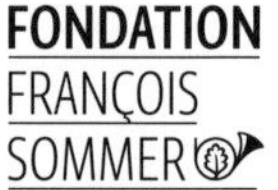

The Endless *Glimmer*

Edi Dubien

JBE BOOKS   MUSÉE DE LA CHASSE & DE LA NATURE

Ah, in this quiet, dark wood...*

Thomas Jolly

Like Orpheus, Edi Dubien knows how to charm animals.
This is the knack he passes on to each of the children
he portrays.
His work takes us into a wood. Sacred, no doubt.
Here, childhood and nature, as if sheltered from the real
world, merge and borrow from each other.
From an old trunk, old-fashioned costumes finished with
leaves, branches, bristles, and feathers. Using a forgotten
makeup palette, flower or root pigments, children
and animals put their faces on, make themselves up.
These getups bring an aura of ancient theater to the
wood. Sometimes fairytales. Possibly a pagan ceremony.
A sanctuary.

It's all so lighthearted. But variously, depending
on whether the encounter is with an animal or a child.

In animals, there's a primal lightheartedness: the one
before the worry. The one that doesn't foreshadow
it. Doesn't consider it. The animals play dress-up.
The dresses, tiaras and hats they adorn themselves with
don't augment them. Makeup doesn't transform them.
As already complete. A reminder that animal nature
is self-sufficient. A mirror, then, for human nature,
of its incompleteness. Whether in tutus or high heels, the

 * First verse of the French libretto of Gluck's opera *Orphée et Eurydice*

animals are not only having fun, they reveal:
they re-enchant our capacity for metamorphosis.

It's one of our strengths—one of our skills—the most
spectacular of all. The power to transform ourselves.
To put on a getup. And thereby recount, fictionalize
and represent us. It is the source of art (theater is king!)
just like our individual and shared existences, intimate
or social: we also dress up our thoughts. We distort words.
We fake feelings. We make up facts.

This talent is innate and above all playful: children, early
on, explore it. But in this wood, unlike animals, children
have a serious and solemn wisdom. It's their eyes that tell
us so.

Though they are costumed and made-up, they carry with
them a silent truth. They saw something they weren't
supposed to see. Not just yet. Not so soon. A damaged look.
A lost sparkle. Is this how the scared gaze comes about?
By losing light, an openness, a hunger for the outside
world, a striving towards the world? Anyone who has seen
photos of oneself over the years can see this slow fading.
But these children are too young and their time too short
to have already cast themselves in shadow.

It's not the prior lightheartedness that can be seen in their
eyes, it's the lightheartedness of after. When the ordeal
is over, the danger has been overcome.
Their adornments, then, don't seem to be mere children's
costumes, but ferine armor, tactical camouflage.
Makeup is war paint to intimidate predators by making
the eyes look big ("look daggers" as the children say).
Jewelry made of feathers or leaves are a few talismans
or magical amulets. Animals and insects complete their

panoply: totemic figures, clan emblems or guardian
deities. Yes, these feral children also look like heroes–
returning from battle.

It's the retrospection of their black-rimmed gazes that
beckons us. Because they create a void between us
and them. A yearning. We approach them all the more
peacefully because, however dark, there's no aggression
in their eyes. Nor threat. Their looks are neither malicious
nor vengeful. Peaceful kids. They have the calm of those
who know. And the insolence or modesty to remain silent
when we stand before them. In their costume of leaves
and twigs, they won't say anything about what they've
seen. The hells from which they have returned.

From the silence between them and us emerges the power
of Edi Dubien's work. In the interstice that our eyes
come to fill in theirs. What do we see then? Self. We see
ourselves. We find ourselves. Their eyes give us room,
the space to see ourselves. Facing one of these children,
a unique loop of images, of memories, of projections is set
in motion. Standing before a work by Edi Dubien, I have
my unique loop. I will keep my words to myself, because
my loop is not more worthy than another. And because it's
a secret, between each of these kids and me. Between my
kid and me.

In his work, Edi Dubien, likely, refers to himself.
But he talks about me. And about you. And about you.
And about you. About us really. This is how we recognize
great works, when the personal expression of the maker
and the singularity of the viewer come together.

Like Orpheus, Edi Dubien has traversed the Underworld
and returned. His strength, he transposes to all the

children he portrays. No matter if they have left behind
their Eurydice, their innocence, their childhood perhaps.
Ah, in this quiet, dark wood, as if in a sweet Elysium, they
now savor rest. That of living having triumphed over fears.
To no longer dread danger. To live free. Heros of leaves,
feathers and twigs, accomplices of the animals to whom
they owe their greatest feat: that of even knowing how
to pacify the Cerberus.

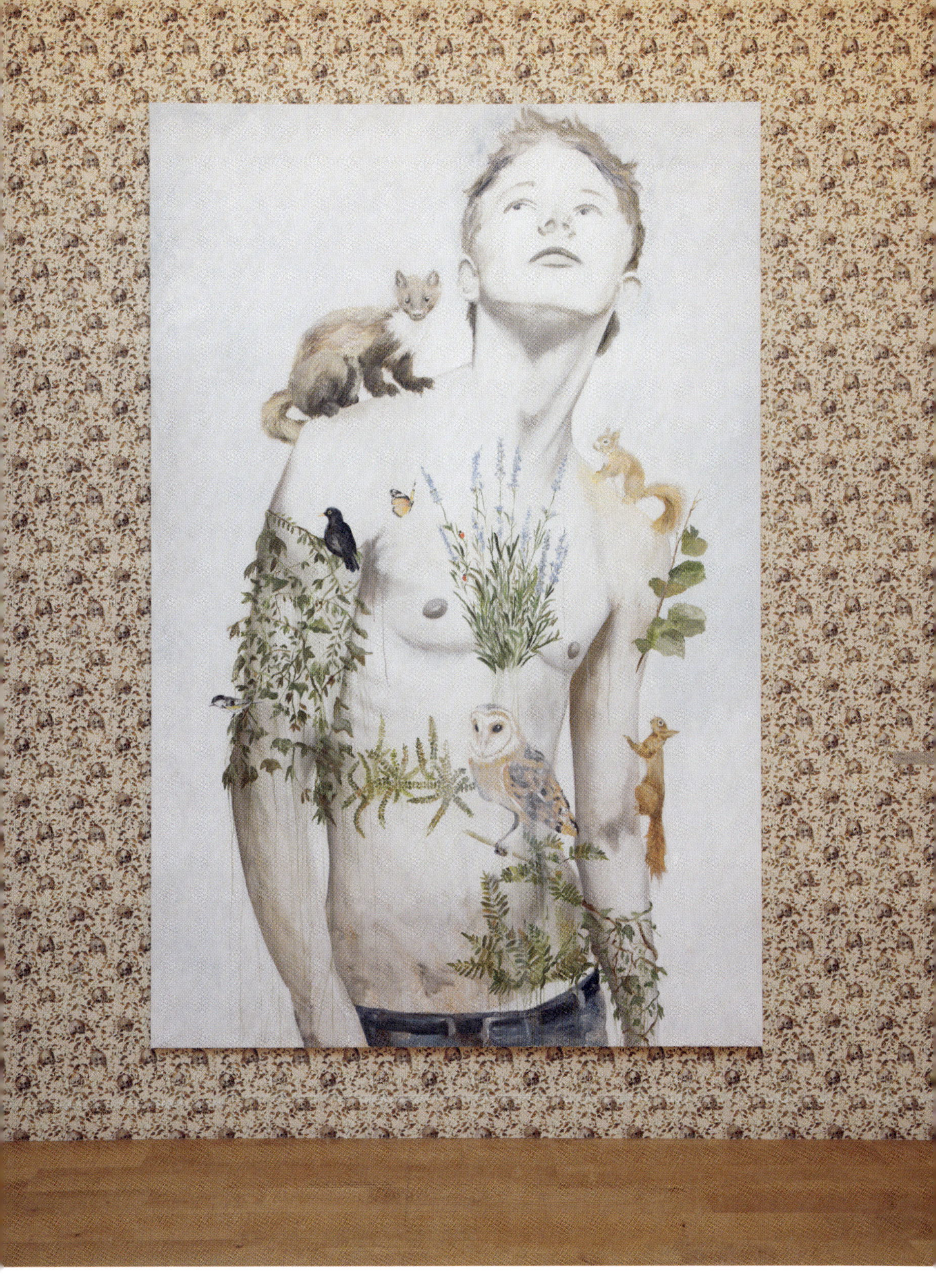

Résistant, 2024

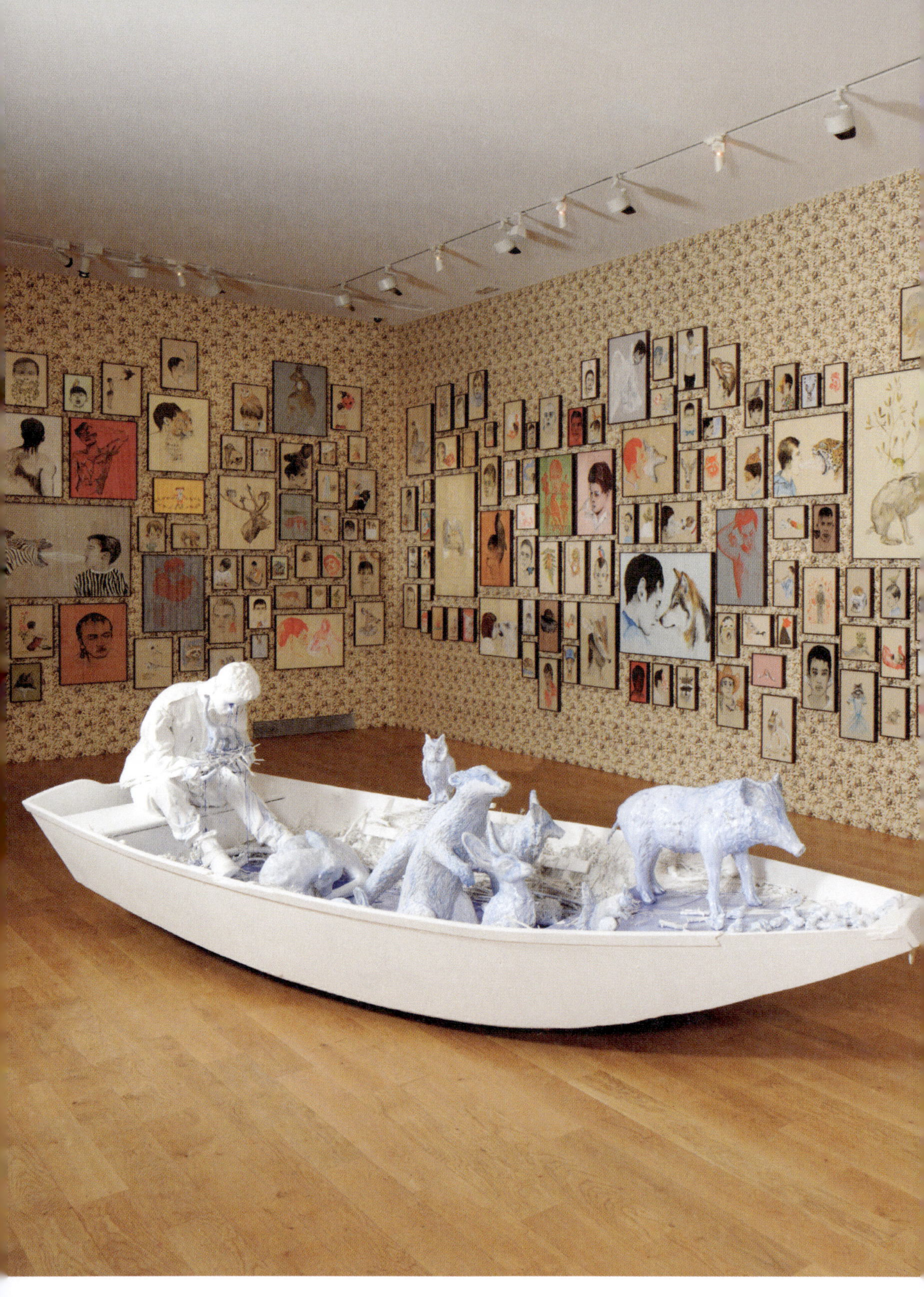

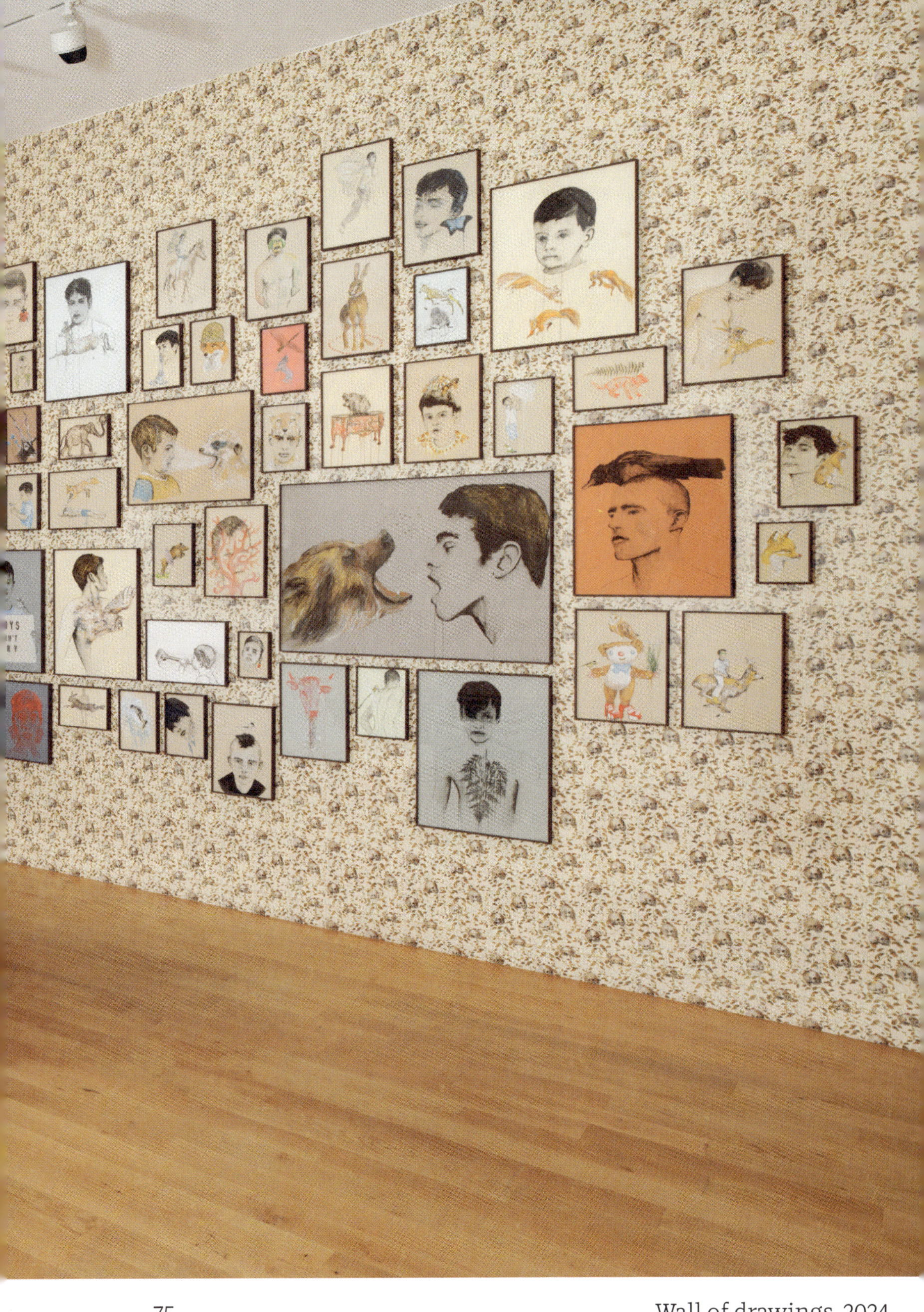

Wall of drawings, 2024

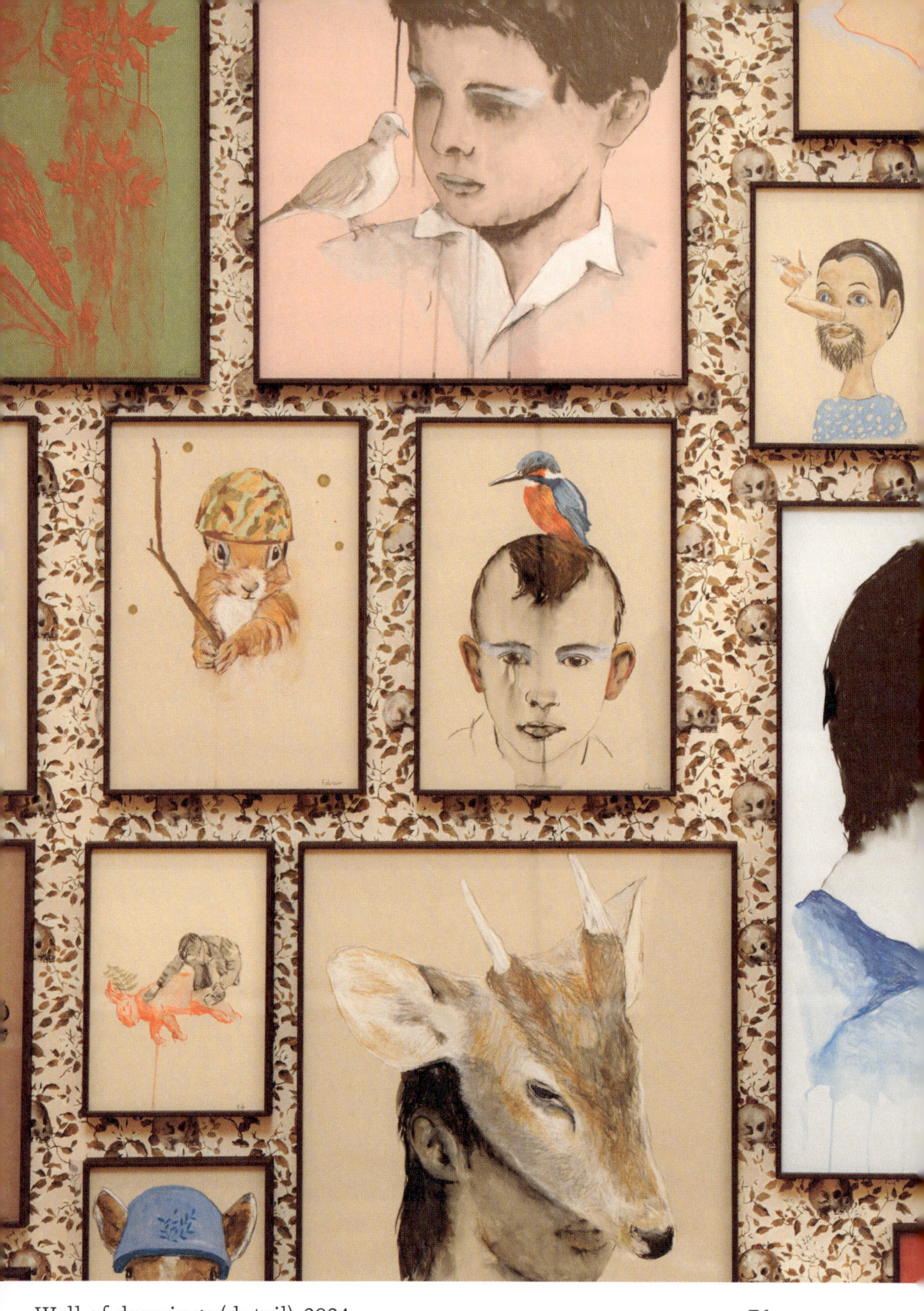

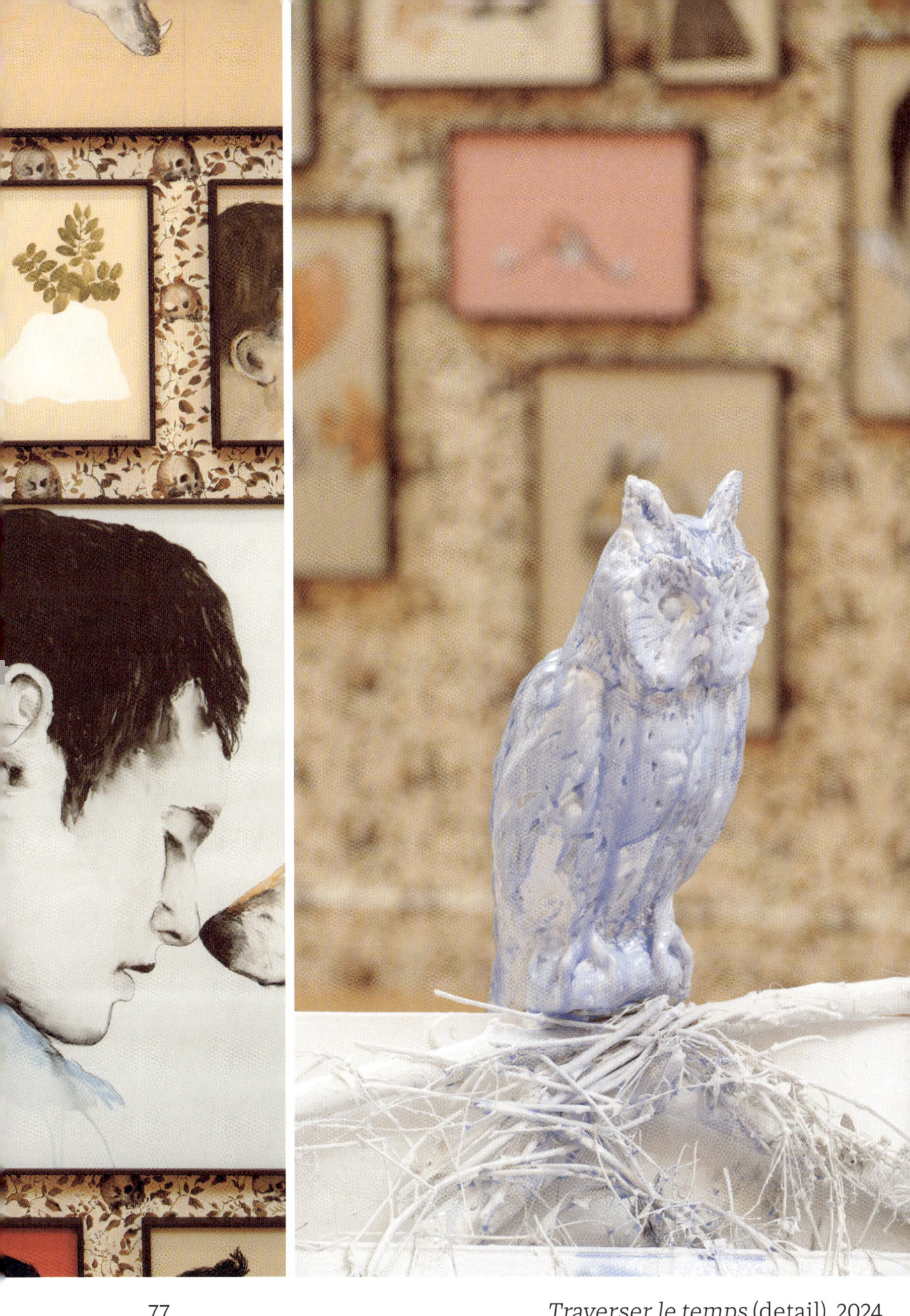

Traverser le temps (detail), 2024

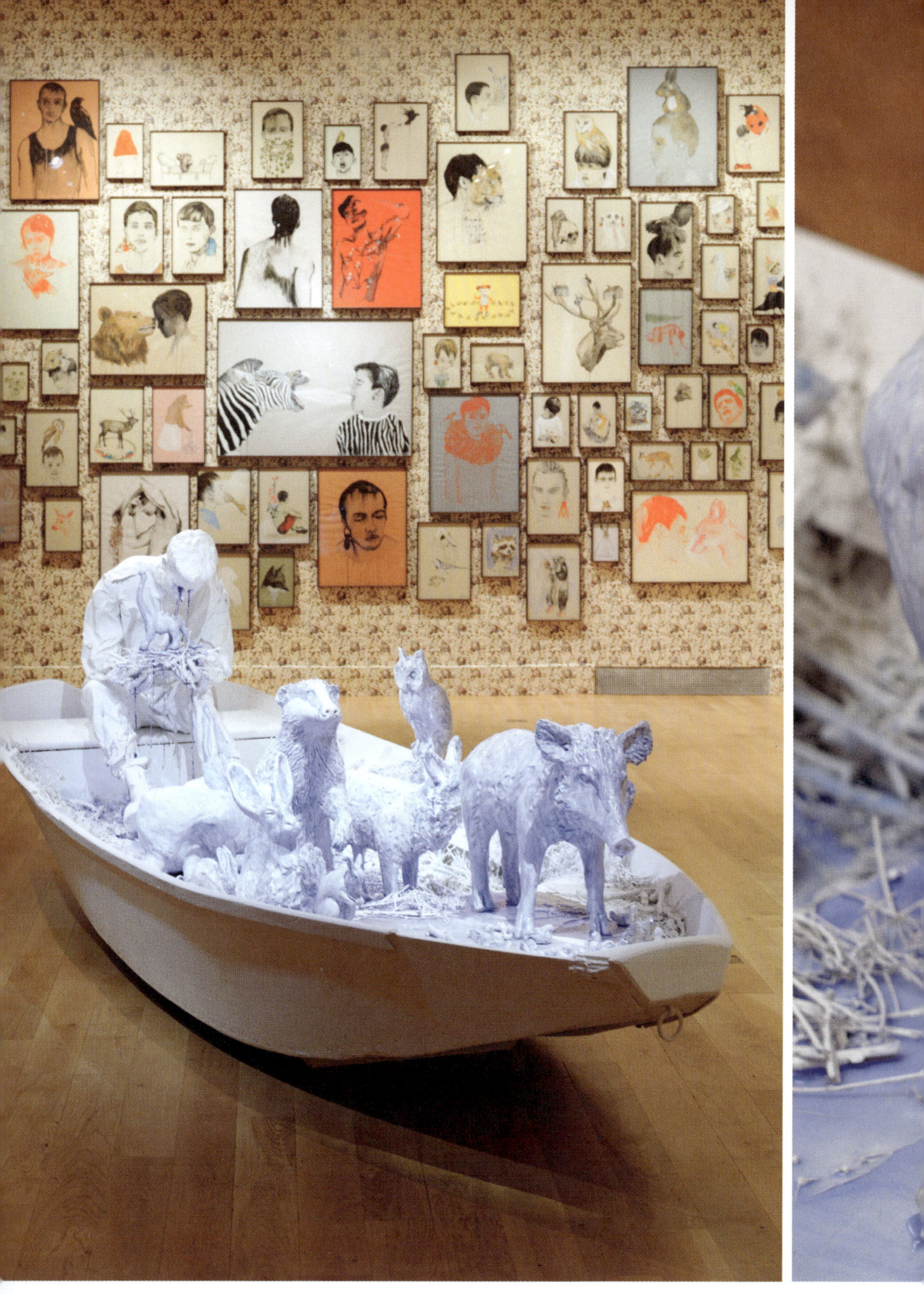

Traverser le temps, 2024

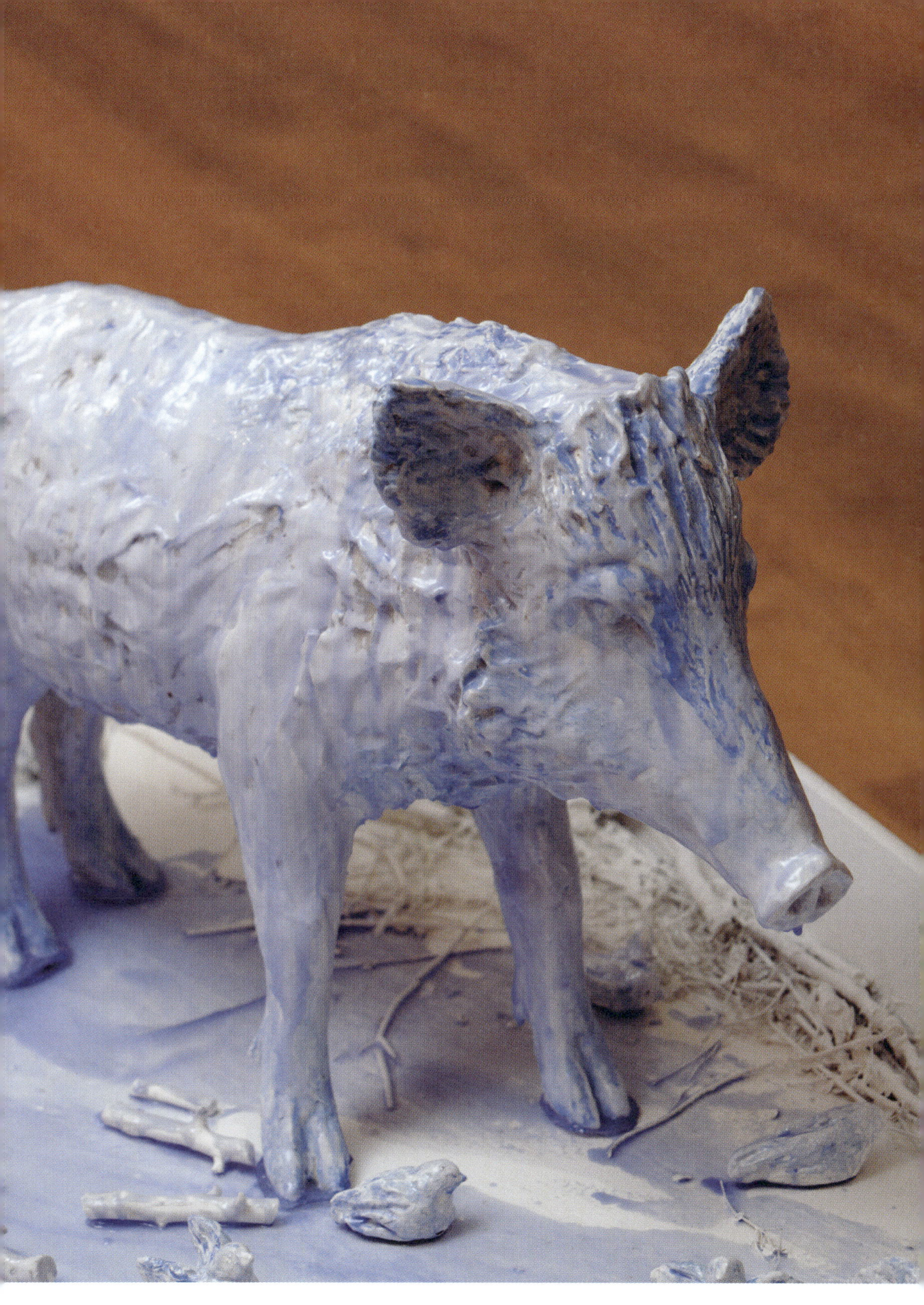

Traverser le temps (detail), 2024

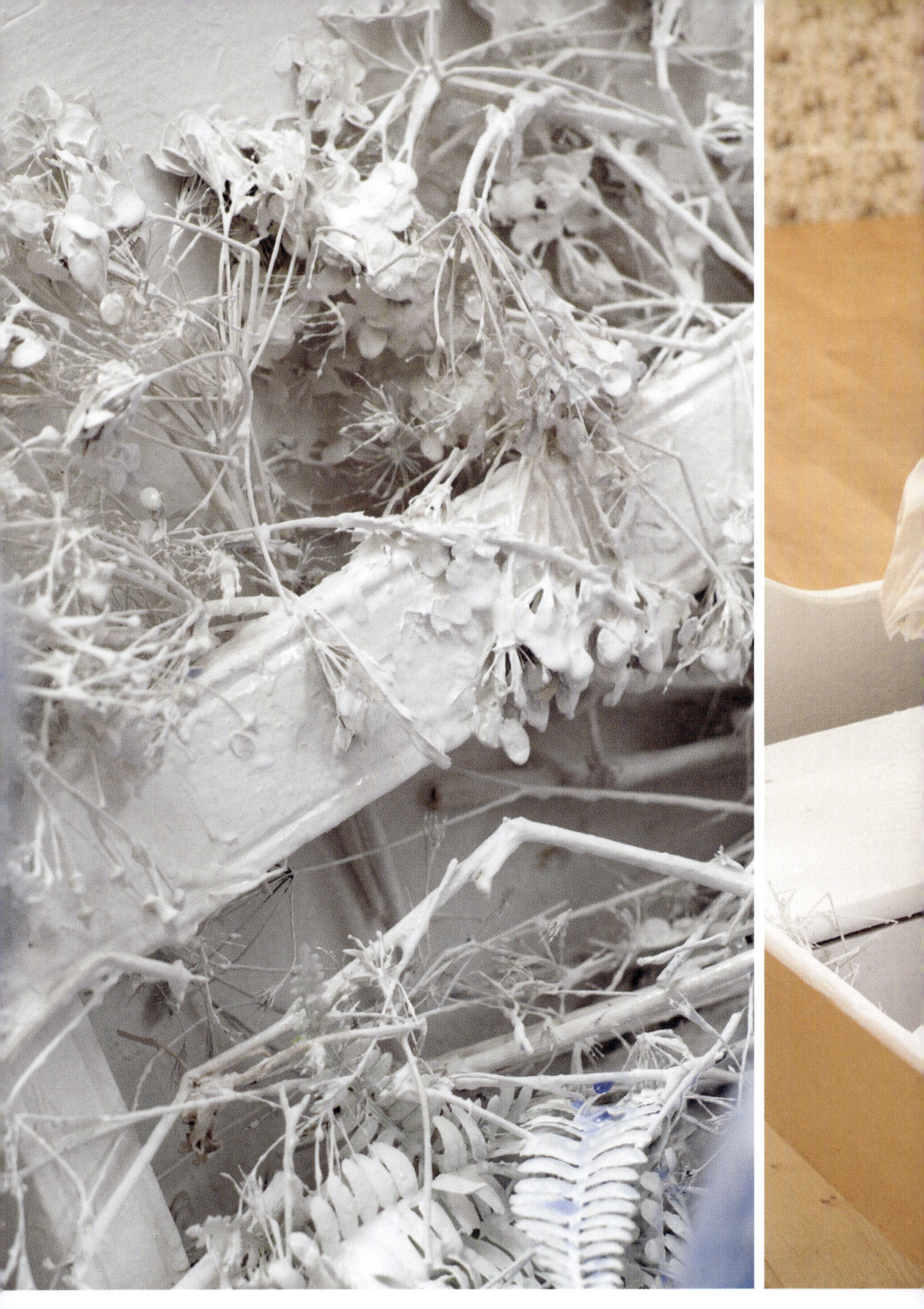

Traverser le temps (detail), 2024

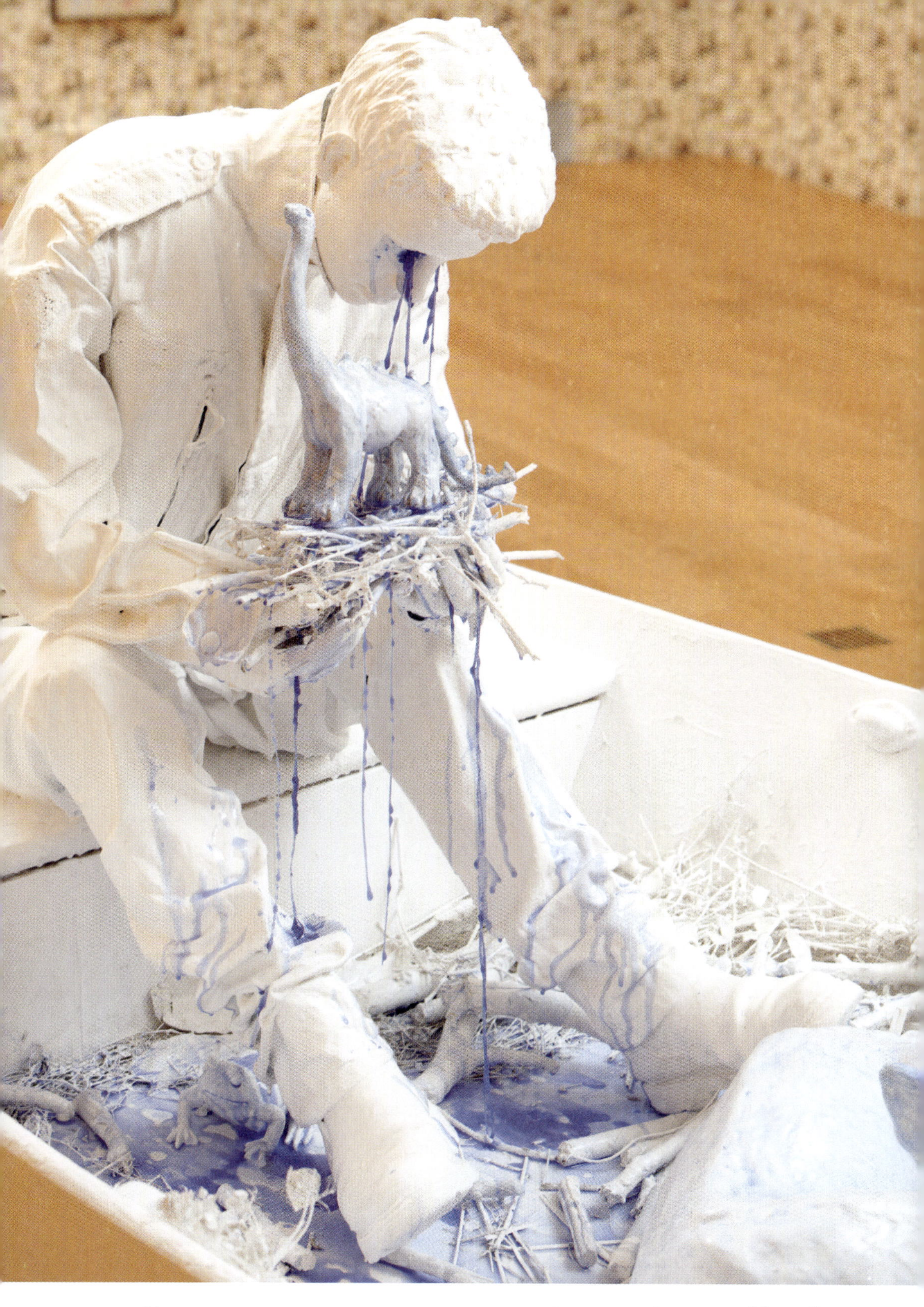

Traverser le temps (detail), 2024

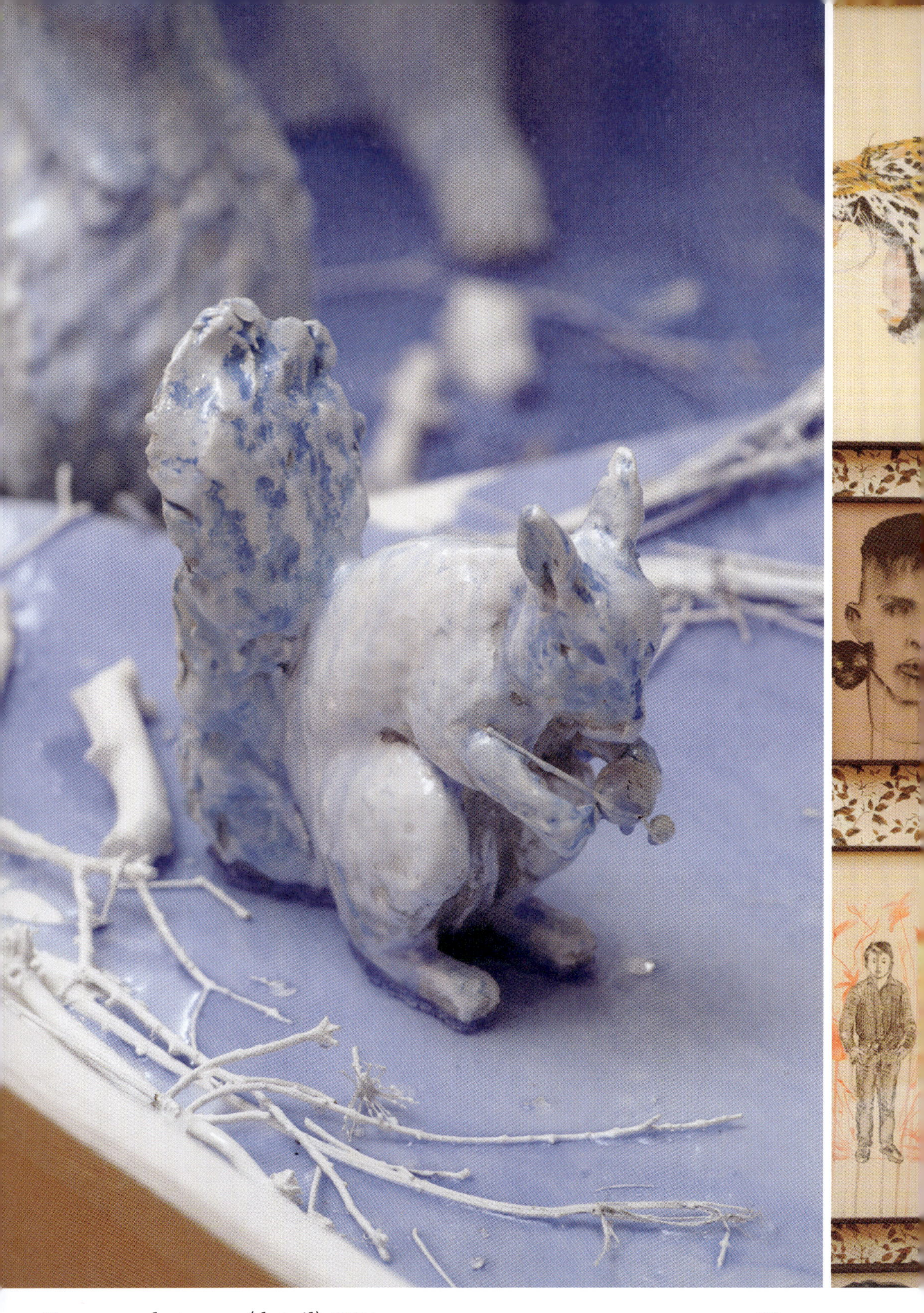

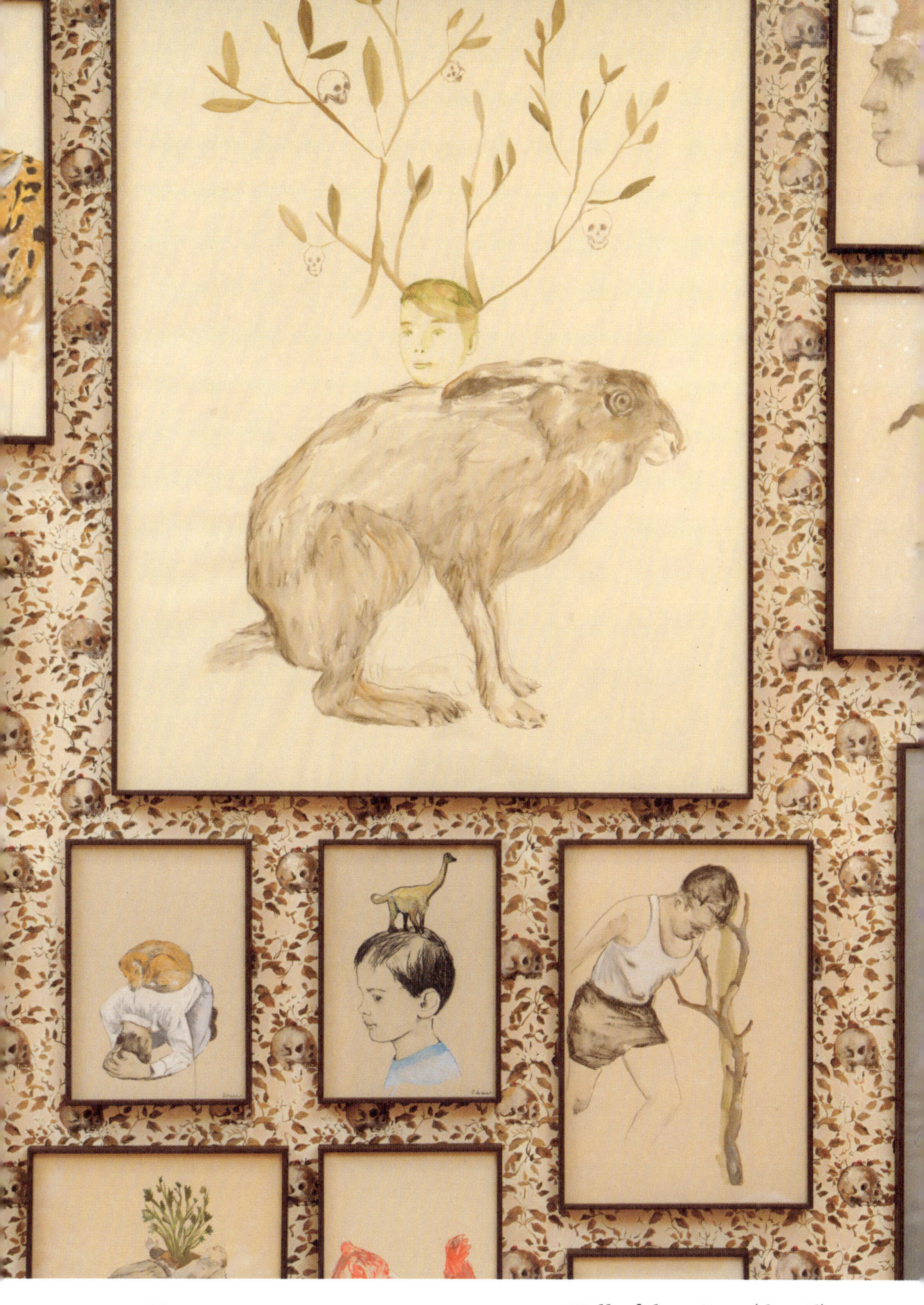

Wall of drawings (detail), 2024

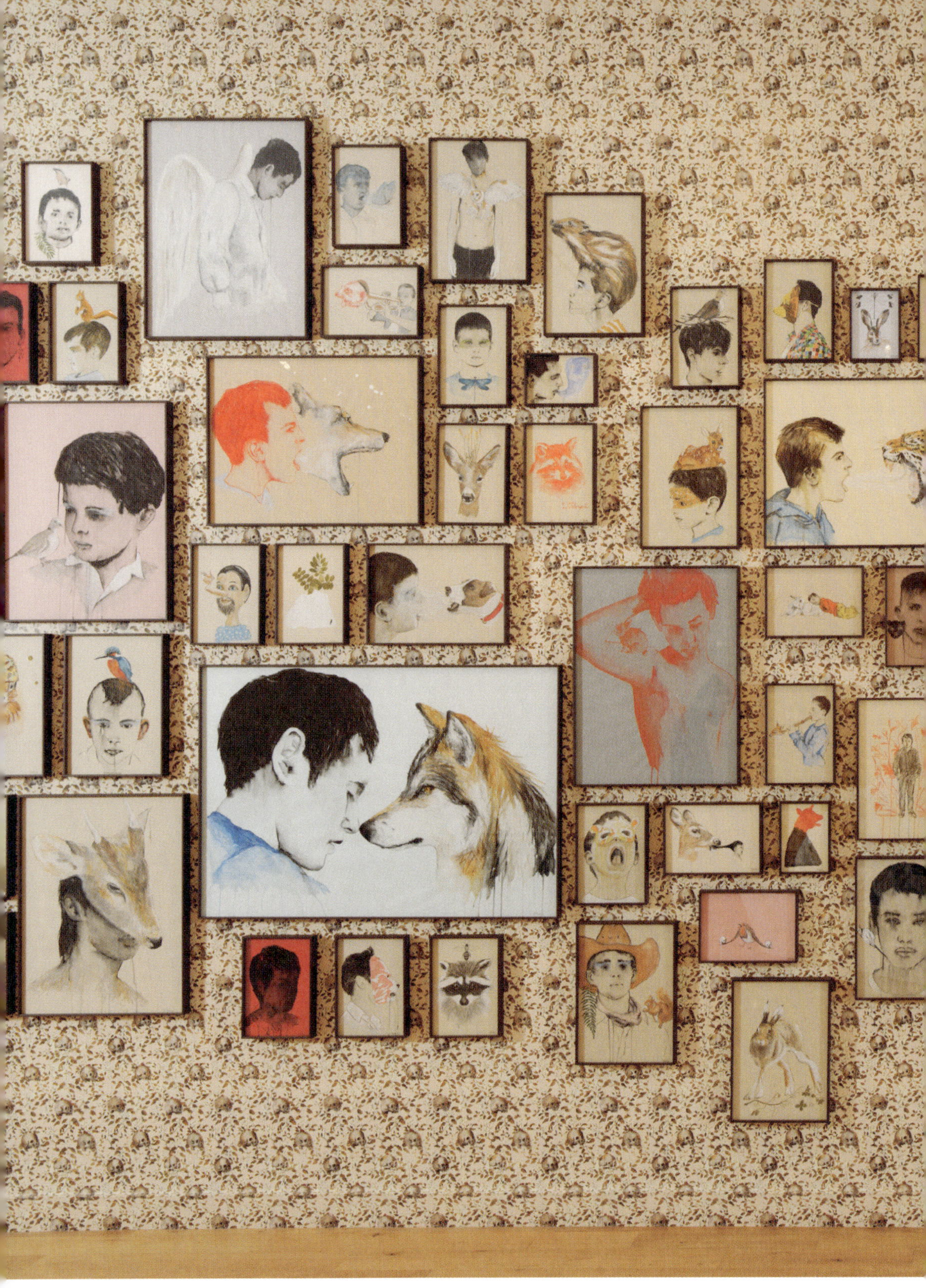

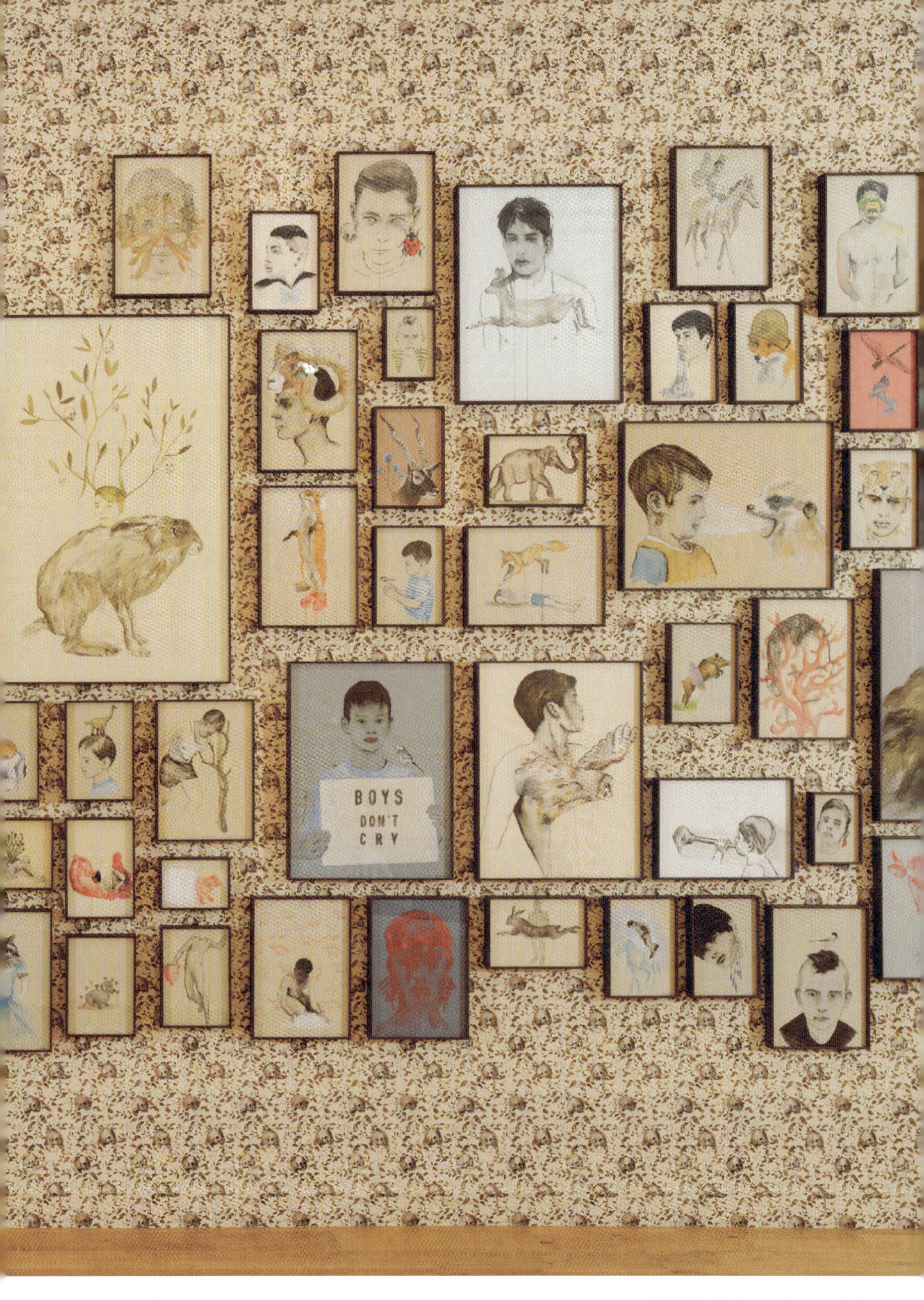

 Wall of drawings, 2024

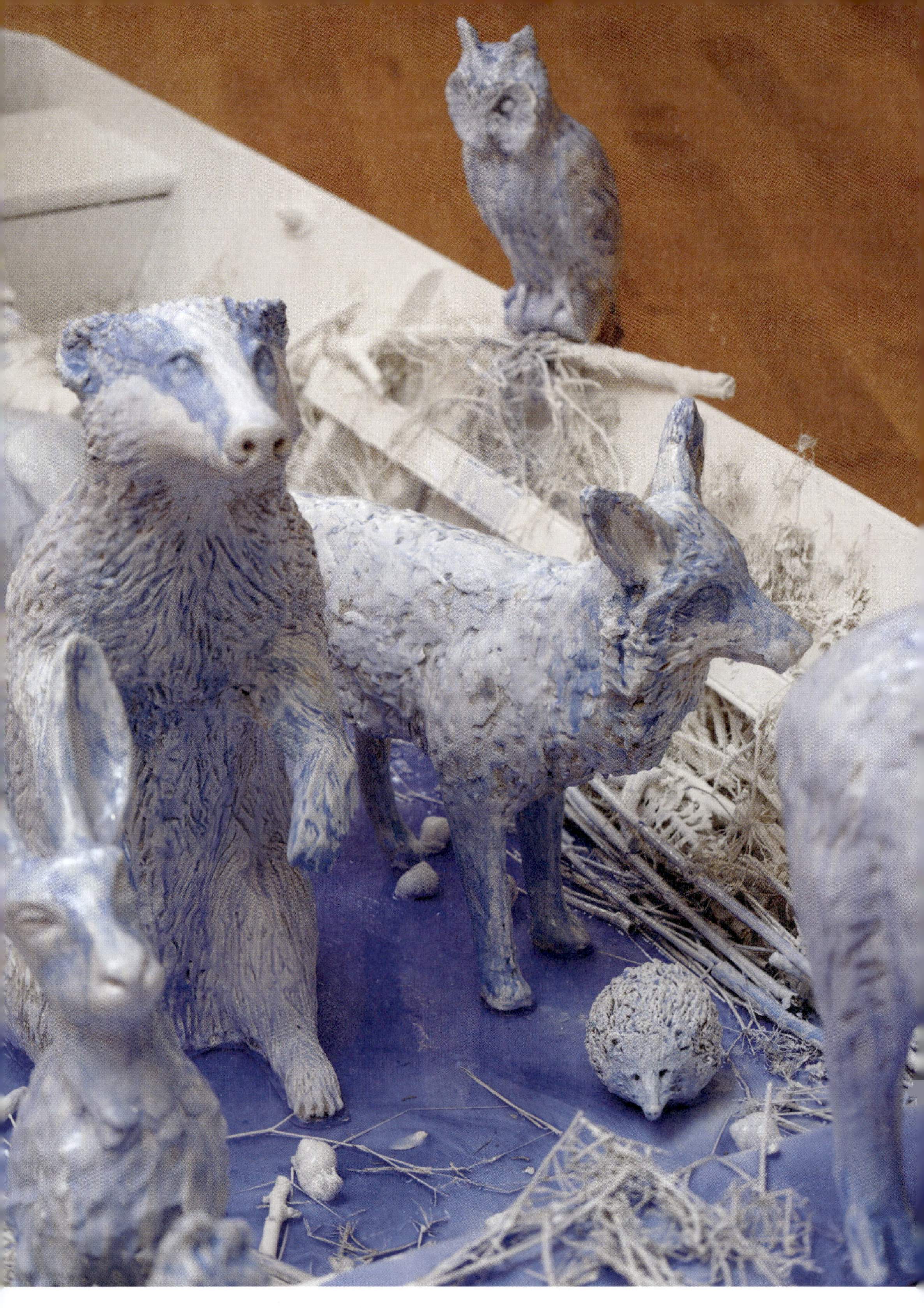

Protect others to protect yourself and *protect yourself* to protect others.

A consistent theme in the work of Edi Dubien is the idea of protection and repair. The animals portrayed often take on the appearance of protective totems or warriors, defending a vulnerable childhood. Young wild boar and badgers become helmets, while squirrels and ravens become epaulets, reinforcing the image of armor against a hostile world. These animal figures also appear as extensions of self, symbolizing a resilience that is embodied in the animal kingdom. Like a small voice on our shoulder, these animals and insects become a projection of the soul or aura, sometimes evoking the daemons of the saga *His Dark Materials* by Philip Pullman (1995-2000). Makeup and the accessories that adorn them are not limited to aesthetics as here embellishing also means strengthening.

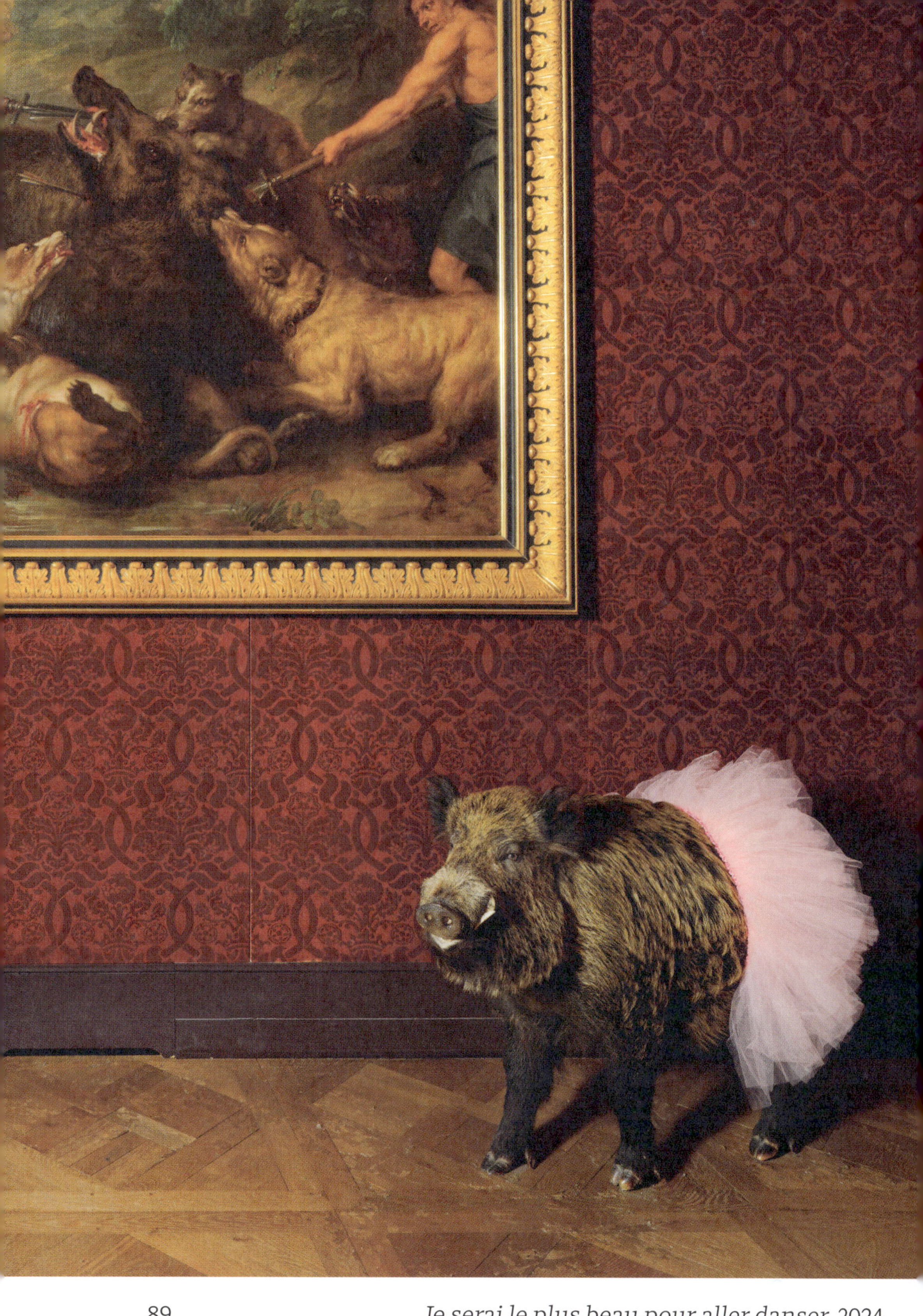

Je serai le plus beau pour aller danser, 2024

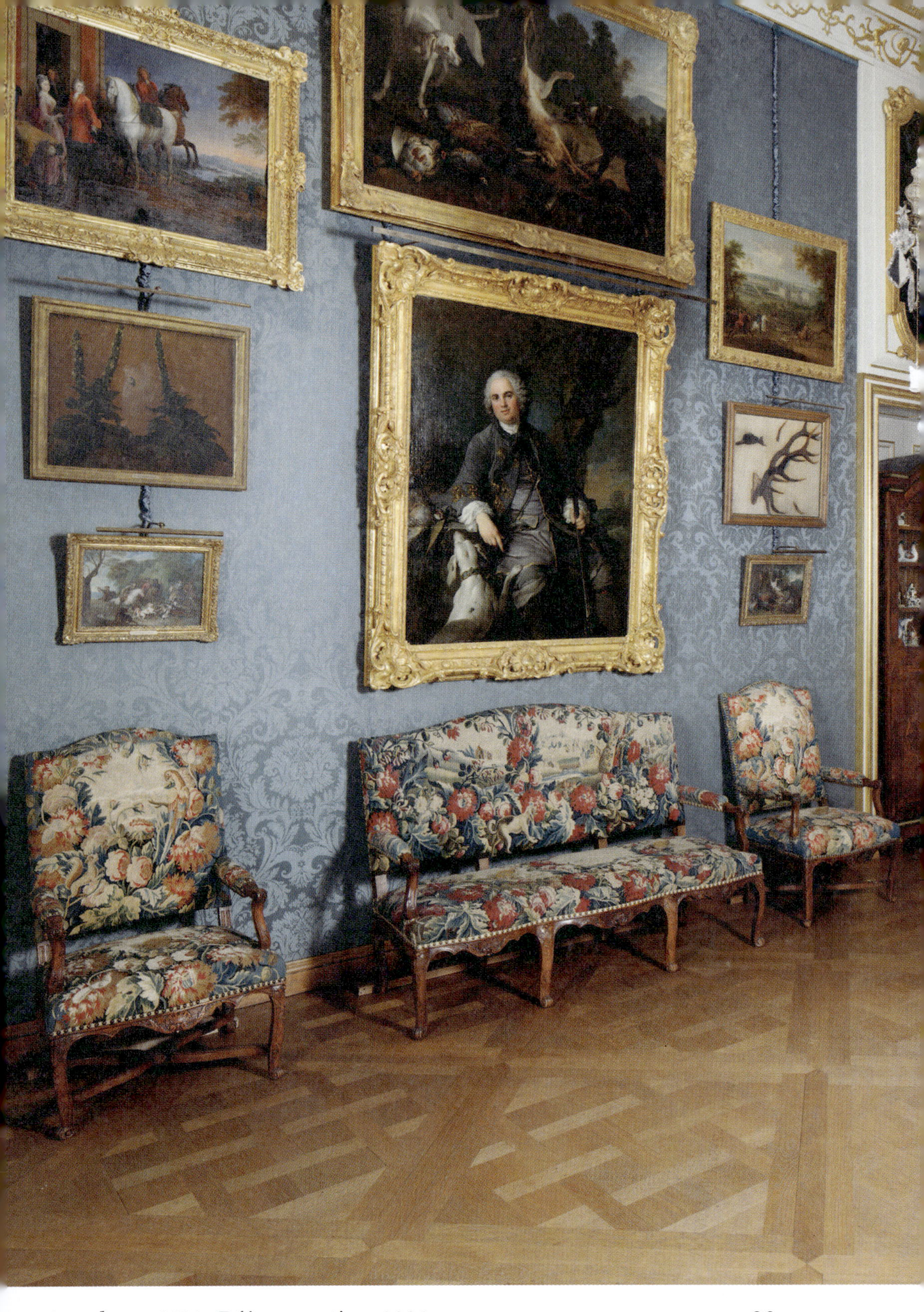

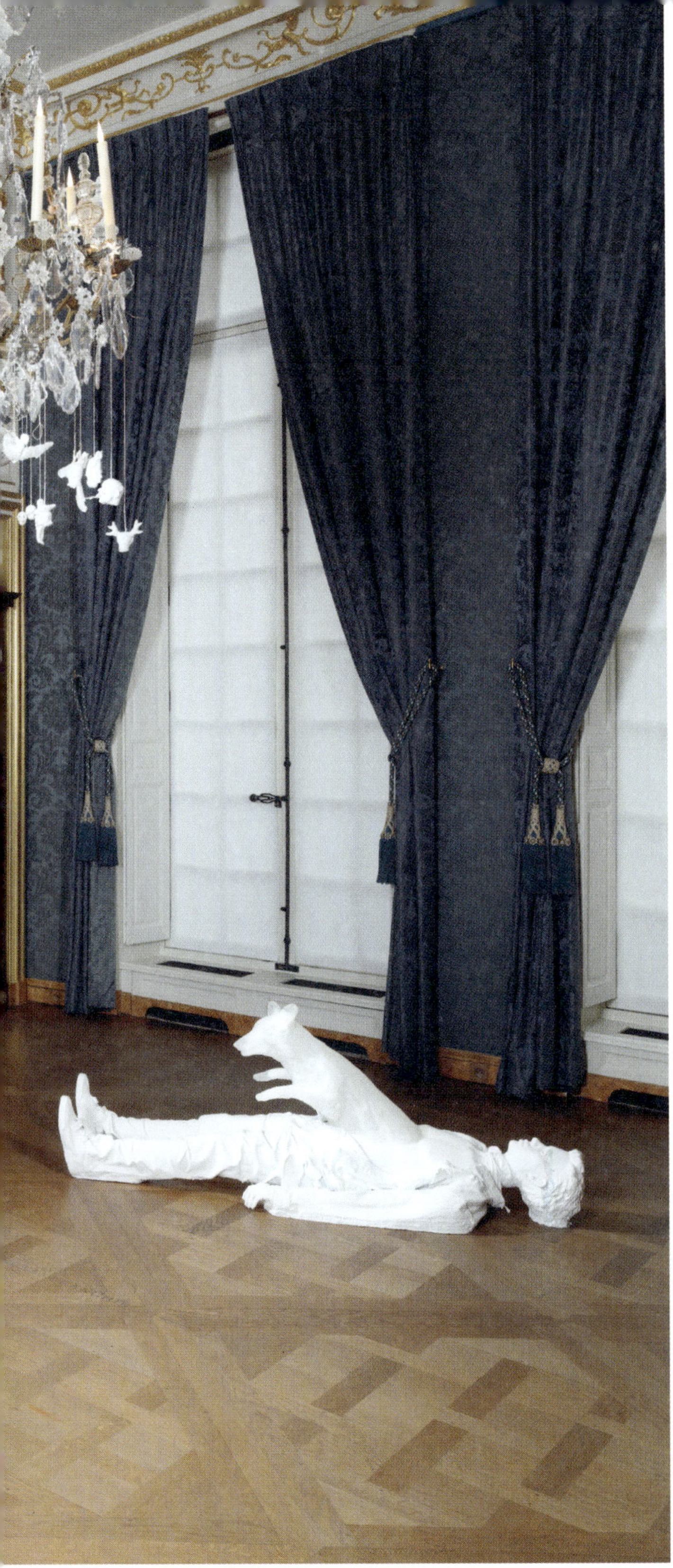

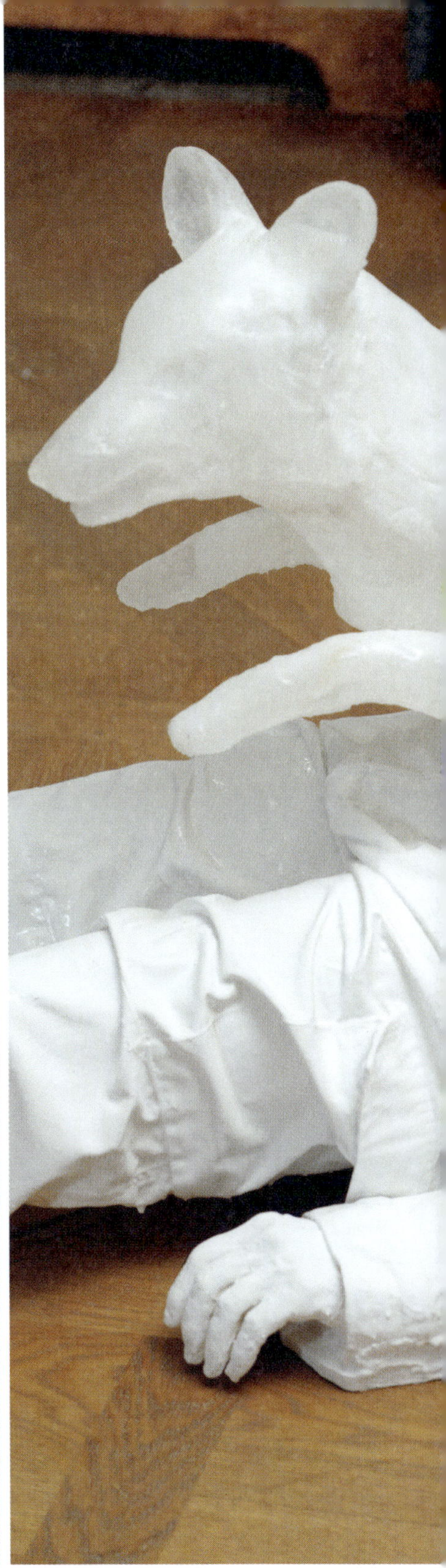

Réincarnation (detail), 2024

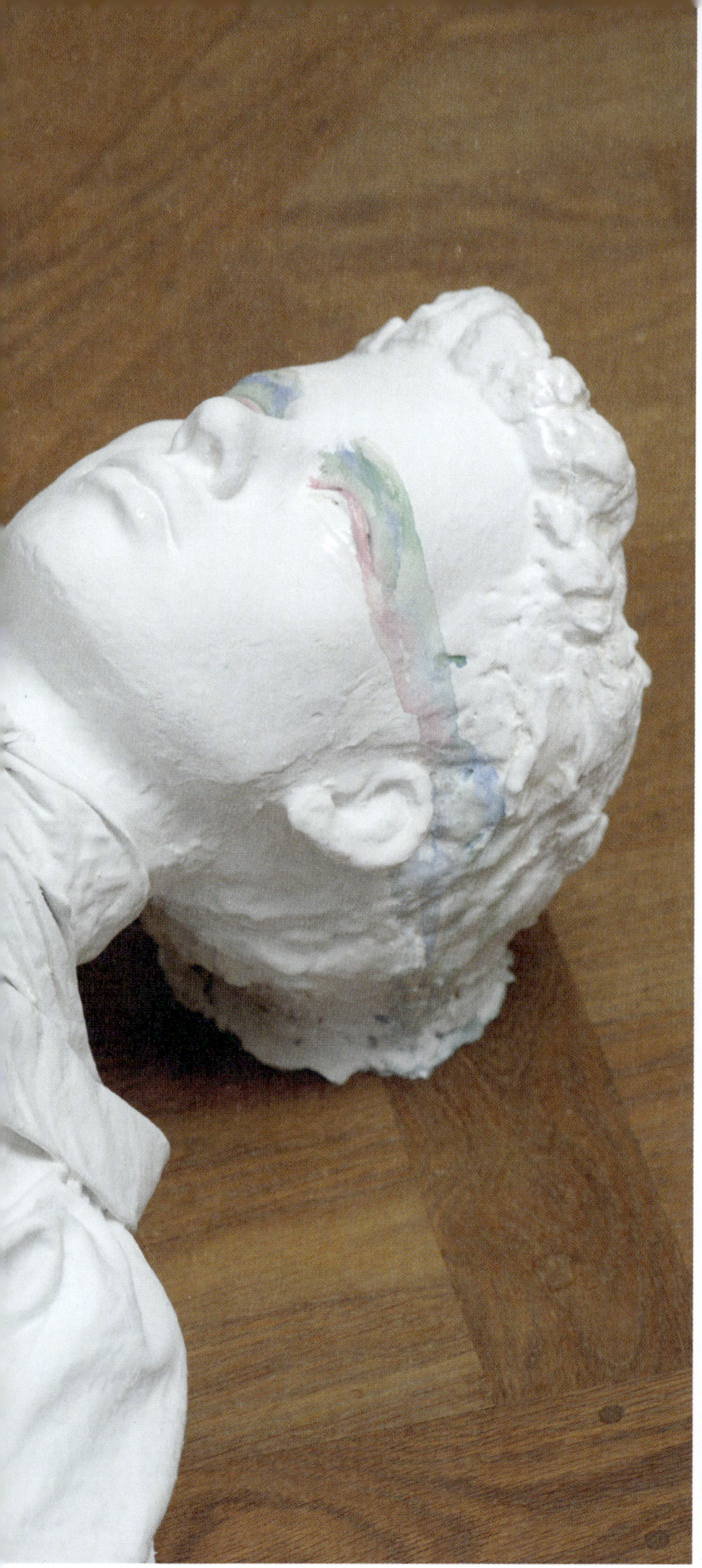
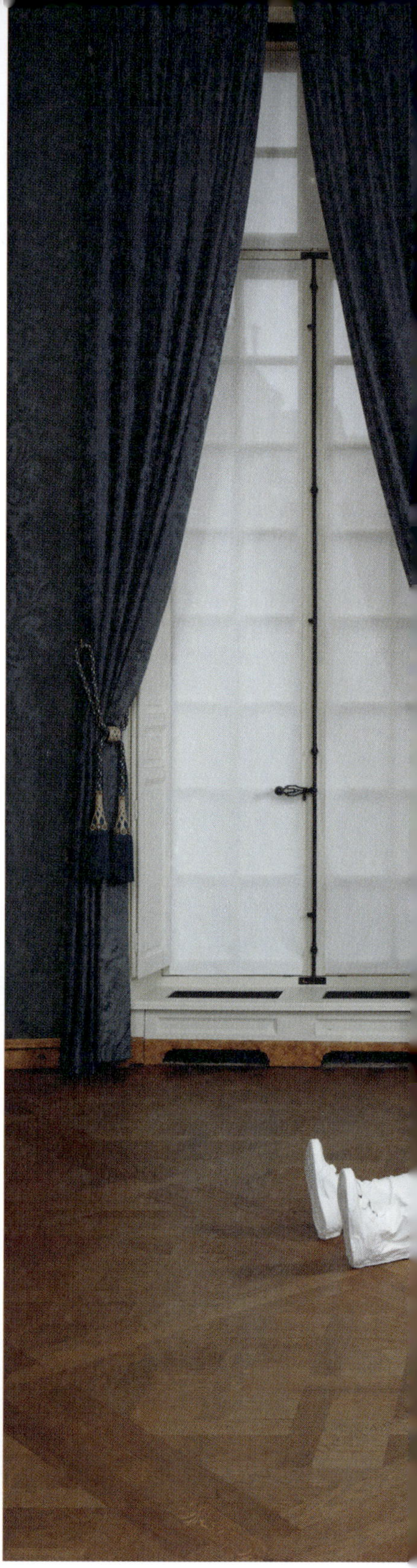

Réincarnation (detail), 2024

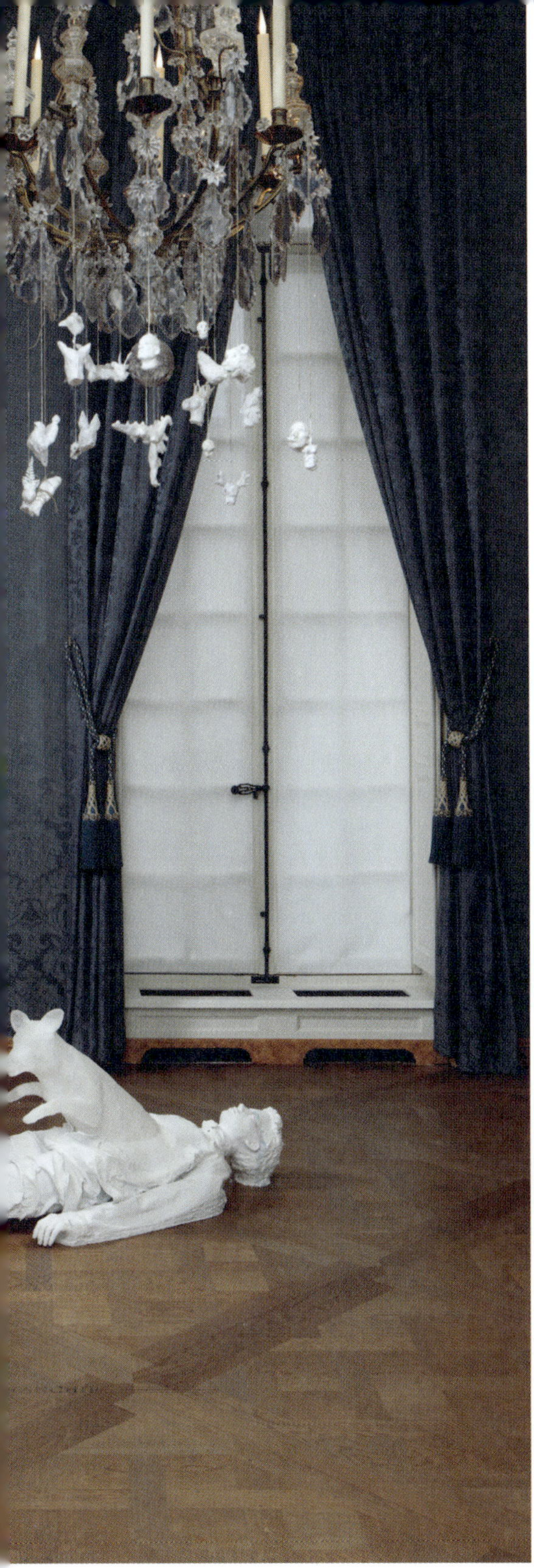

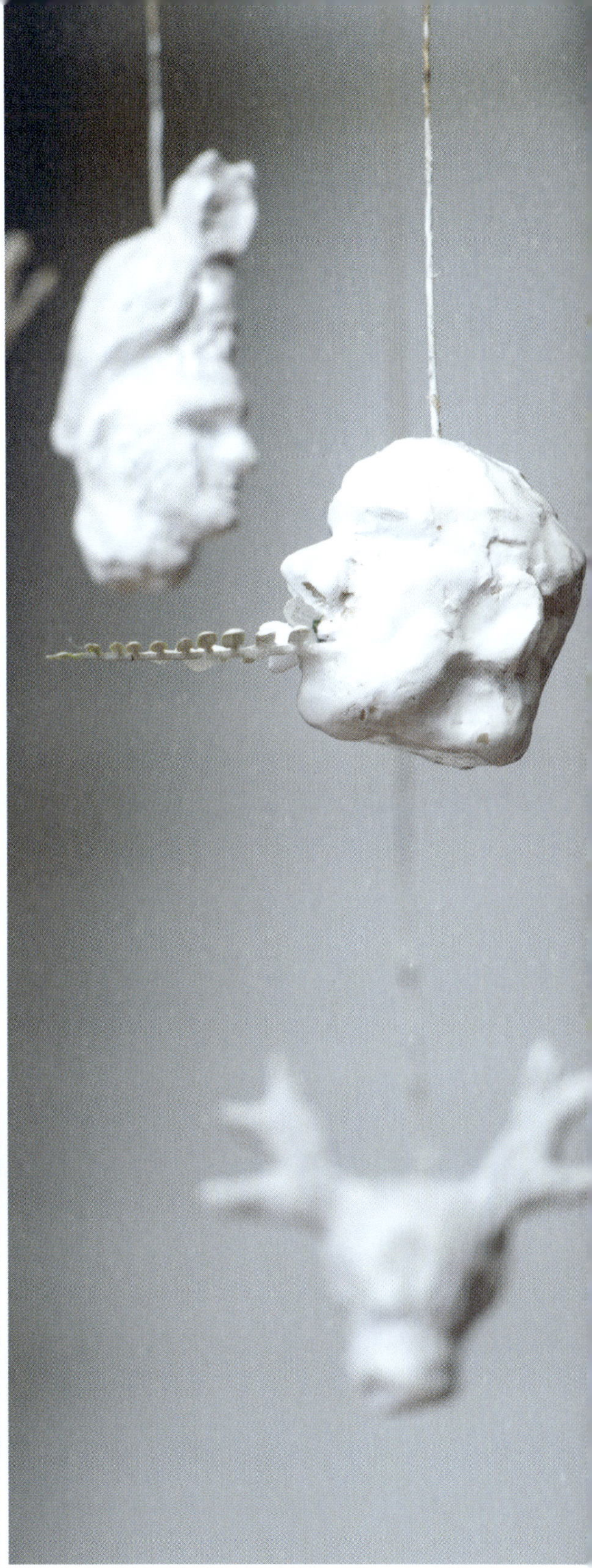

Amulette (detail), 2024

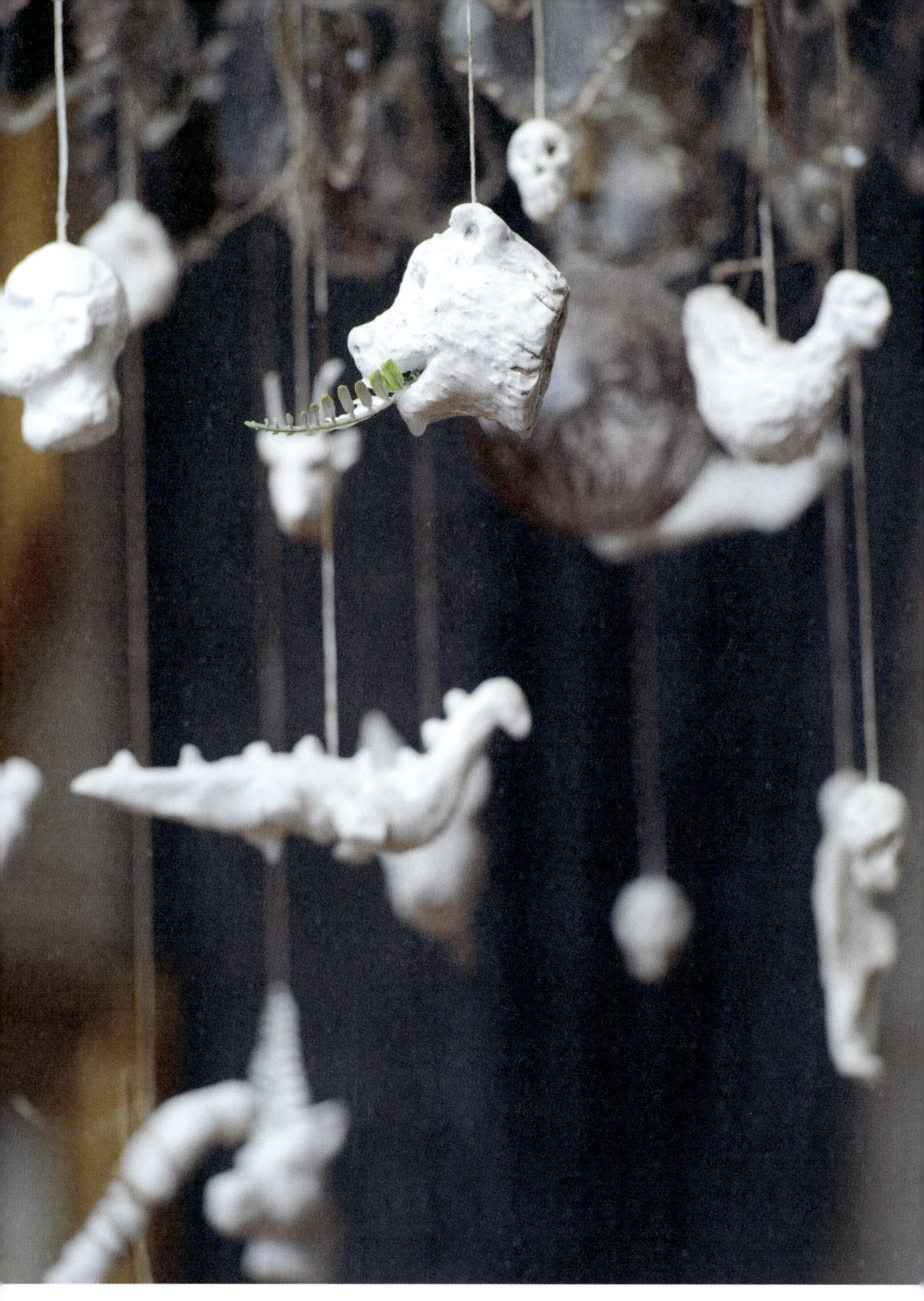

"**I give my hope** *my heart like an ex-voto*. **I give my hope** *the entire future* **that trembles like** *a small glimmer in the forest*". **Guillaume Apollinaire,** *Poèmes à Lou*, **1955**

Many of the recurring motifs in Edi Dubien's work have a deep and singular meaning. On wallpaper, for example, the skull does more than evoke death: it refers to vanity or the Christian ex-voto, symbolizing a spiritual or physical rebirth, like Edi's journey. It becomes a emblem of protection and hope. The ladybug, nicknamed in French "God's bug", regains its role as a good-luck charm as it straddles the skull, uniting two wishes in one. These ex-votos take on other forms and motifs, such as the tear, which transcends sadness to become a creative force, a bearer of renewal. The blue butterfly, the morpho, goes beyond the simple evocation of ordinary biodiversity to symbolize rarity and transformation. As in some Latin American traditions, it embodies the cycle of life, carrying a message of rebirth.

Edi Dubien reinvents these symbols to question our link with life and metamorphosis, inviting us to rediscover what is meaningful in our existence.

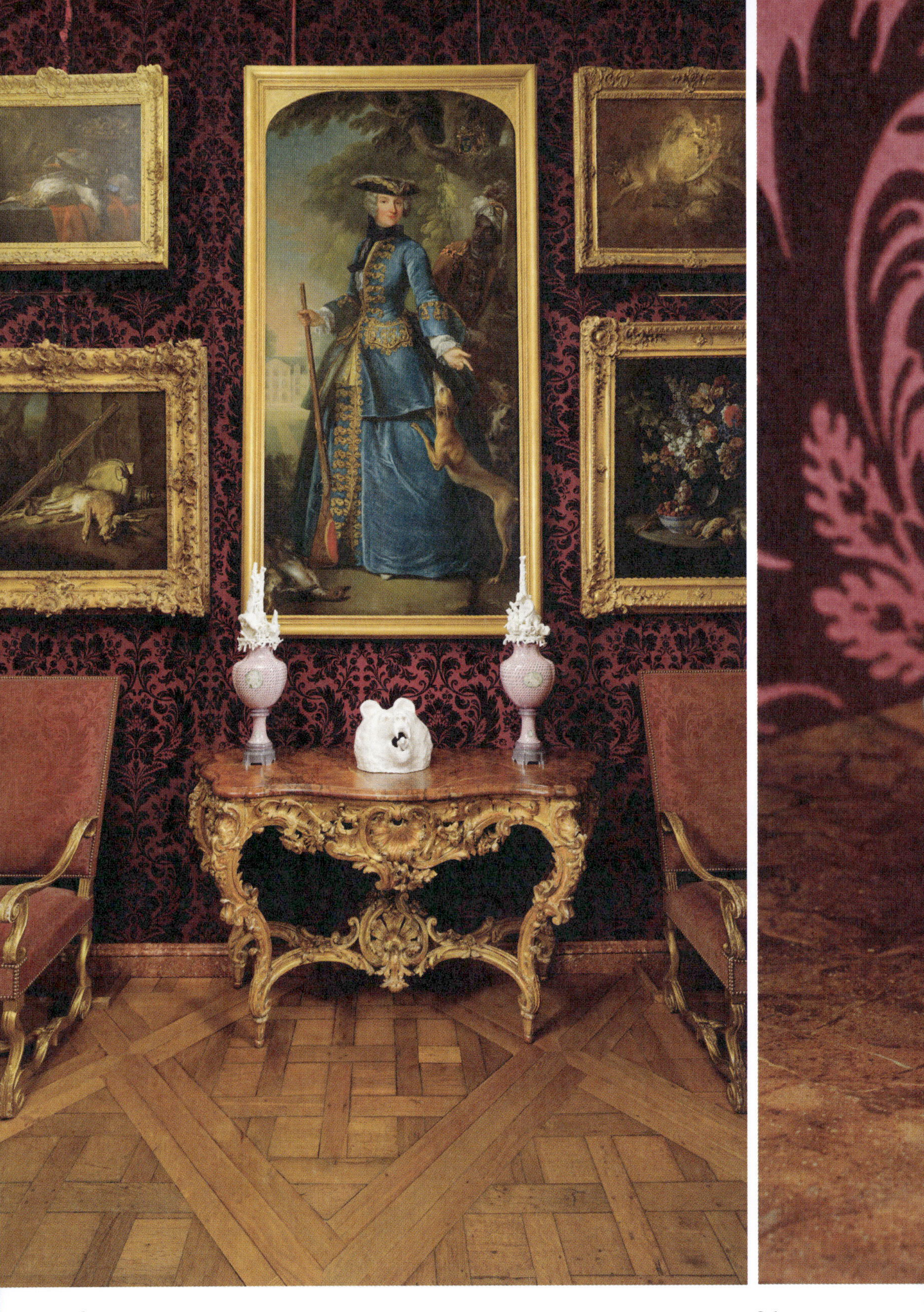

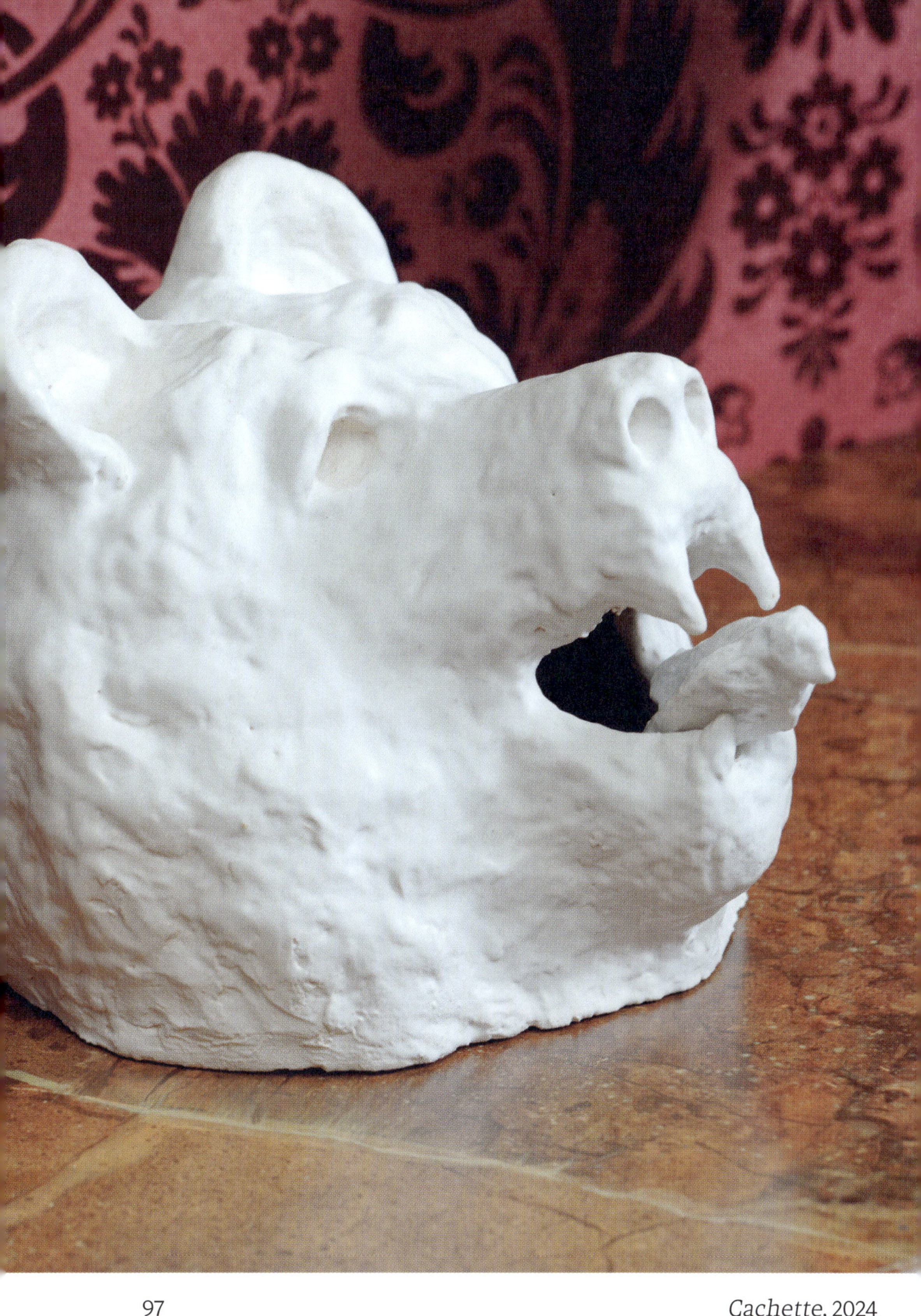

Cachette, 2024

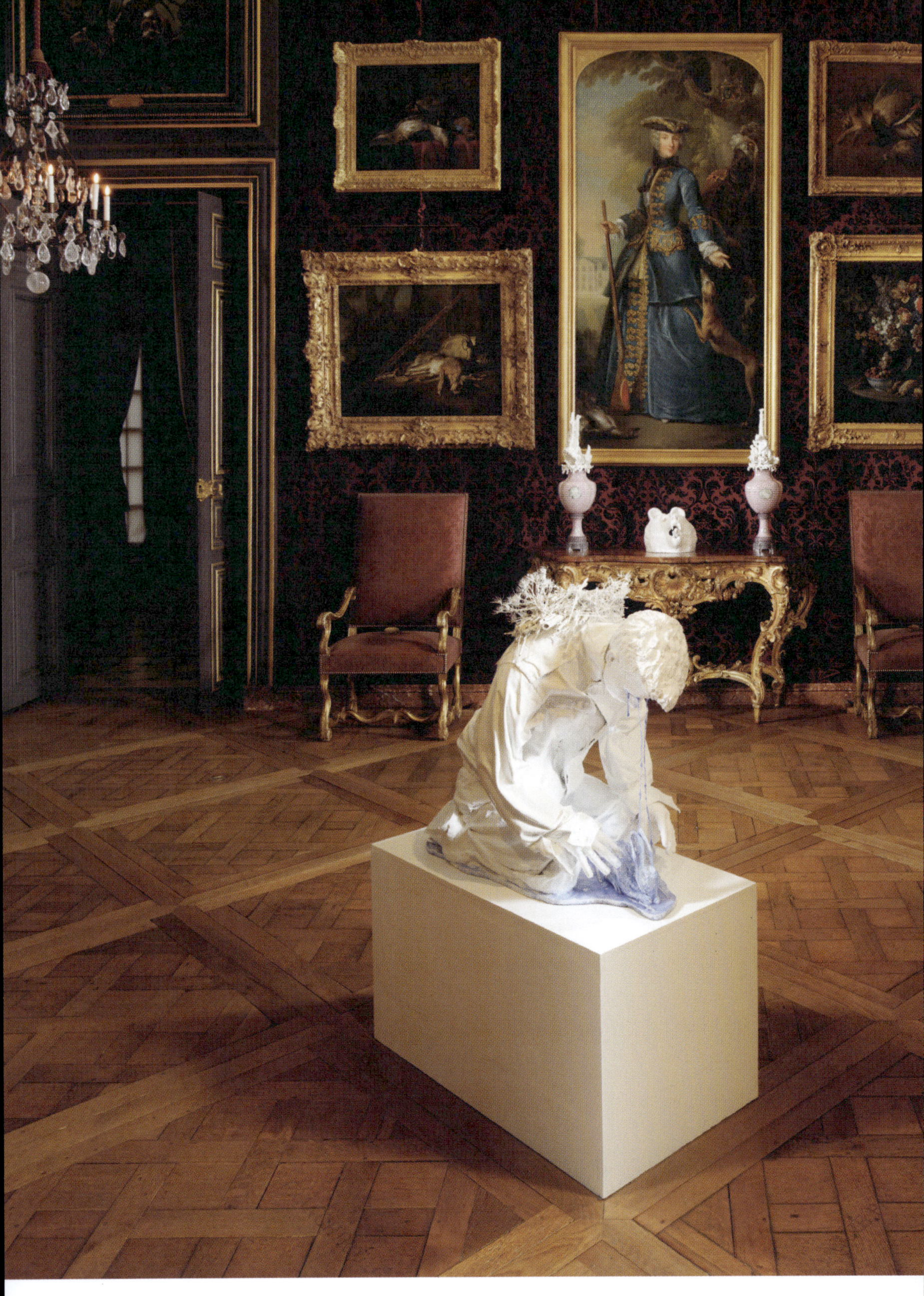

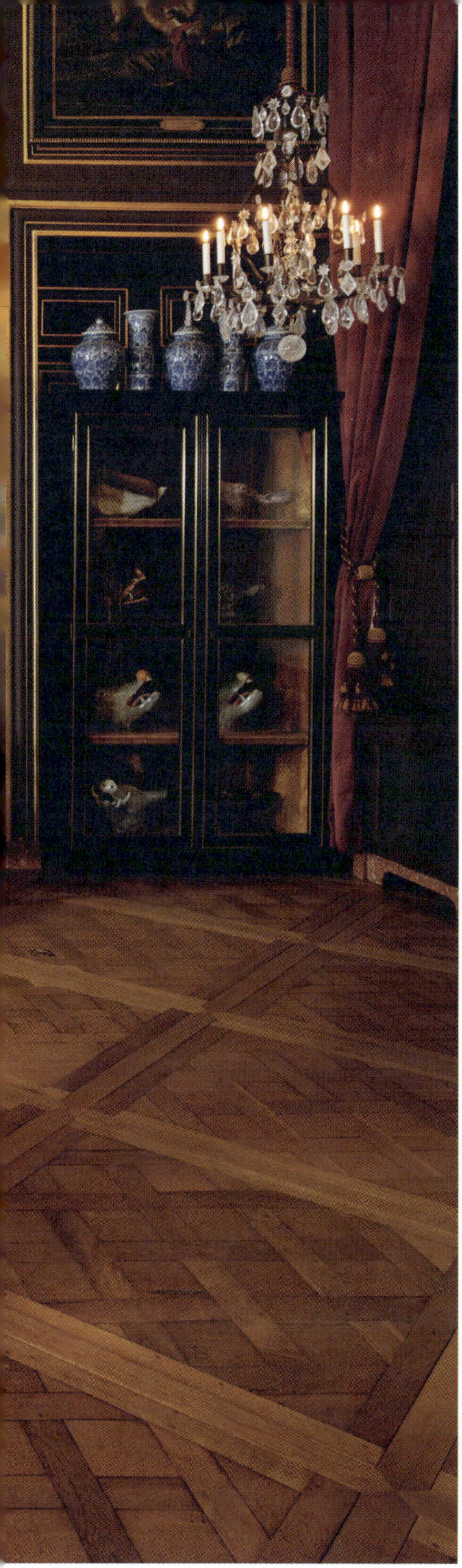

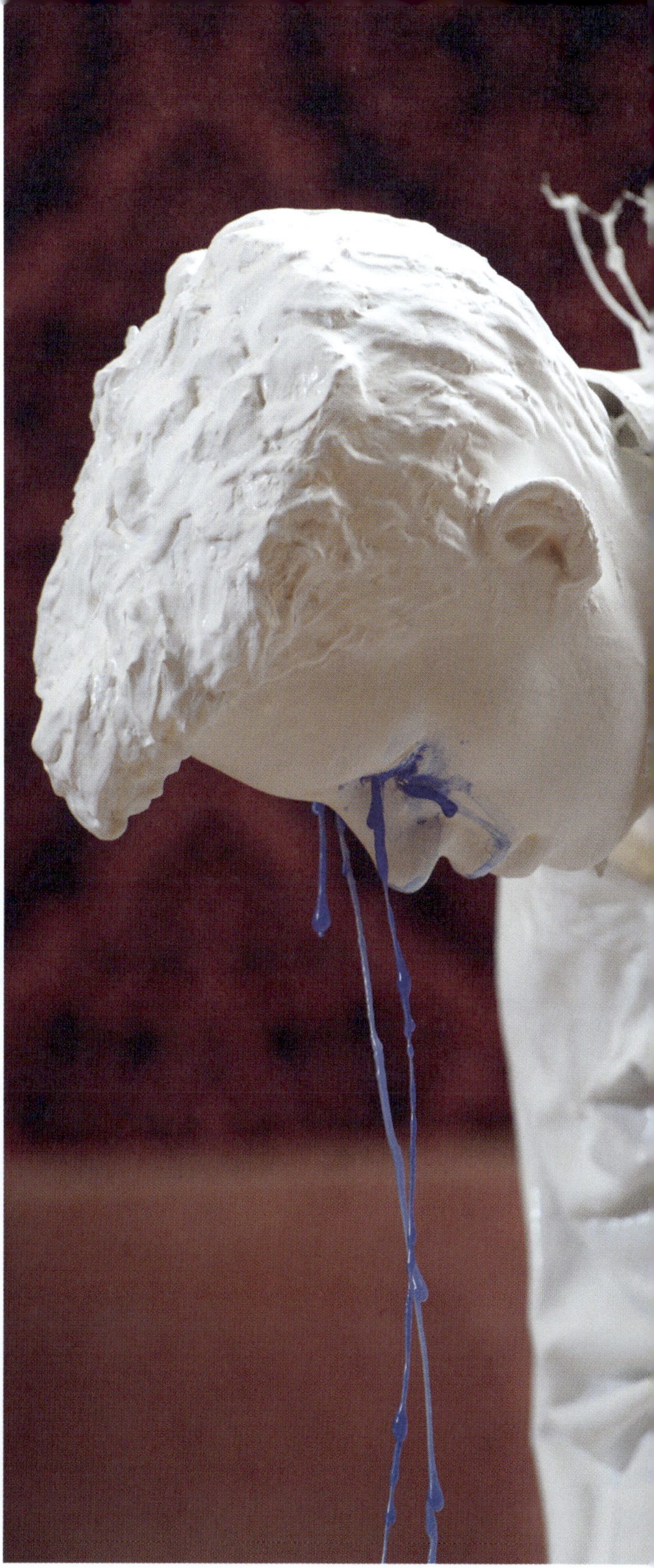

Pleurer des lapins (detail), 2024

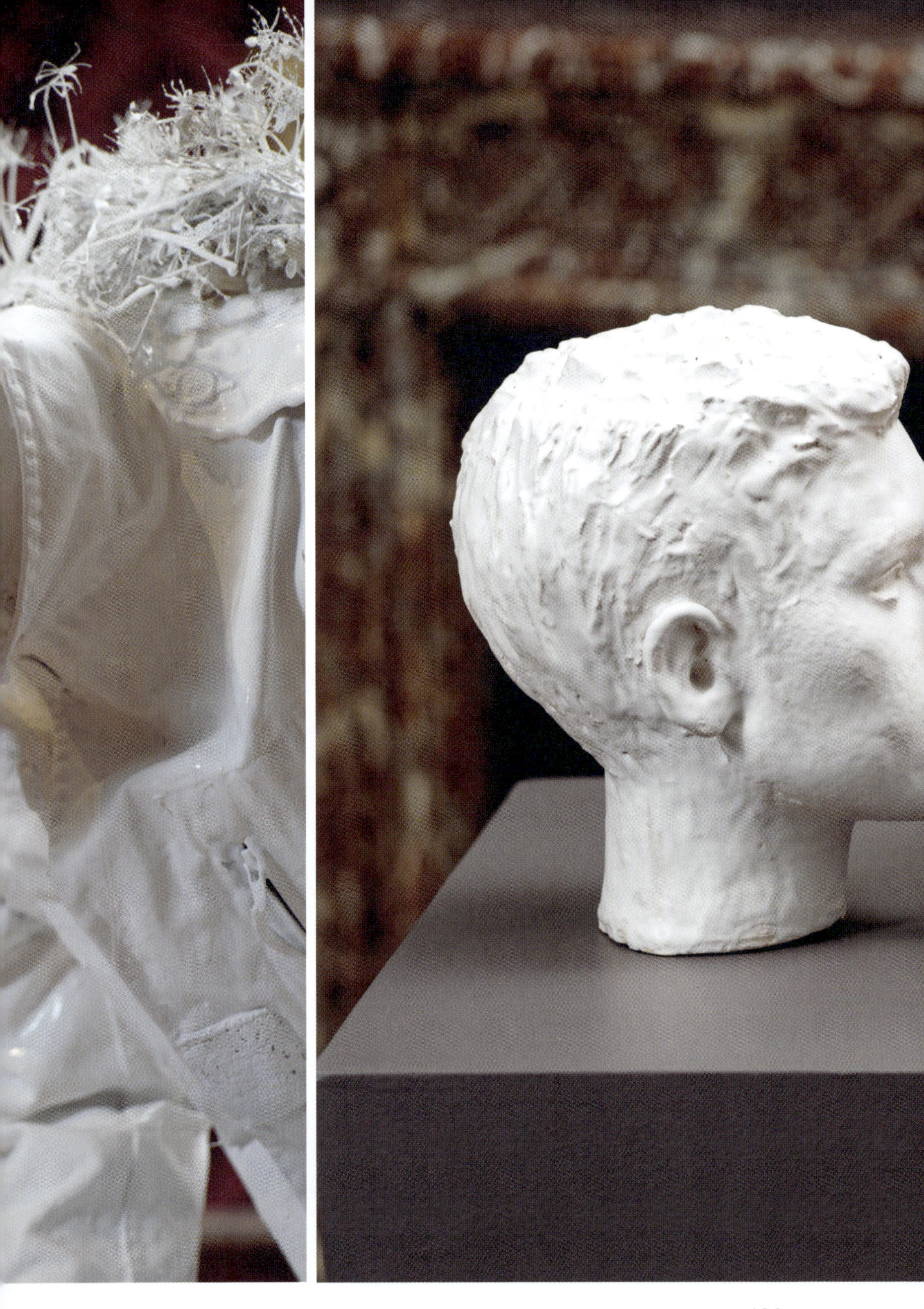

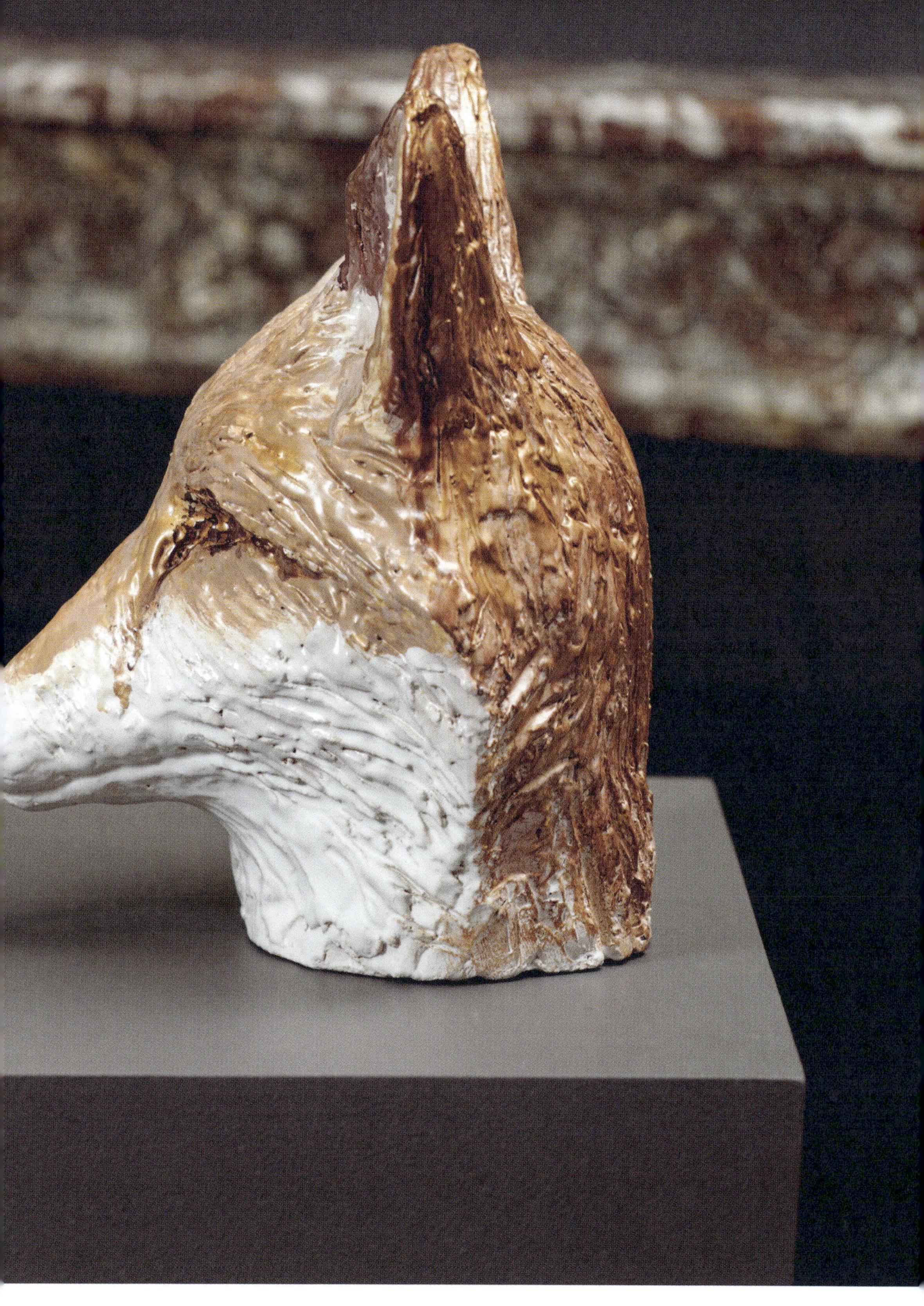

Romance 2, 2024

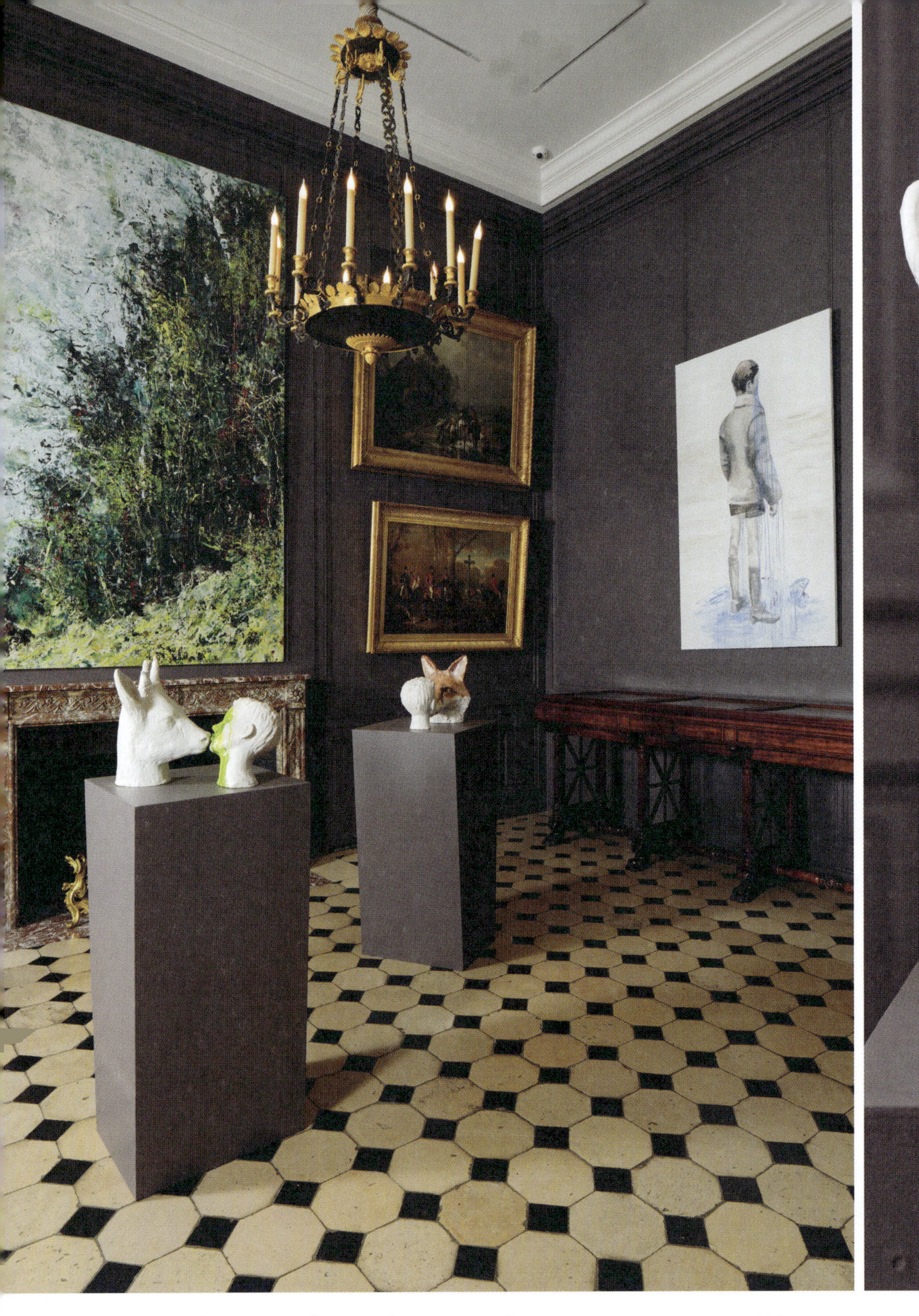

Romance 1 and 2, 2024 ; Pleurer des crapauds, 2024

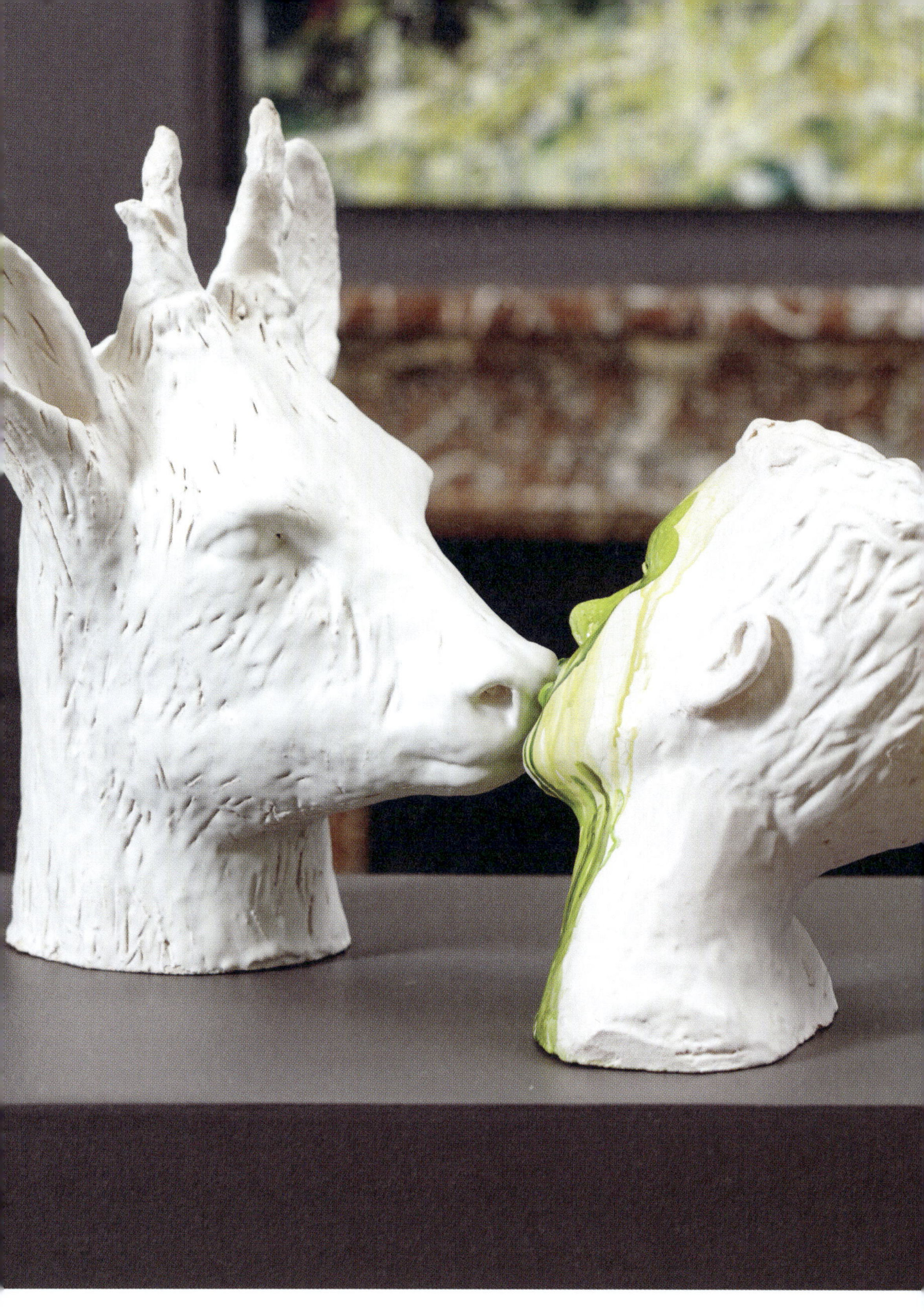

Romance 1, 2024

Edi Dubien's work at the Musée de la Chasse et de la Nature: *like an odyssey*.

Throughout the museum, the relationship between the untamed world and people is explored, sometimes chronologically: wild boar for Antiquity, stag and wolf for the Middle Ages, etc. The museum visit is also likened to an initiatory journey through a forest. This idea is echoed in the pieces by Edi Dubien: the more we progress, the more we discover and learn. As in fairy tales, when Little Red Riding Hood enters the forest, she undergoes a transformation marked by her encounter with the wolf. The myth of Actaeon also illustrates this metamorphosis when after surprising Artemis, he is turned into a stag and hunted by his own dogs. These stories reflect a journey from which we never return unchanged, like a boat that carries its passengers towards a point of no return.

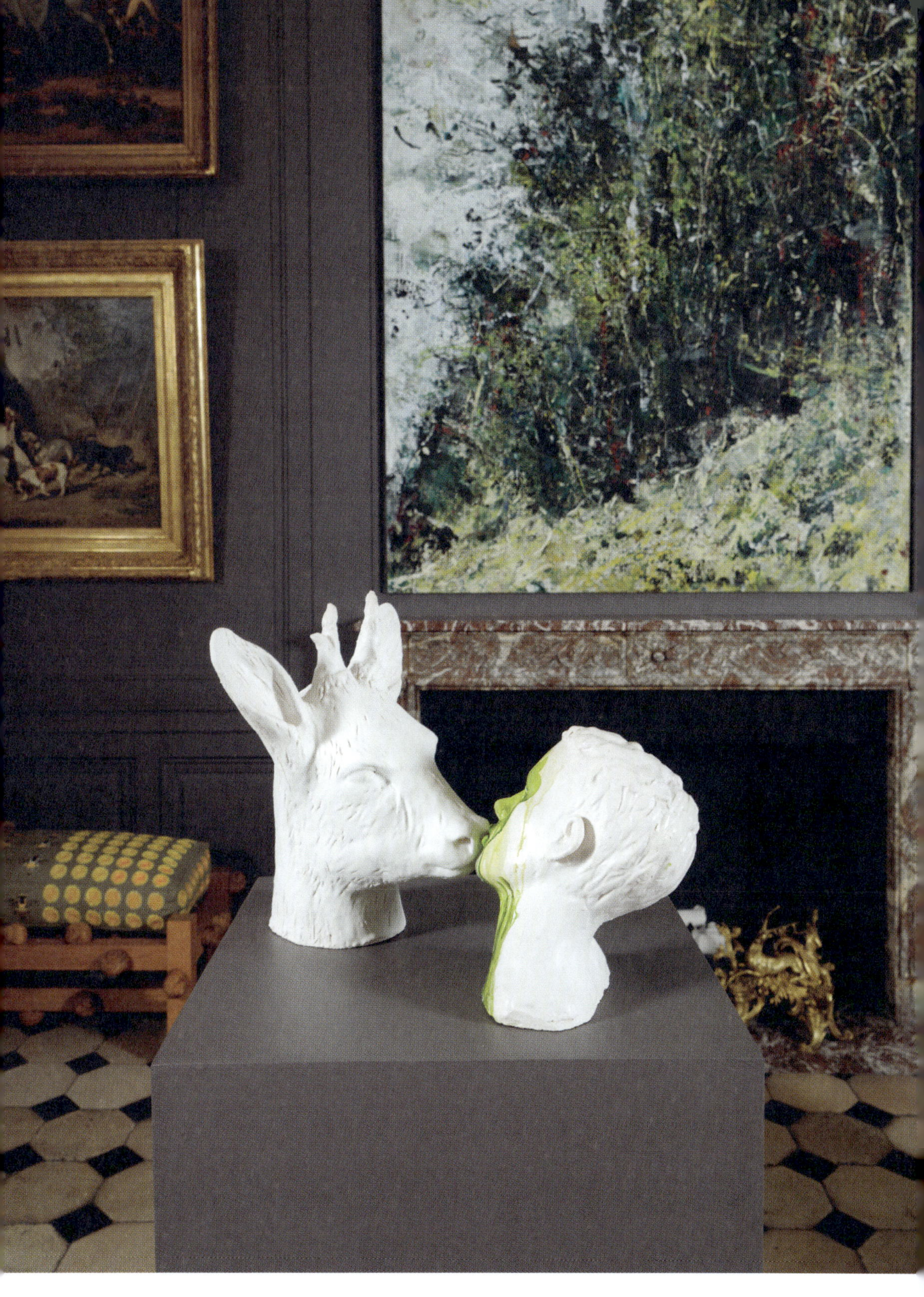

Romance 1, 2024

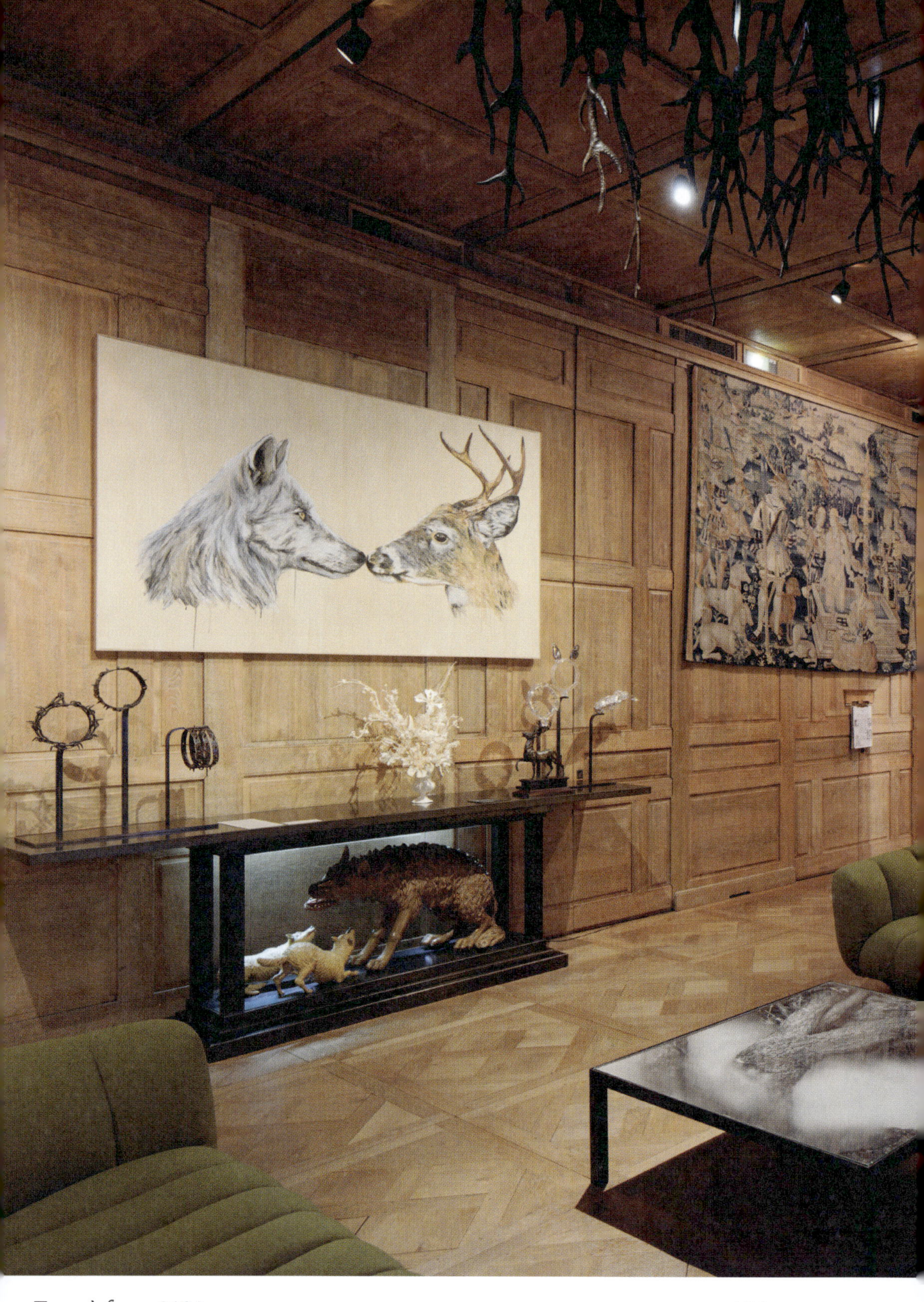

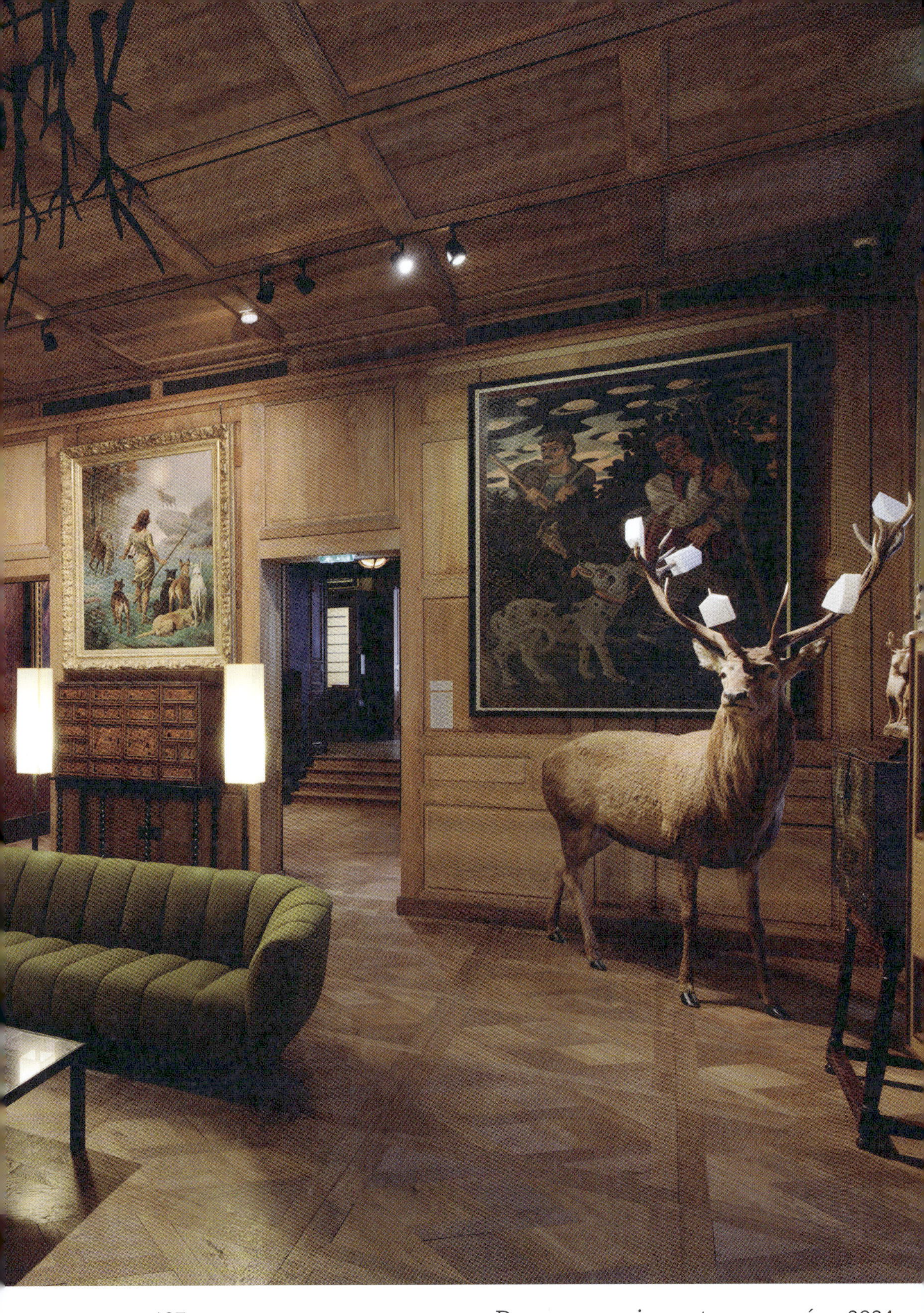

Dans nos maisons transpercées, 2024

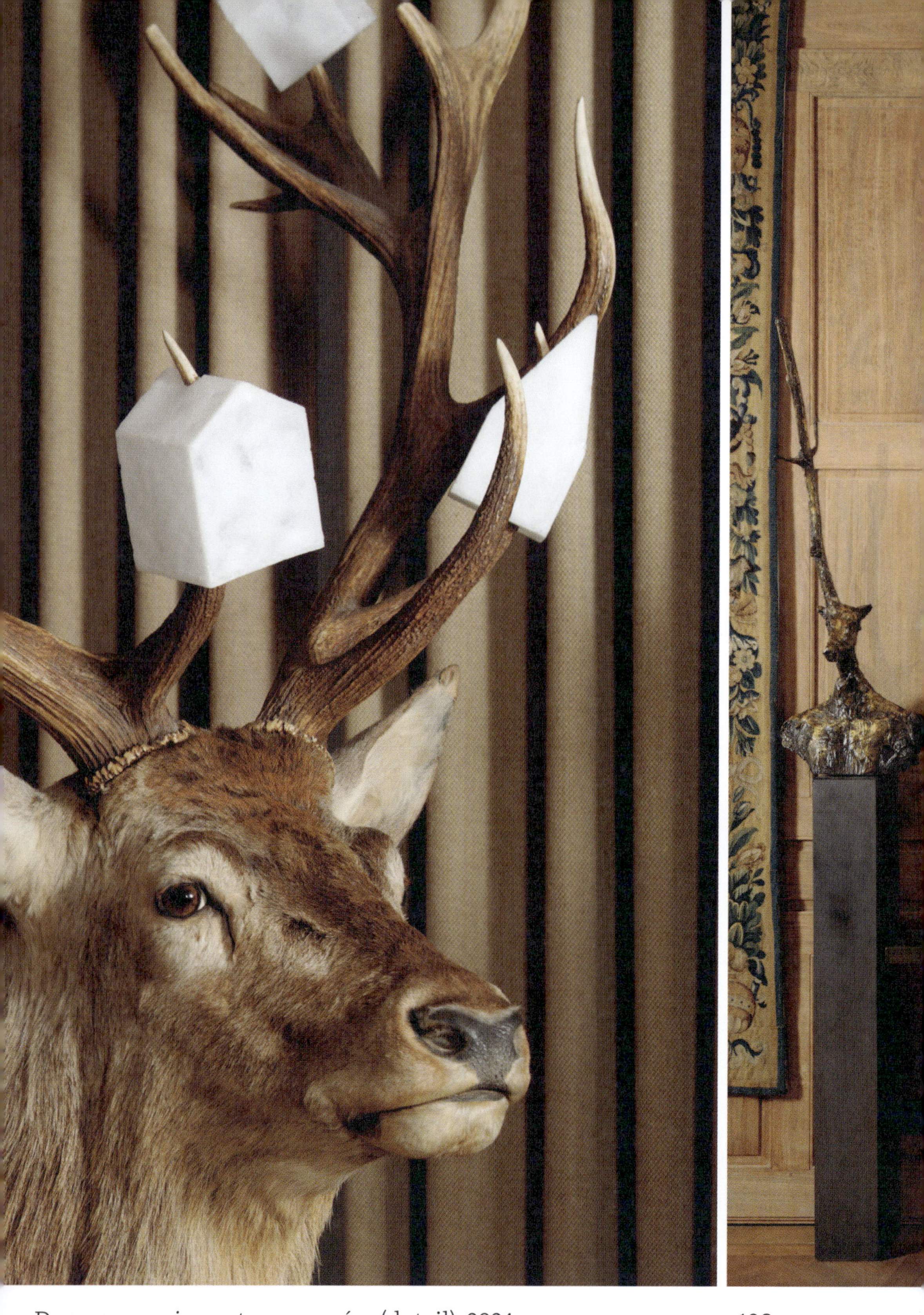

Dans nos maisons transpercées (detail), 2024

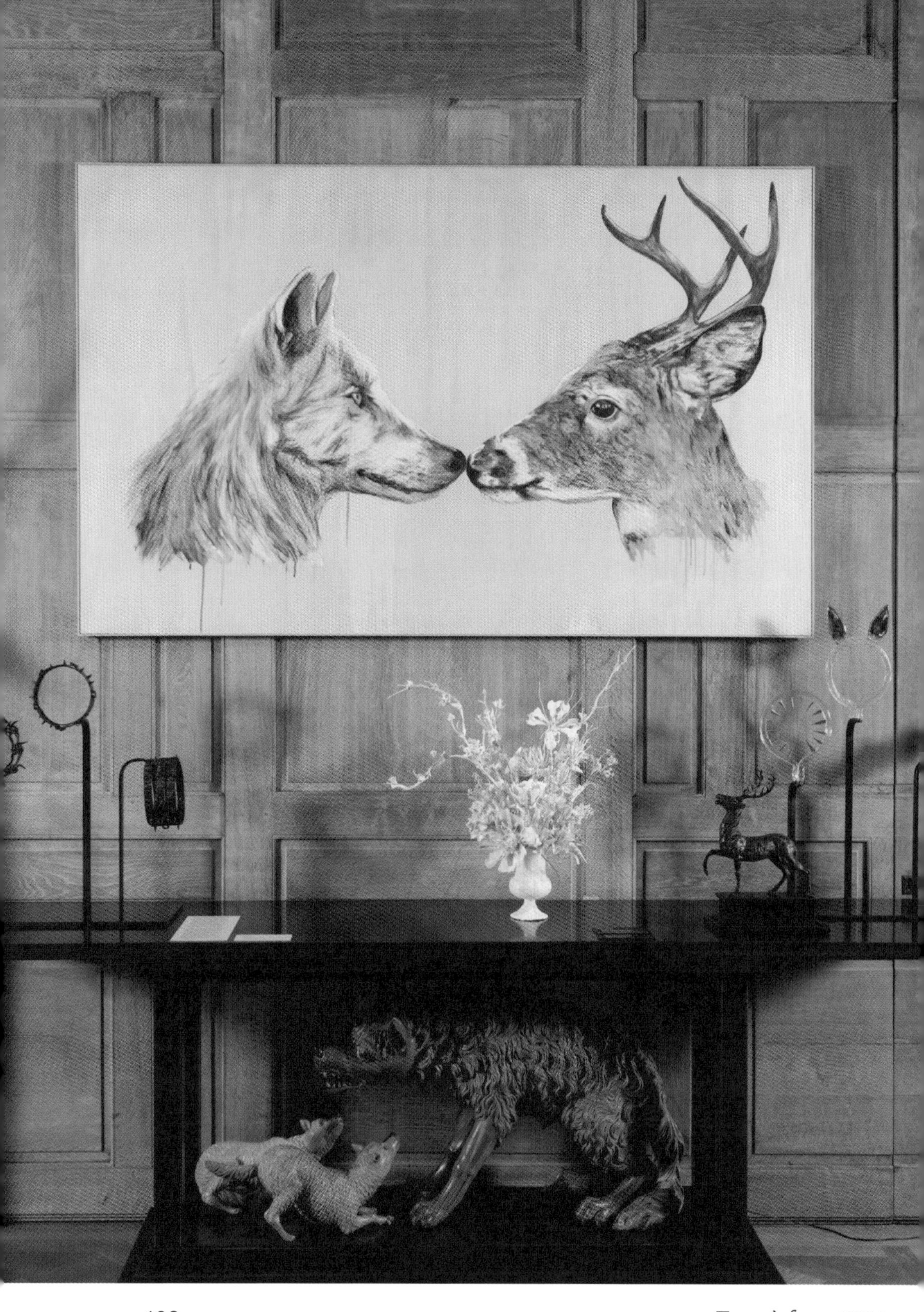

Face à face, 2024

Between Human
and Animal:
Redefining Identities

The deep connection with flora and fauna, present
in Edi Dubien's life and in his drawings, highlights
animosities that are deeply rooted in our society,
such as depictions of masculinity and femininity,
and the question of gender assignment and identity.
In Europe, for example, aesthetics and gentleness are
often associated with femininity, while strength and
competition are associated with masculinity. This fusion
sometimes gives rise to rebirth, as in the sculpture of the
same name, where a young man is transformed into a fox.
These tender, gentle encounters question our relationship
with others, with animals and with humans. A (hu)man
can be gentle, virile, tender, strong, but above all kind.

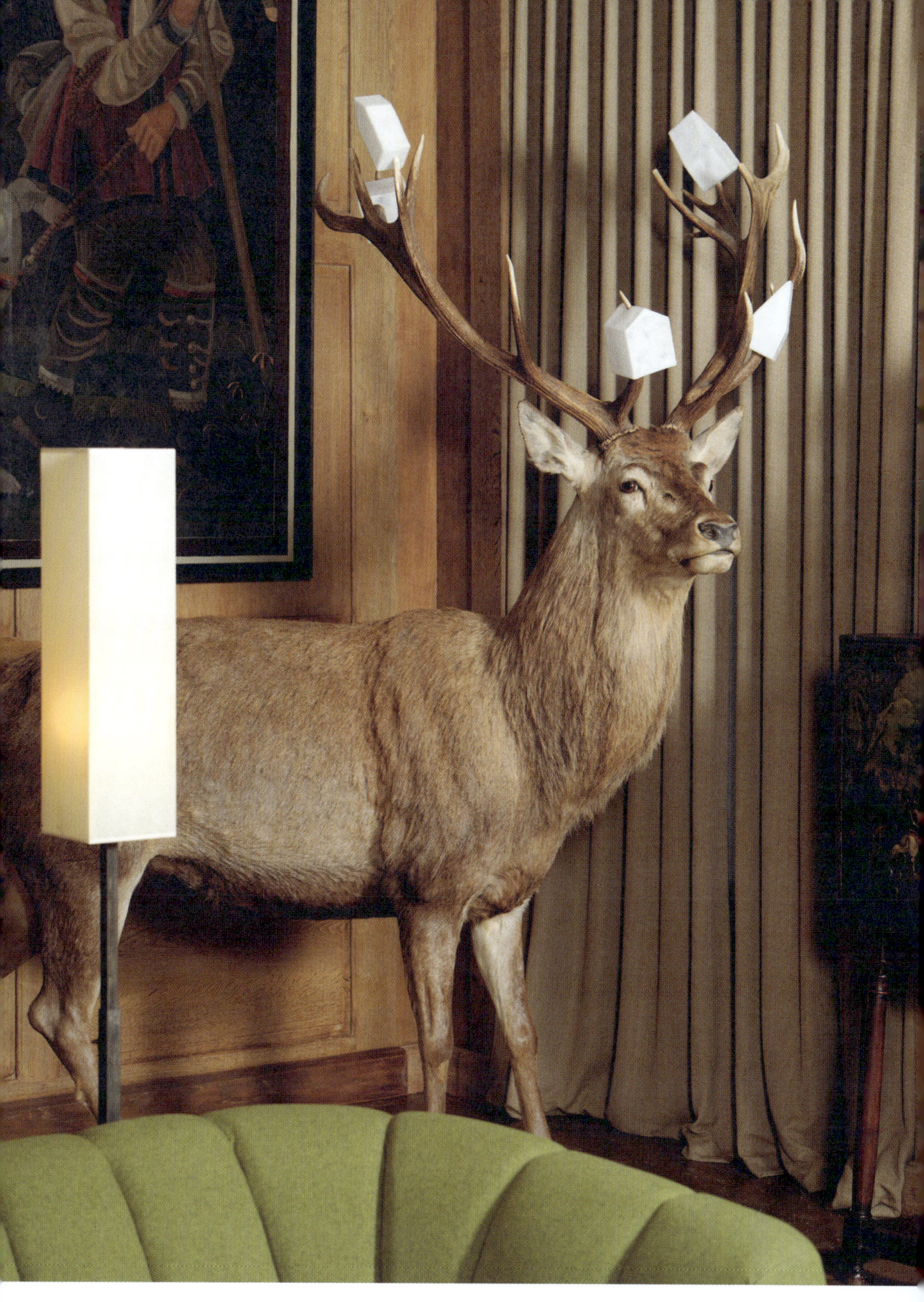

Dans nos maisons transpercées, 2024

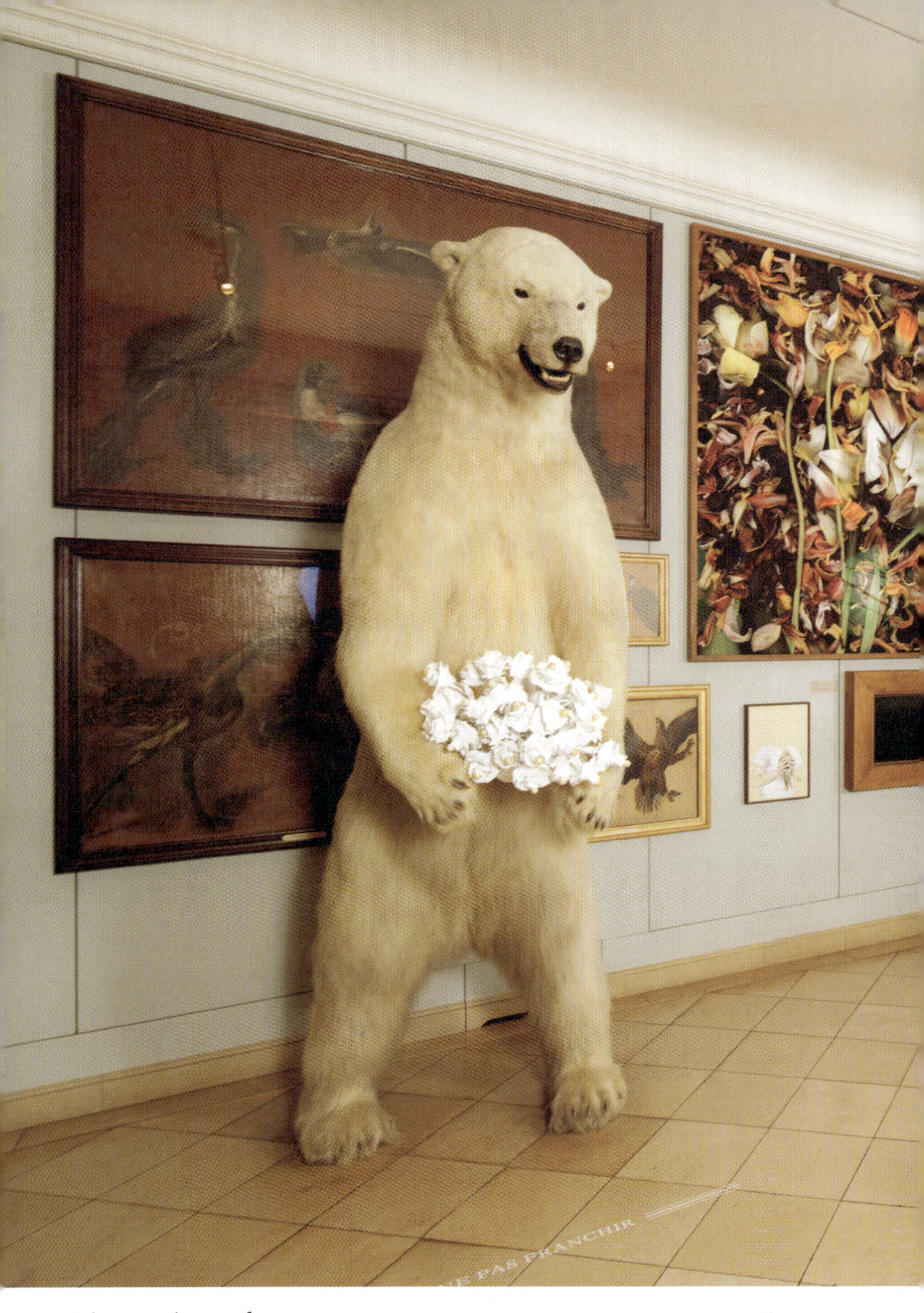

Je t'aime moi non plus, 2024

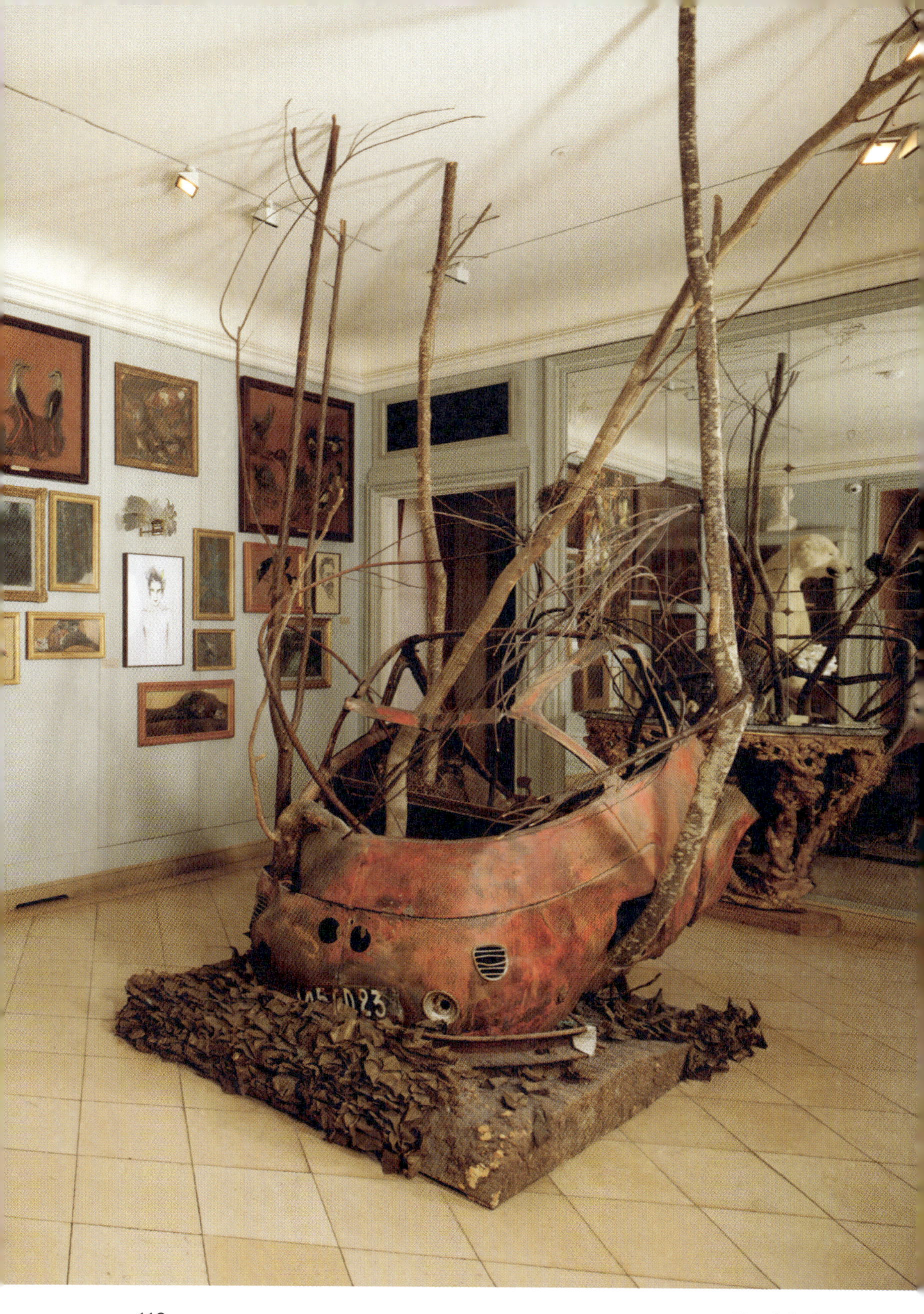

Untitled, 2024

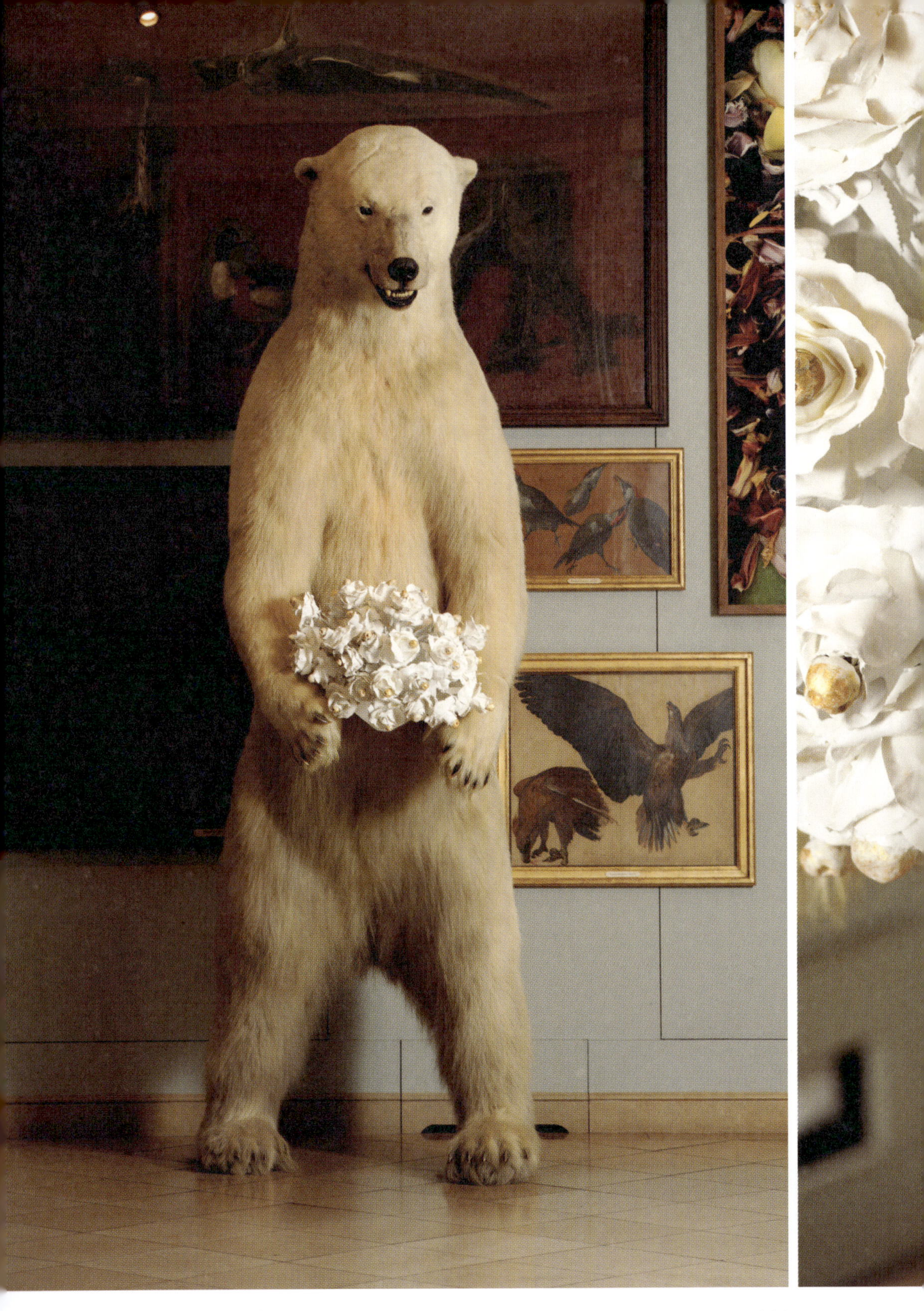

Je t'aime moi non plus, 2024

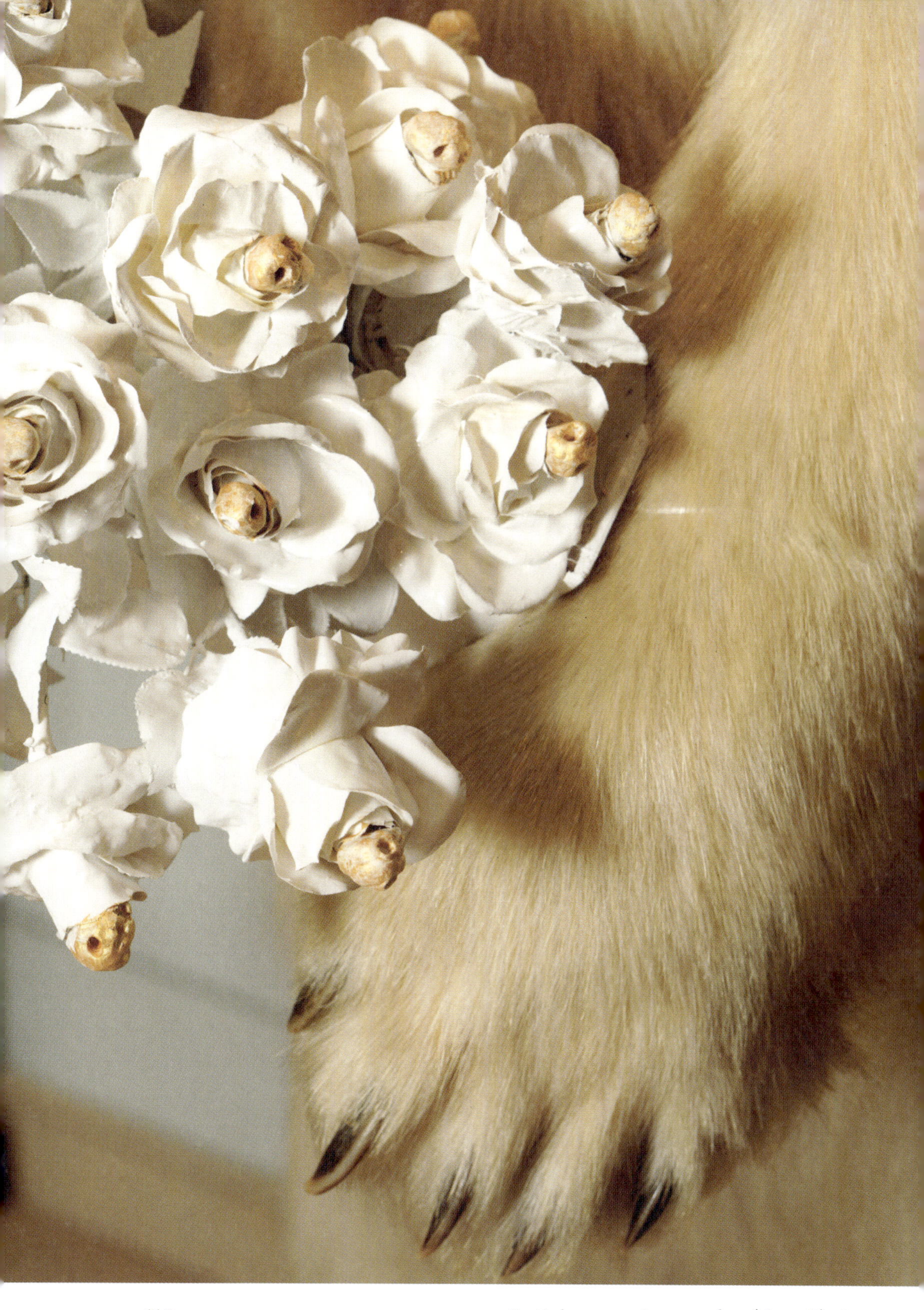

Je t'aime moi non plus (detail), 2024

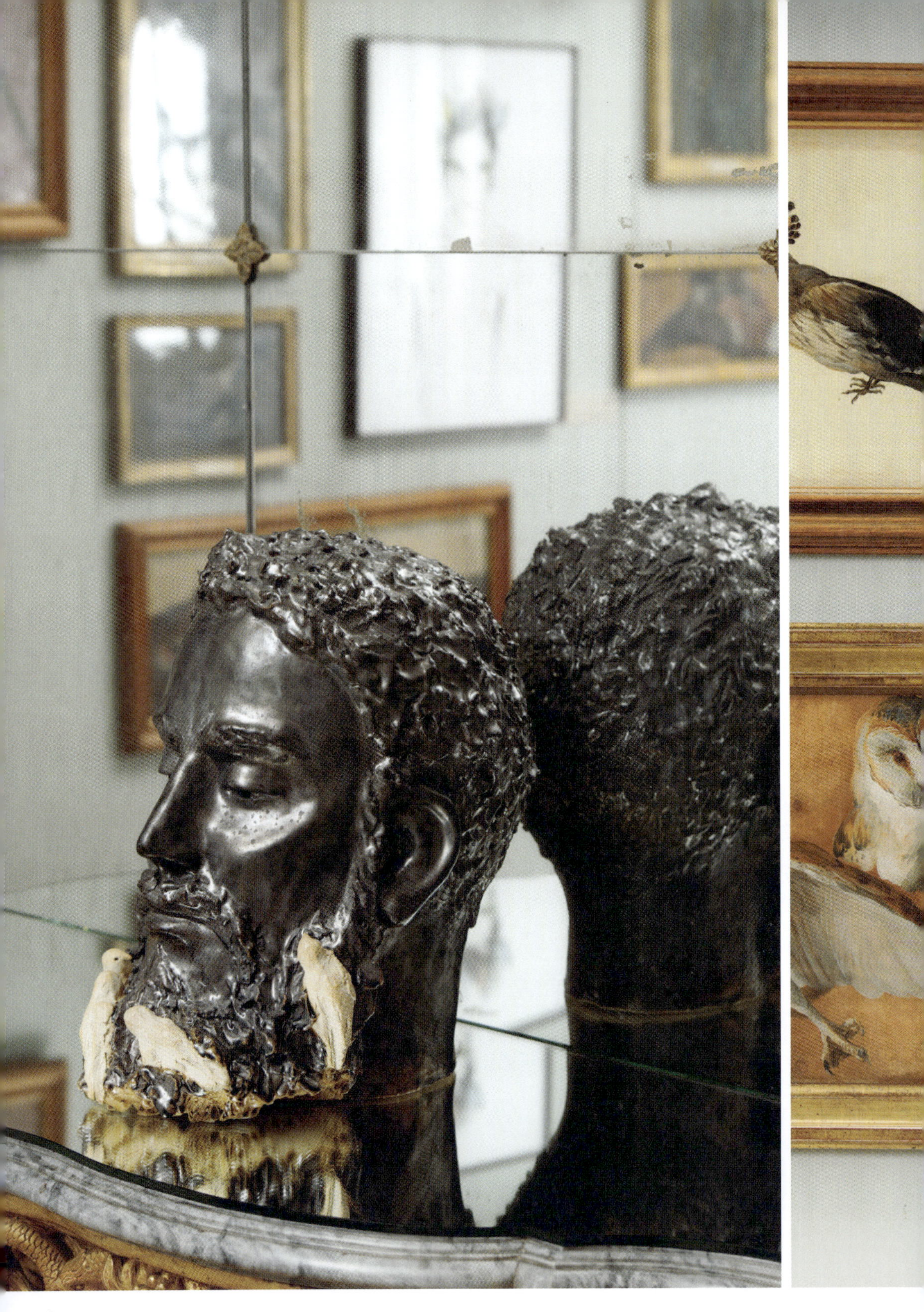

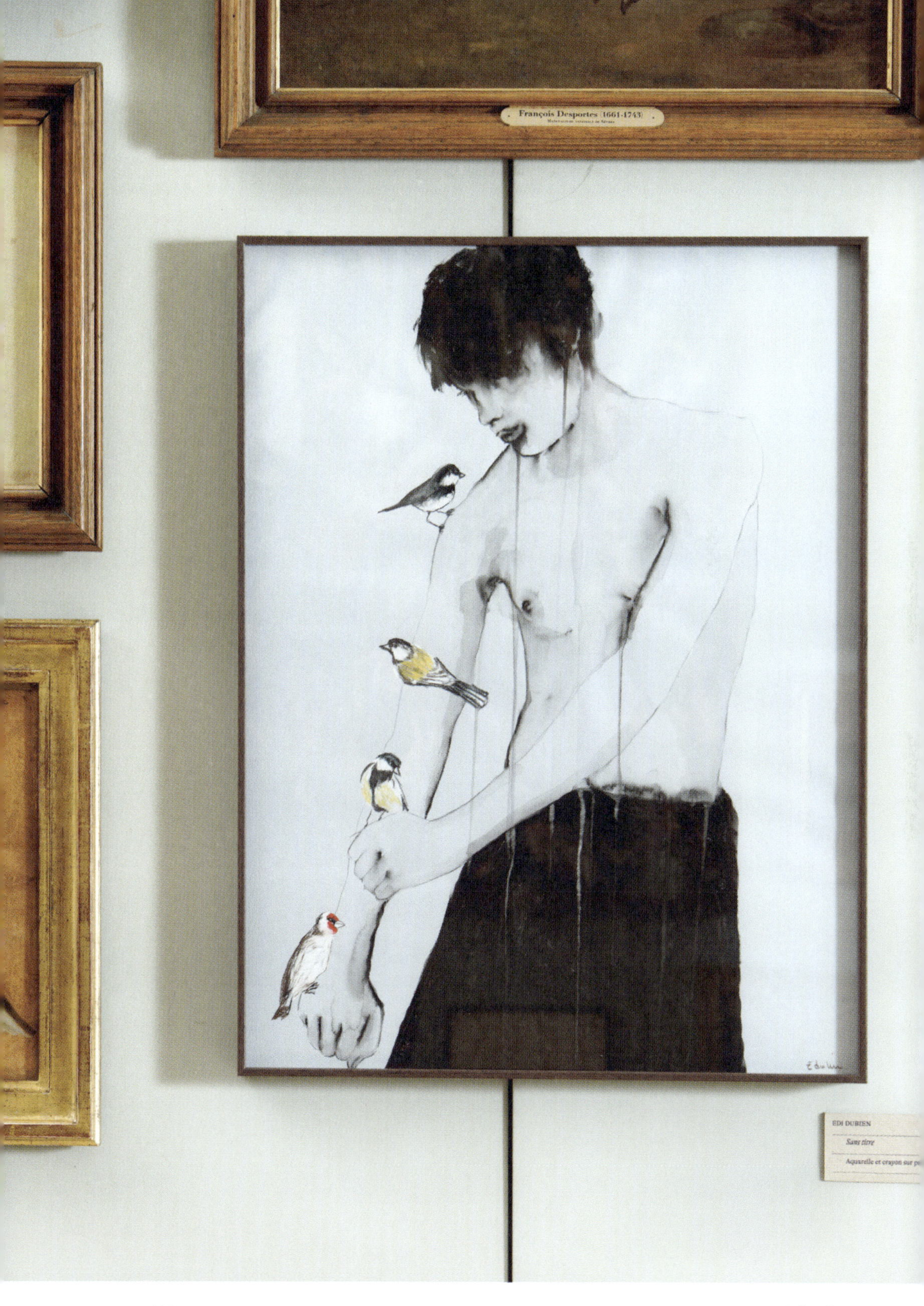

Untitled, 2024

A *committed* anachronism

Often, a bear in heels, a boar proudly wearing a tiara,
a deer in makeup, or Pinocchio riding a crow, are sure
to put a smile on more than one person's face. Hold your
tongue, such is the aim! Why is he acting this way?
What does this mean? Why doesn't this bear look ferocious
or frightening? Through these images, Edi recalls his
childhood, an anachronistic outfit imposed on him,
a forced cross-dressing: little patent leather shoes when
really what he wanted to do was scratch his knees jump
into the haystacks and straw. But Edi speaks to all of us
about the discomfort of that jacket we buy, that we like
so much but know will attract the scrutiny of others.
He speaks of the gaze of others, of self-acceptance,
and Edi Dubien won't give you any answers, other than
the fundamental right to freedom and difference.

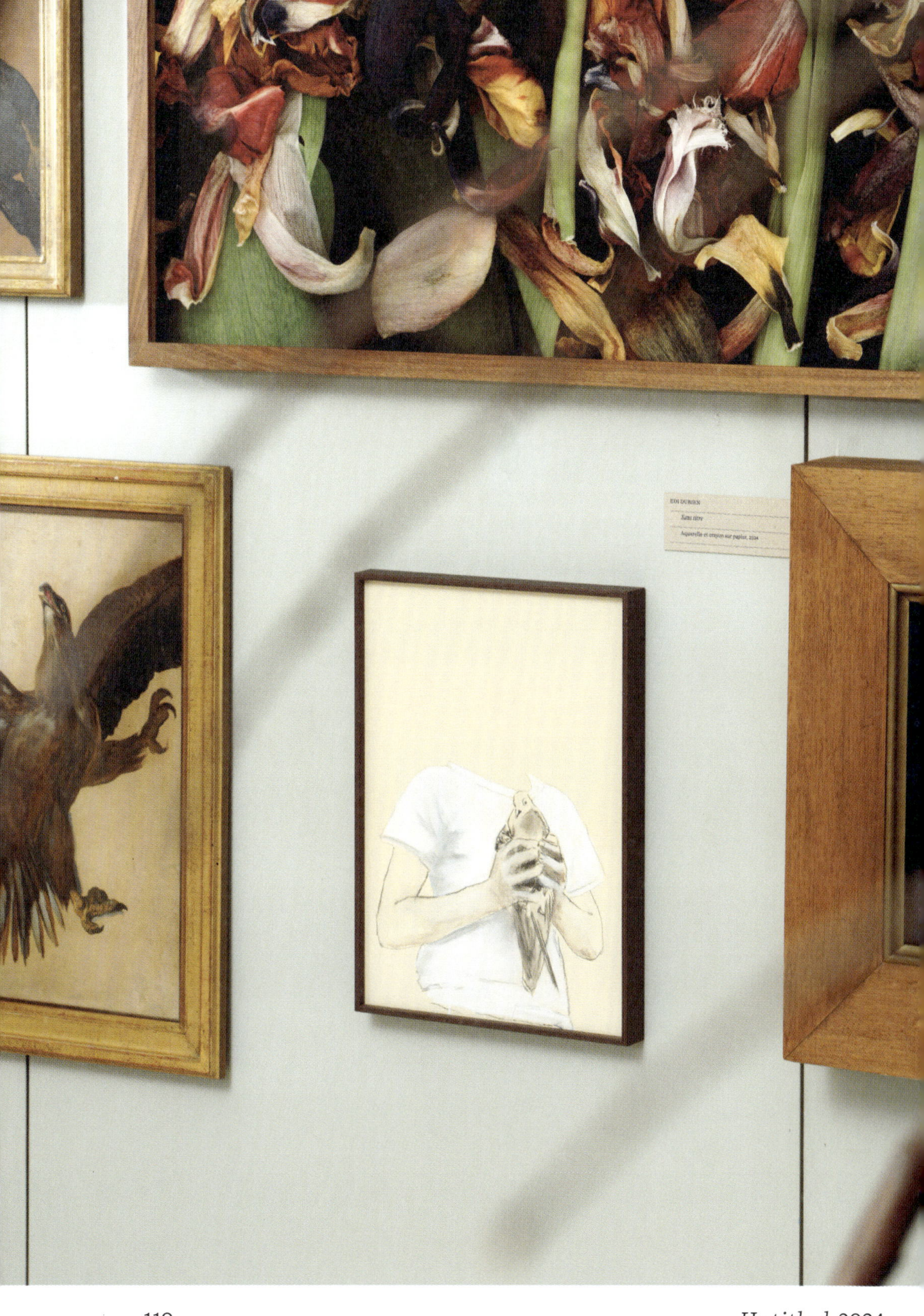

Untitled, 2024

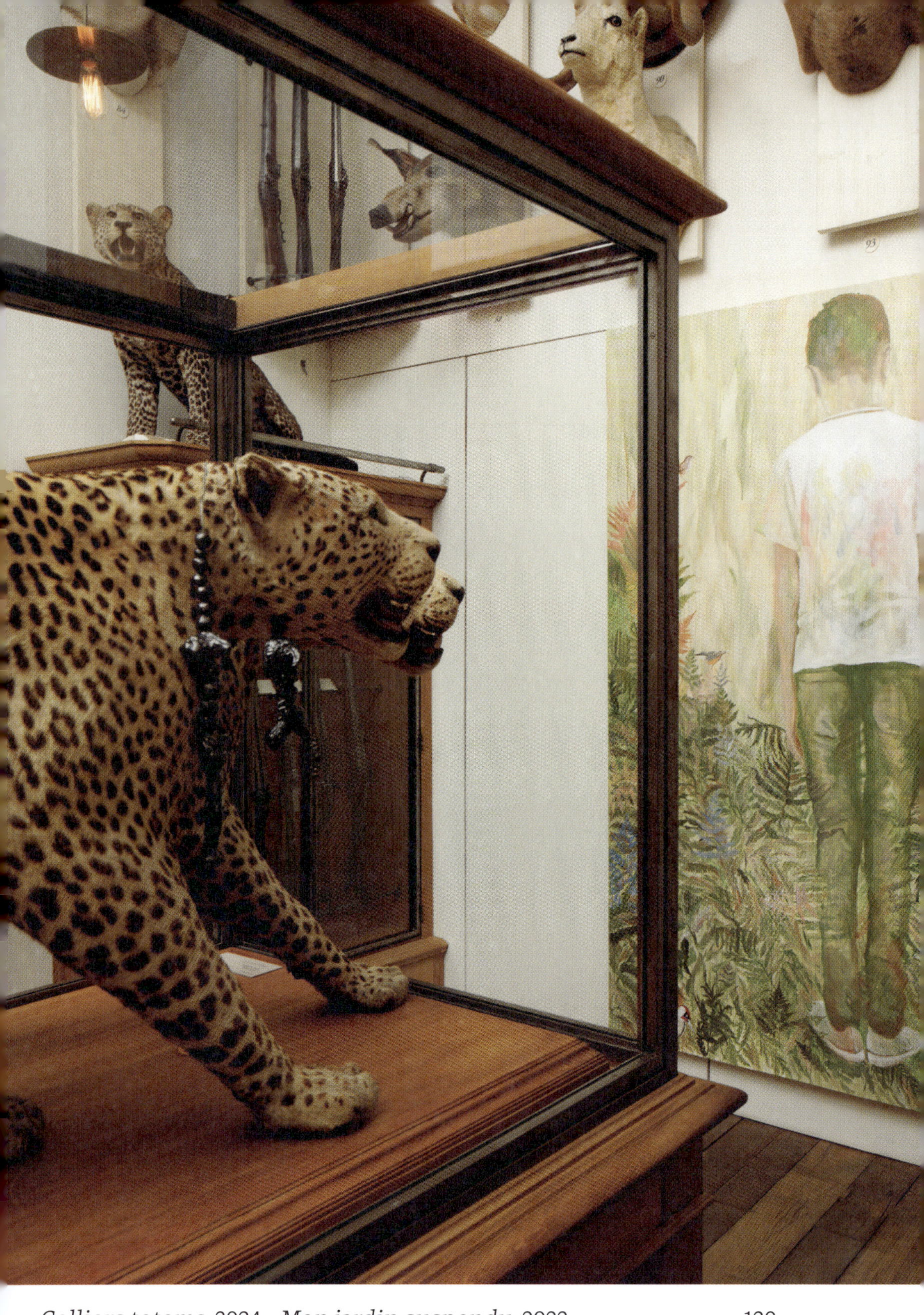

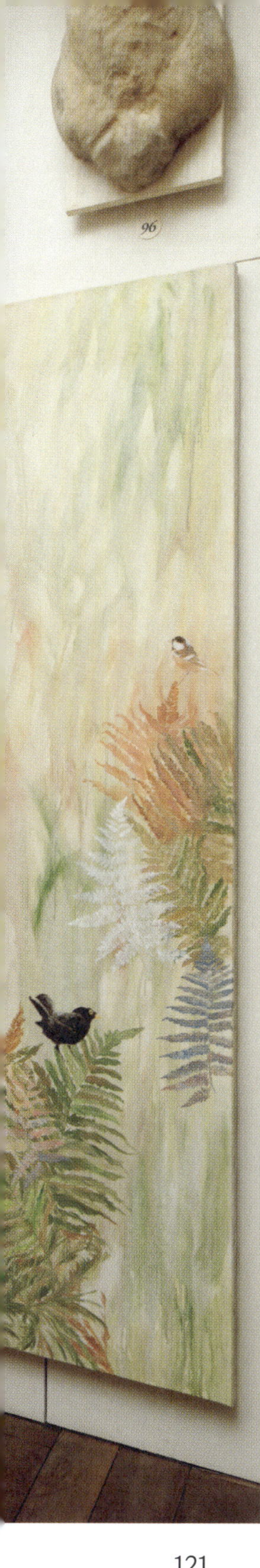

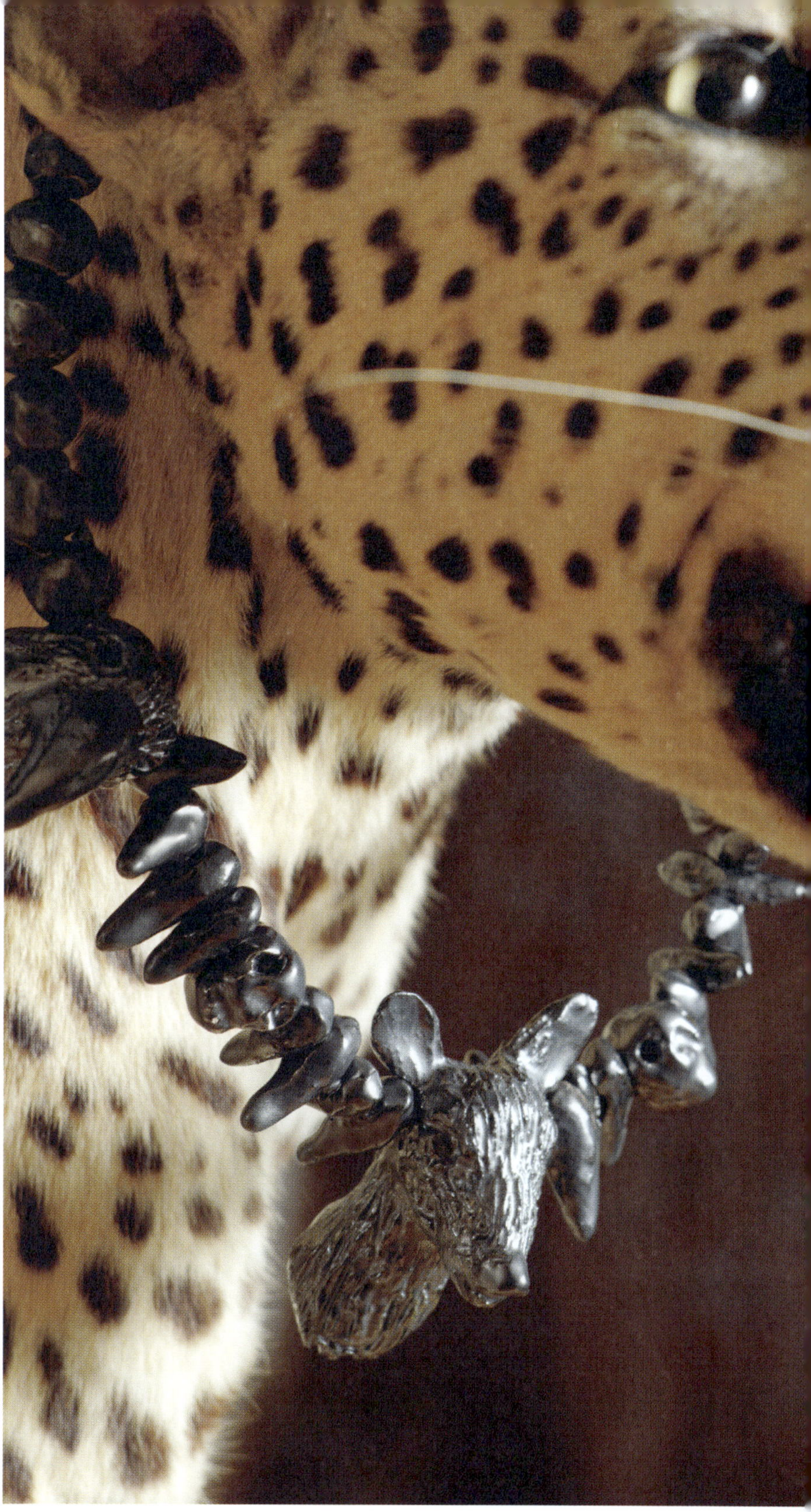

Colliers totems (detail), 2024

A *philosophy* as old as *time*

The relationship between people and animals allows
us, as the artist puts it, to "show things", while exploring
philosophical concepts close to those developed
by Philippe Descola: where is Nature located? And what
exactly is Nature? Do we really belong? When deer antlers
become support structures for tiny houses–in this
drawing, then in the installation in the deer and wolf room
entitled *Dans nos maisons transpercées* (in our pierced
homes)–, this raises the question of sustainable habitat
management between humans and animals. This work
also raises the question of the cohabitation between
two ecosystems often perceived as in opposition and
ambivalent, but deeply interdependent.
Edi Dubien presents a symbiotic vision of these two
worlds, where the boundary between the reigns becomes
a kingdom, a shared space where the Anthropocene
ceases to exist.

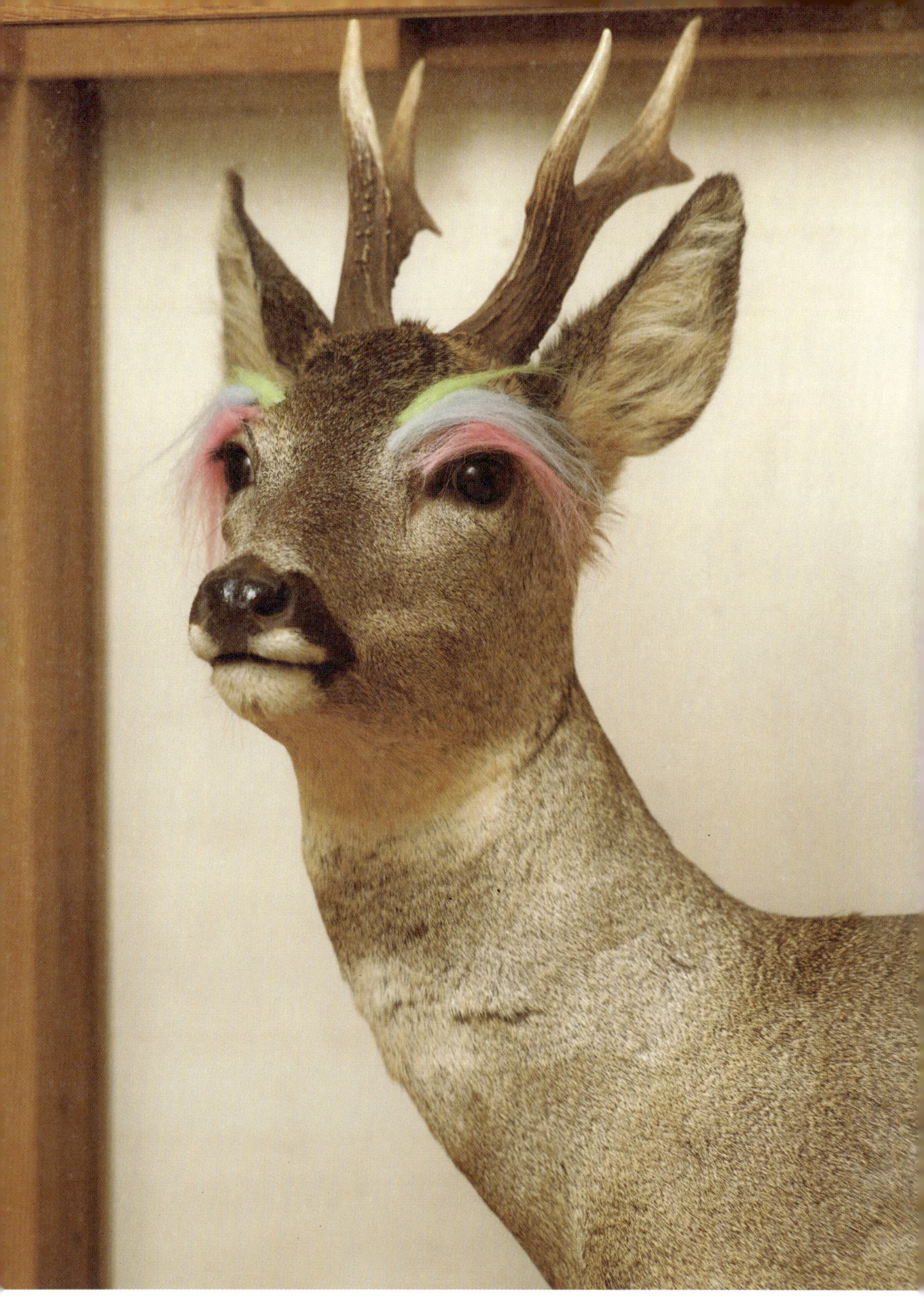

Je vous aime (detail), 2024

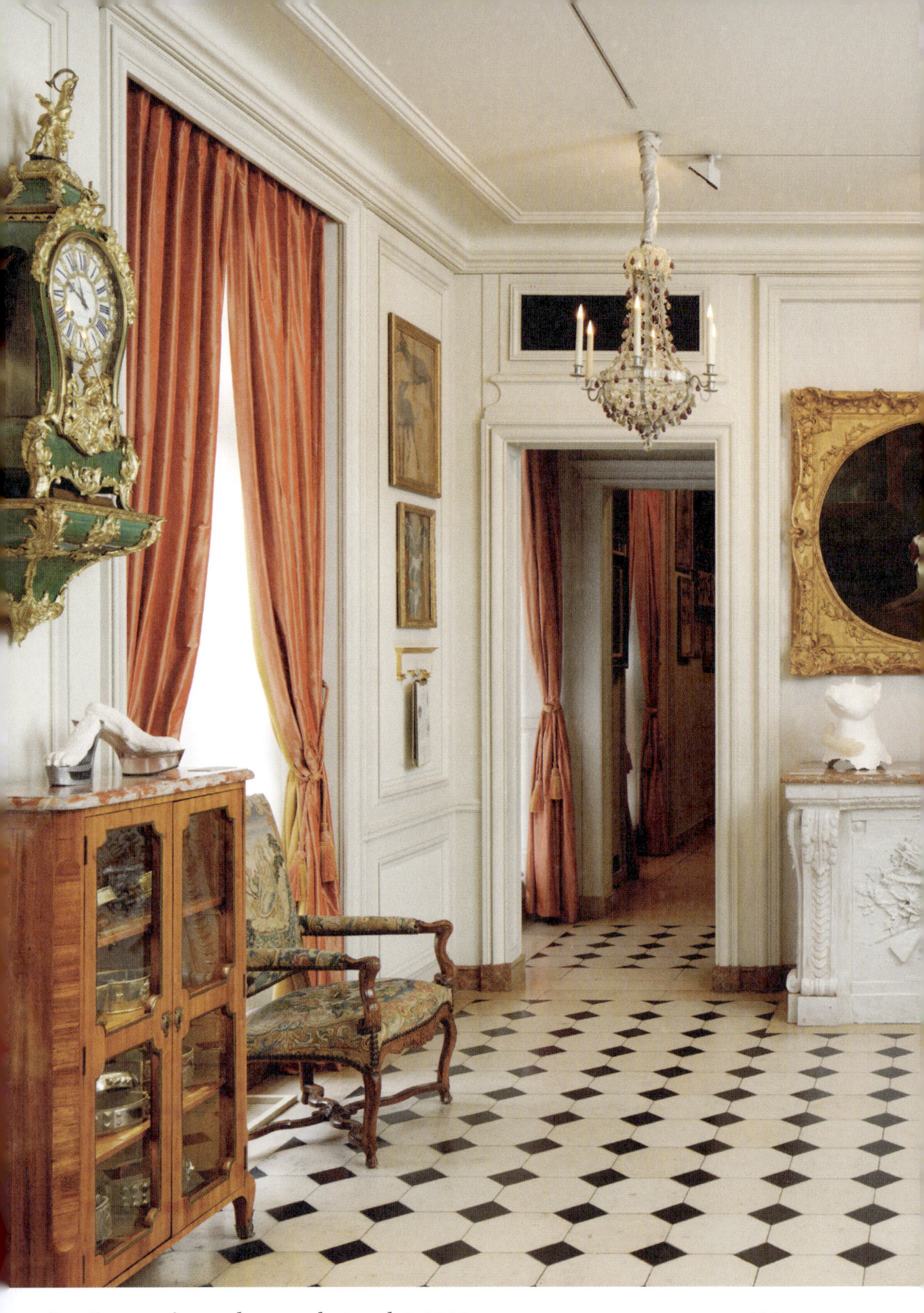

Ça n'ira pas à tout le monde 1 and 2, 2024

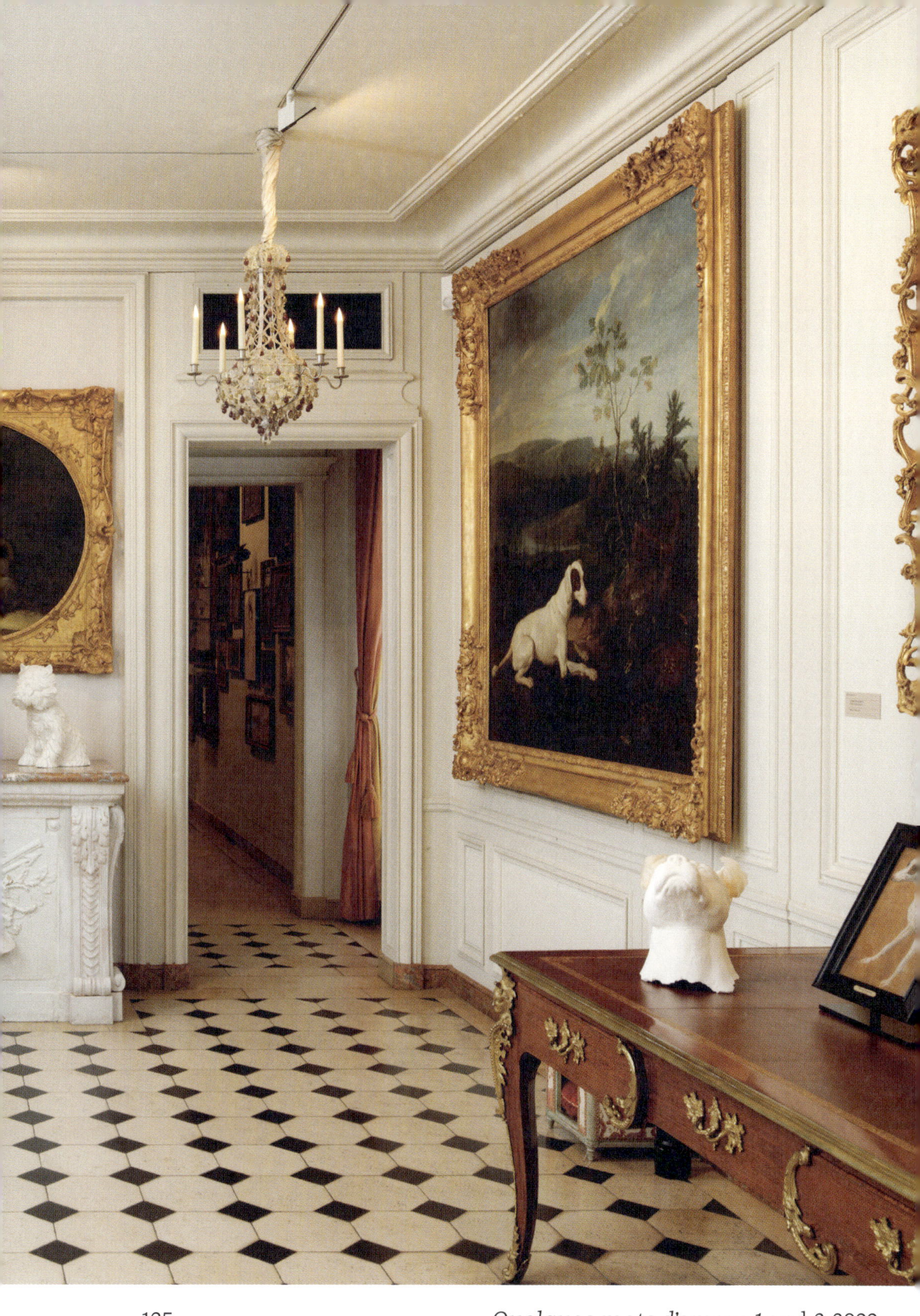

Quelques mots d'amour 1 and *2, 2022*

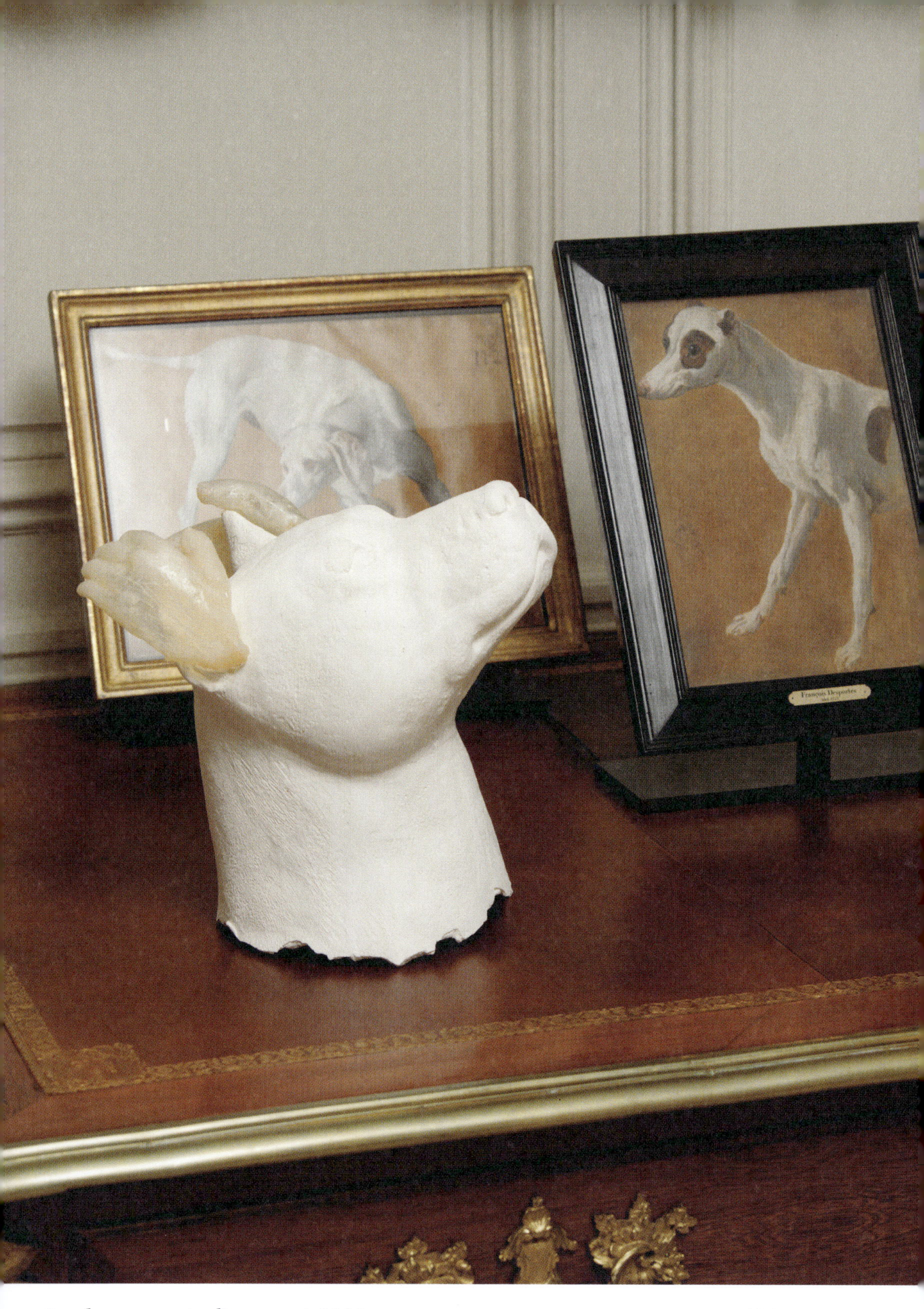

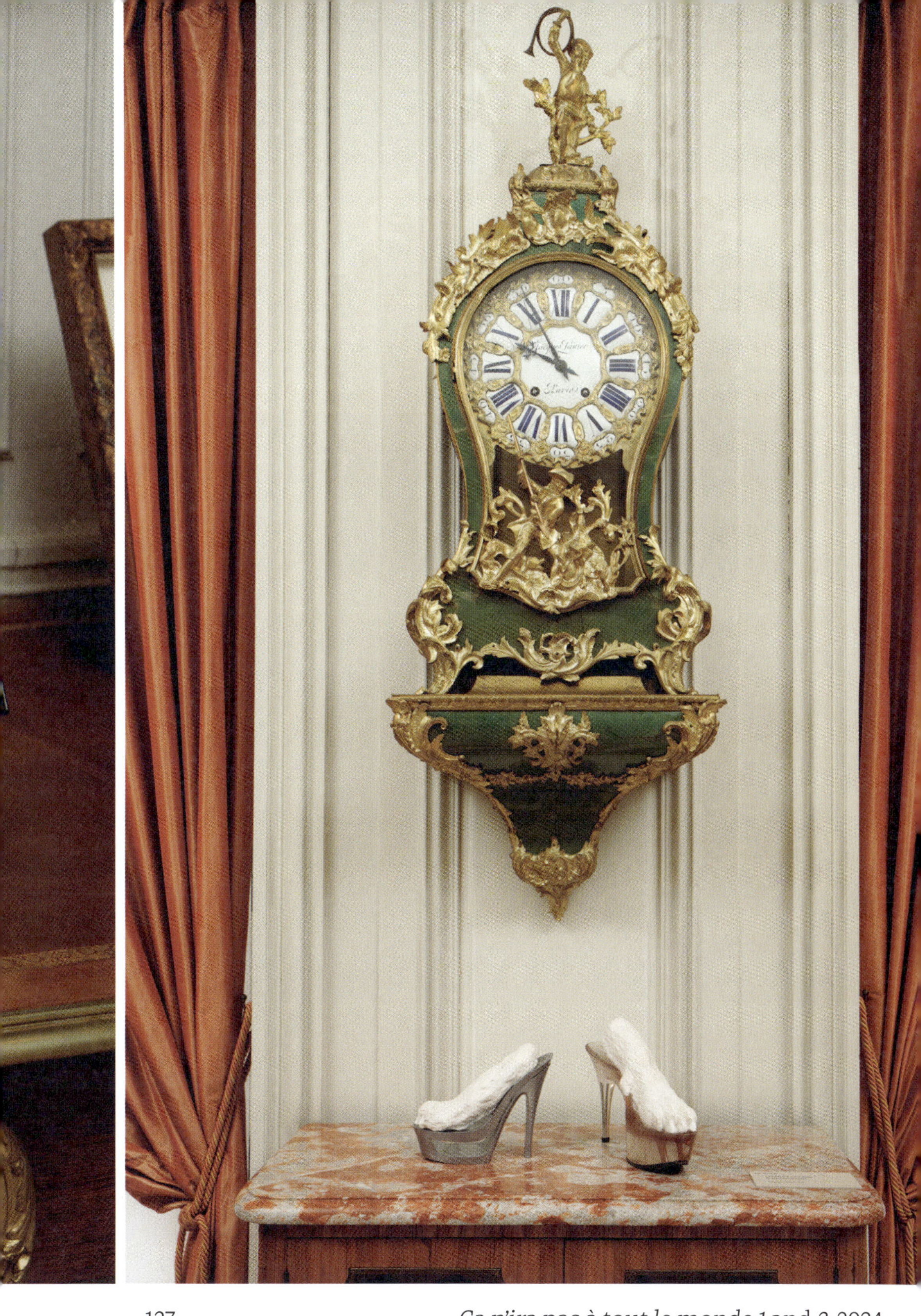

Ça n'ira pas à tout le monde 1 and 2, 2024

Very familiar *animals*

In all this nuance and gentleness, a realism that
is sometimes overwhelming unfolds. The animal
portraits that Edi Dubien draws or paints are imbued
with a singular force, carried by the intensity of their
expressions. Those expressive eyes seem to question us,
awakening in us a strange sense of déjà-vu. And for good
reason as these animals are not so far removed from us.
What sets them apart is the wild freedom that eludes us.
Looking at them, we recognize, as if in a photo yellowed
by time, an old friend, a family member, perhaps even
a reflection of ourselves.
In fact, it's a part of our own animality, our own
nature, that is visible through these works. This subtle
anthropomorphism is an invitation to reconnect with
the living, with each other, and with what surrounds us.
These reconciliations, like the "kisses" between the people
and the animals Edi portrays, question our common place
on this earth, and call for mutual protection, between
humans and non-humans.

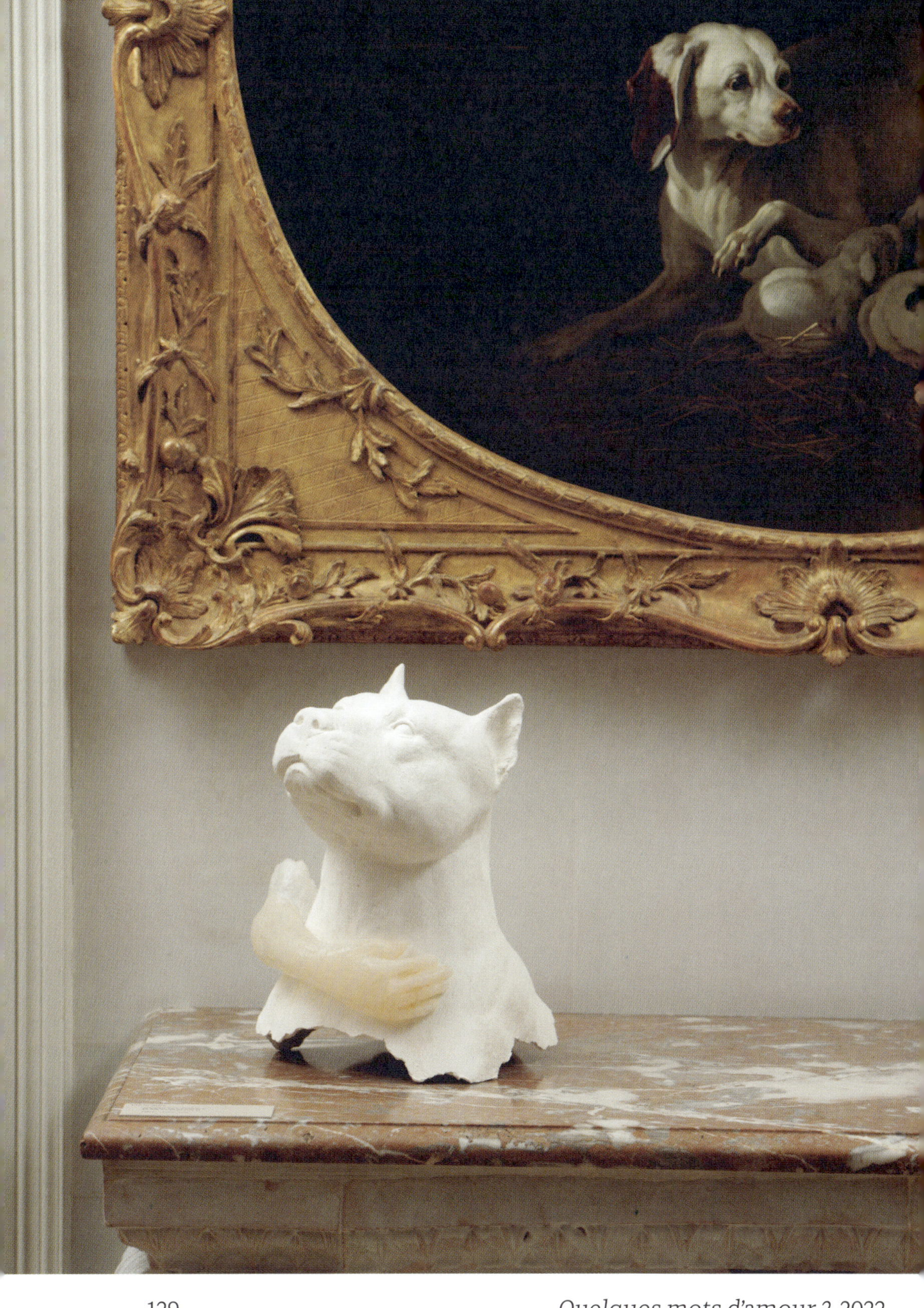

Quelques mots d'amour 2, 2022

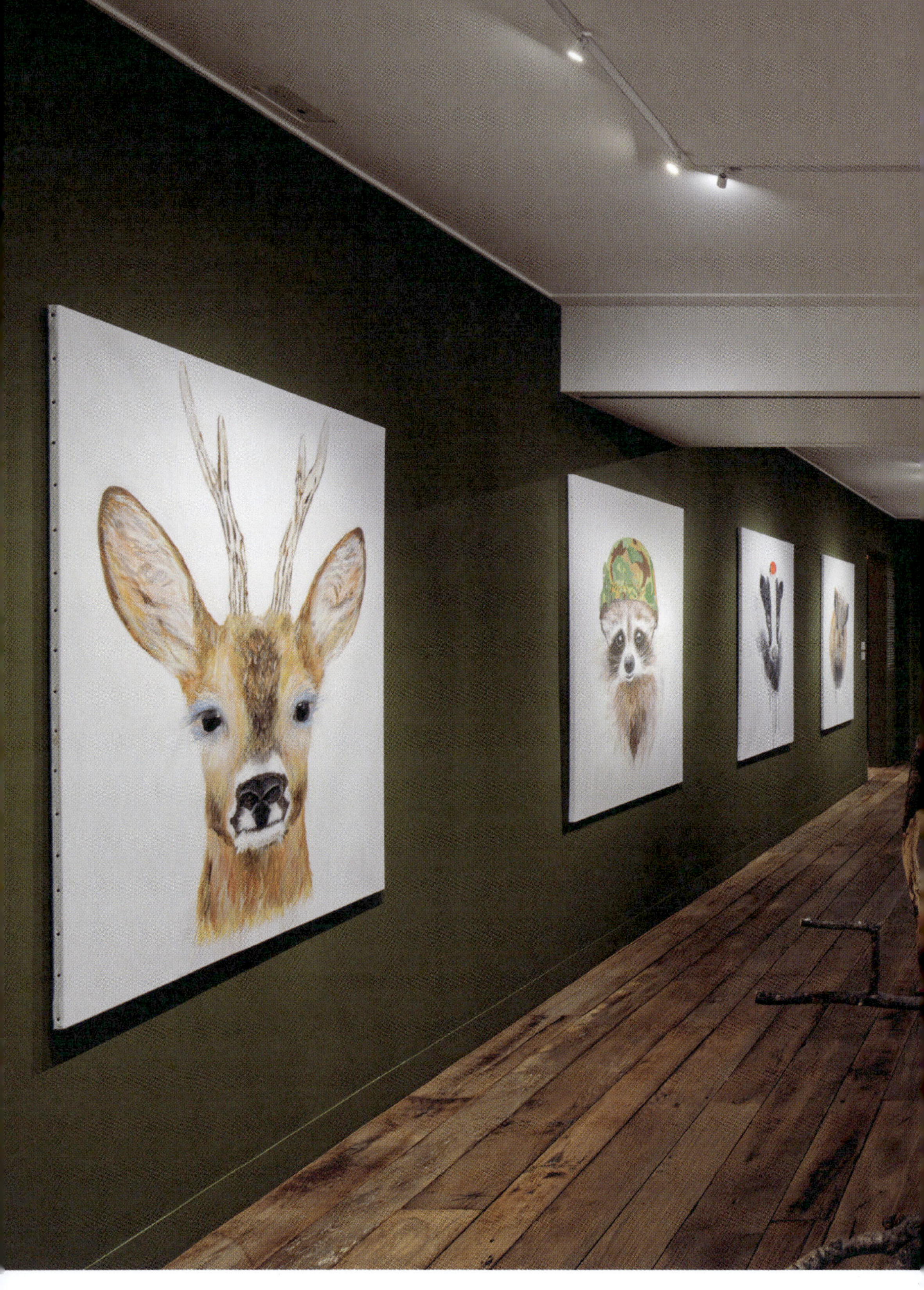

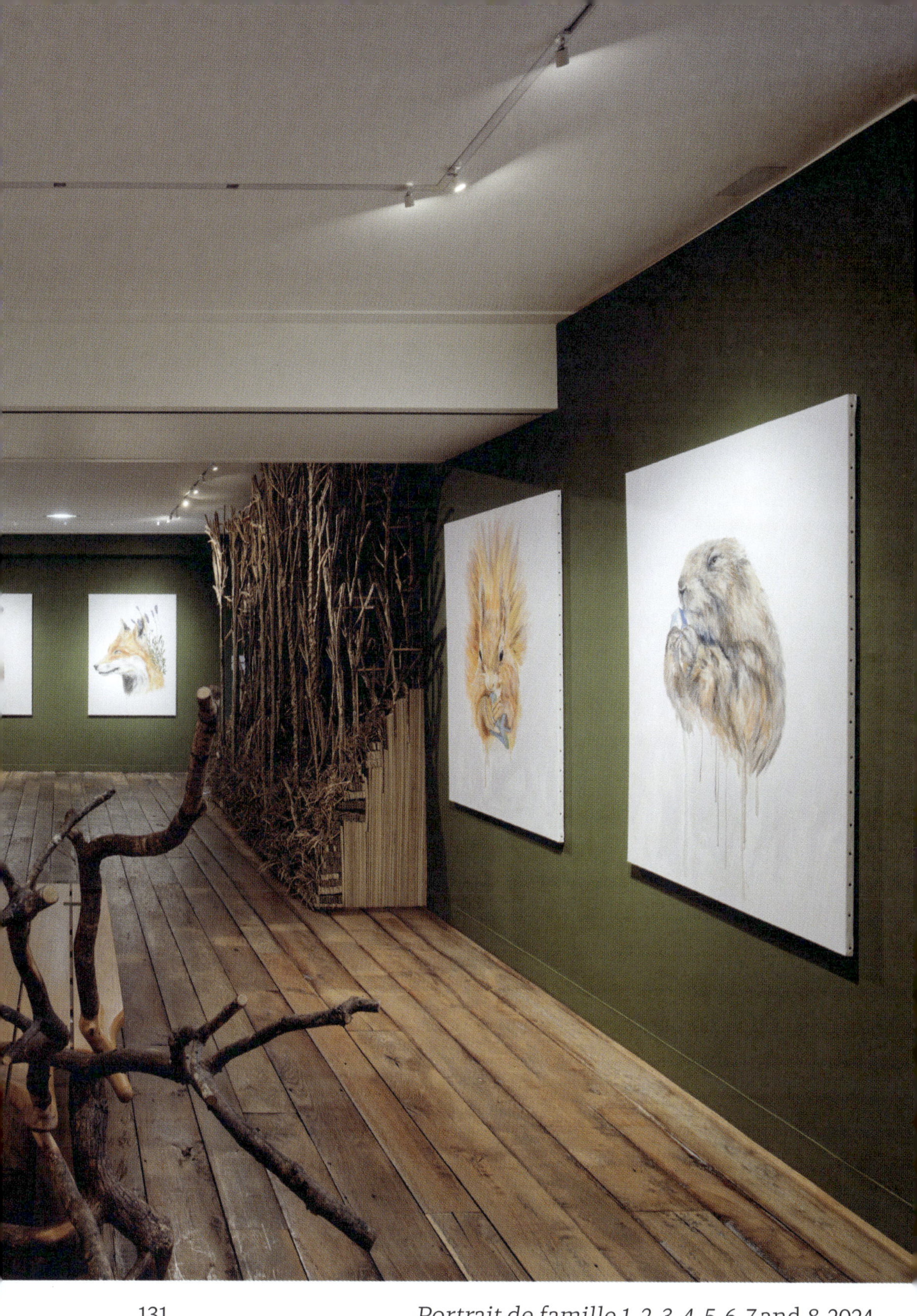

Portrait de famille 1, 2, 3, 4, 5, 6, 7 and 8, 2024

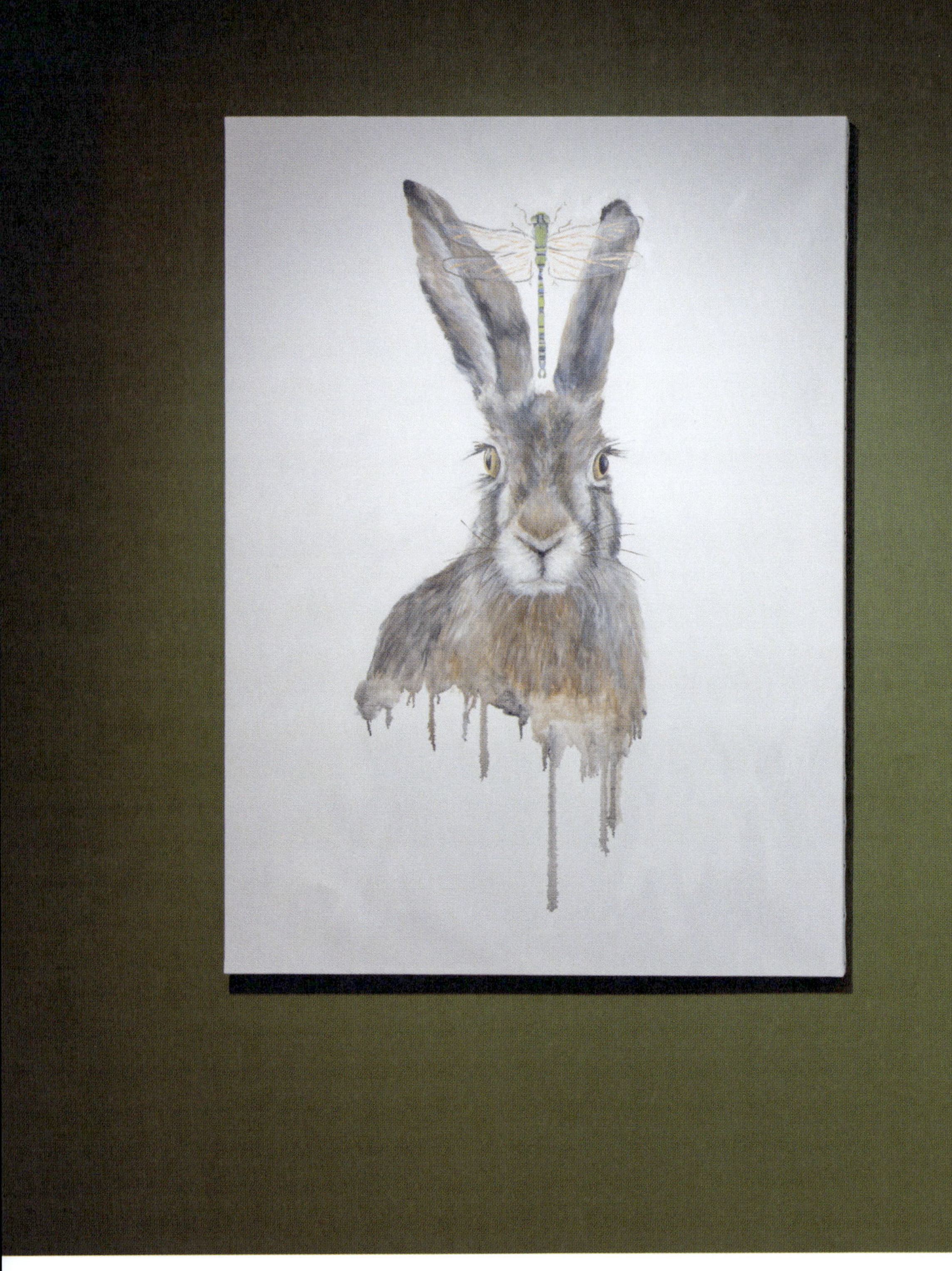

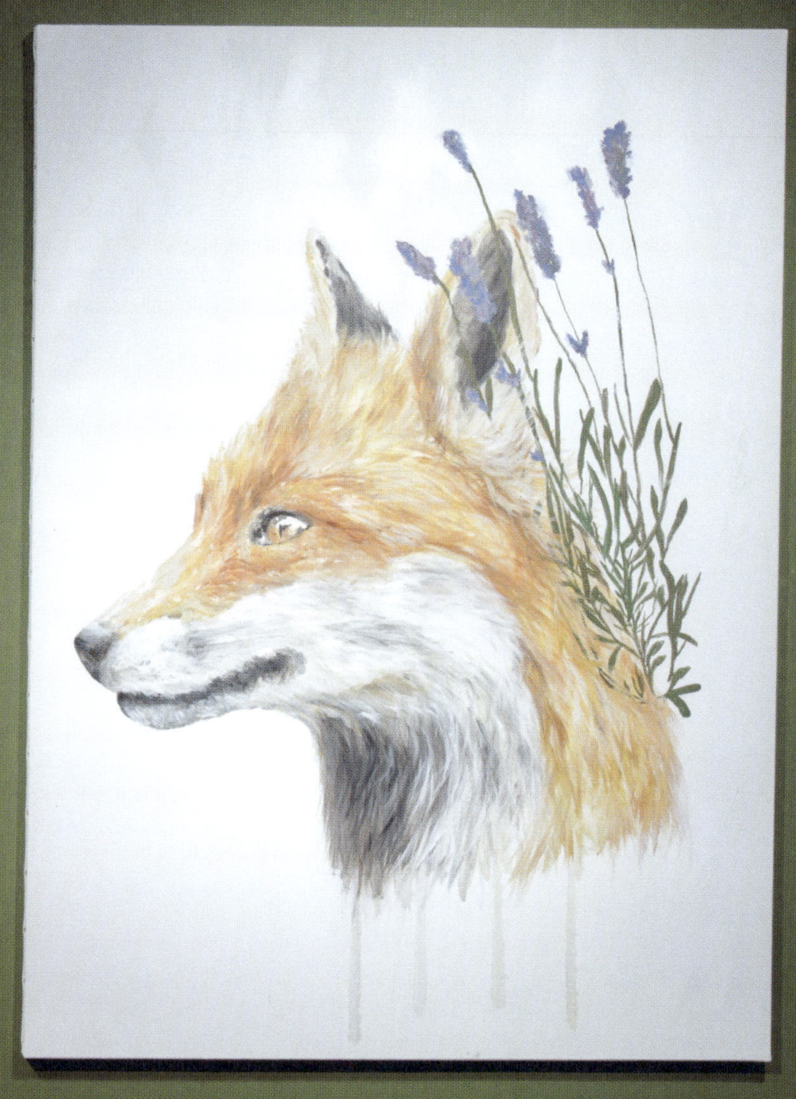

Portrait de famille 1, 2024

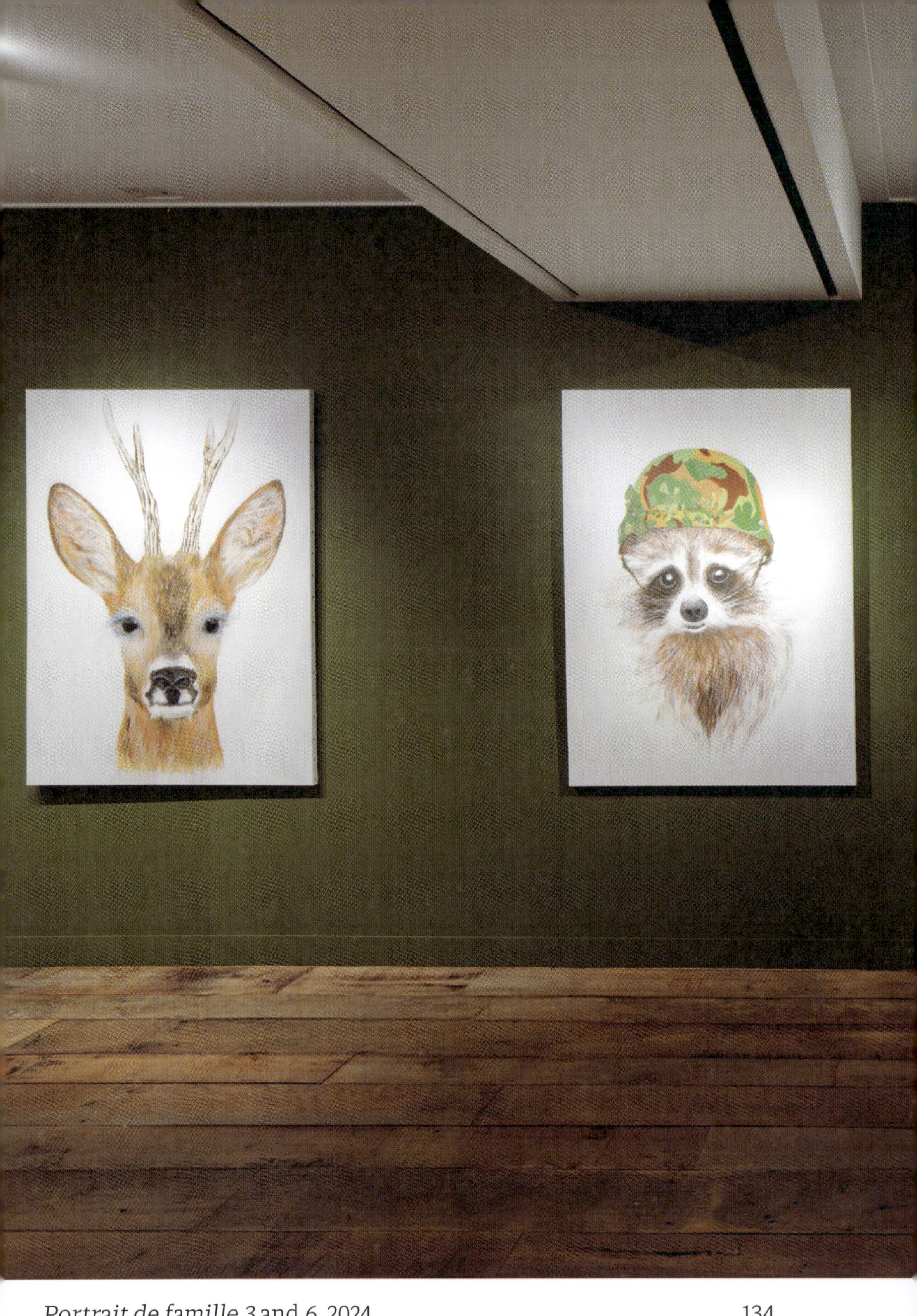

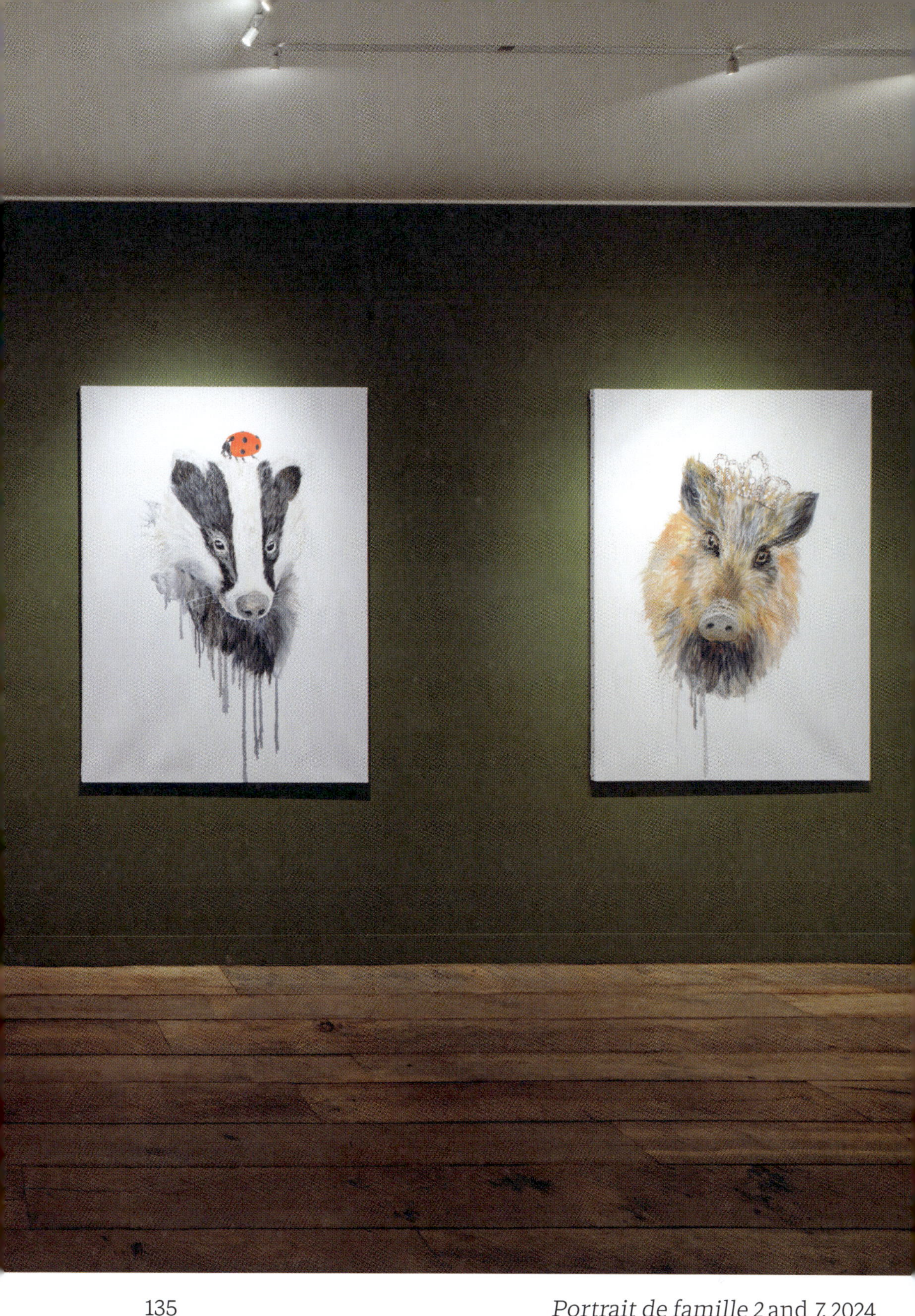

Portrait de famille 2 and 7, 2024

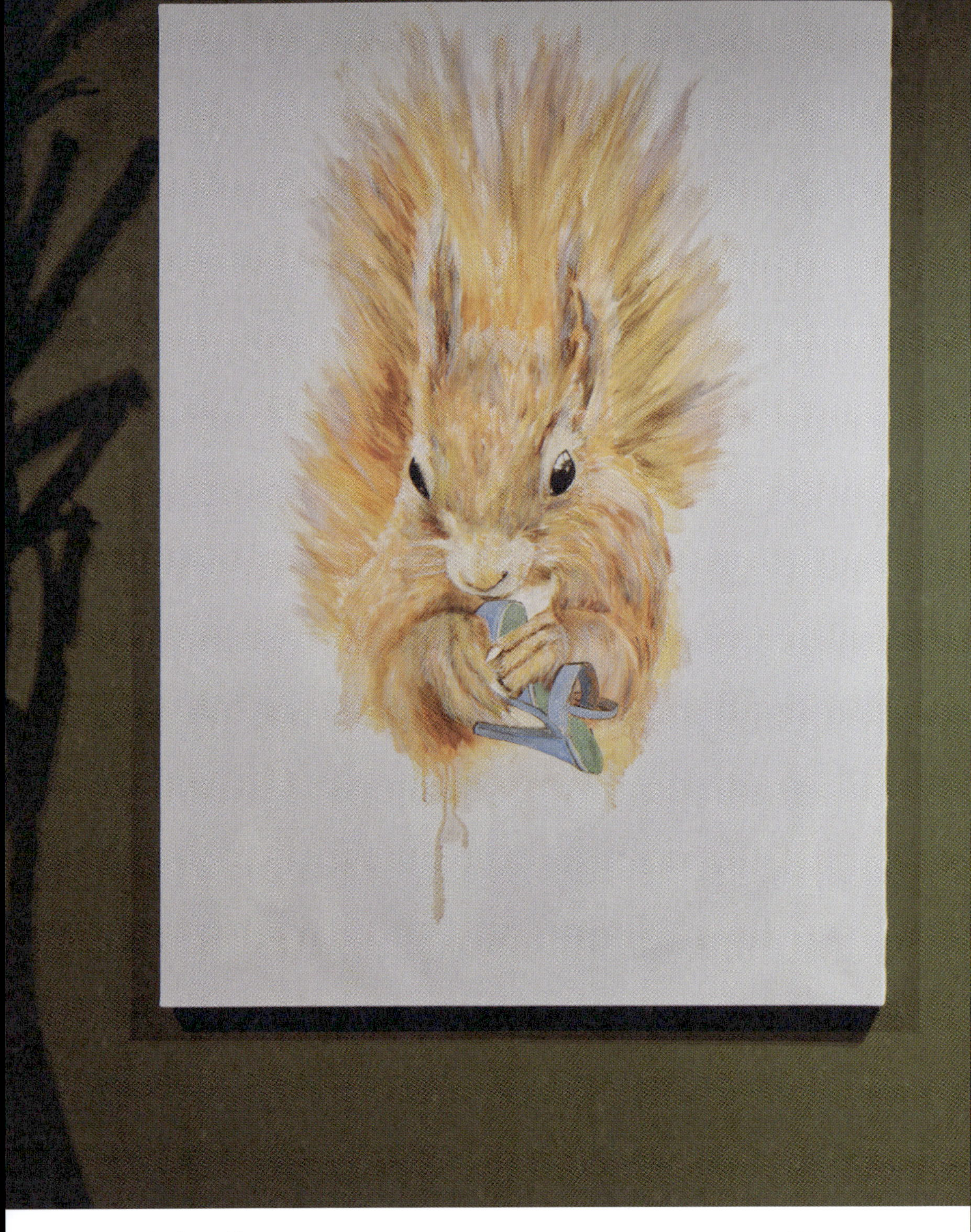

Portrait de famille 4, 2024

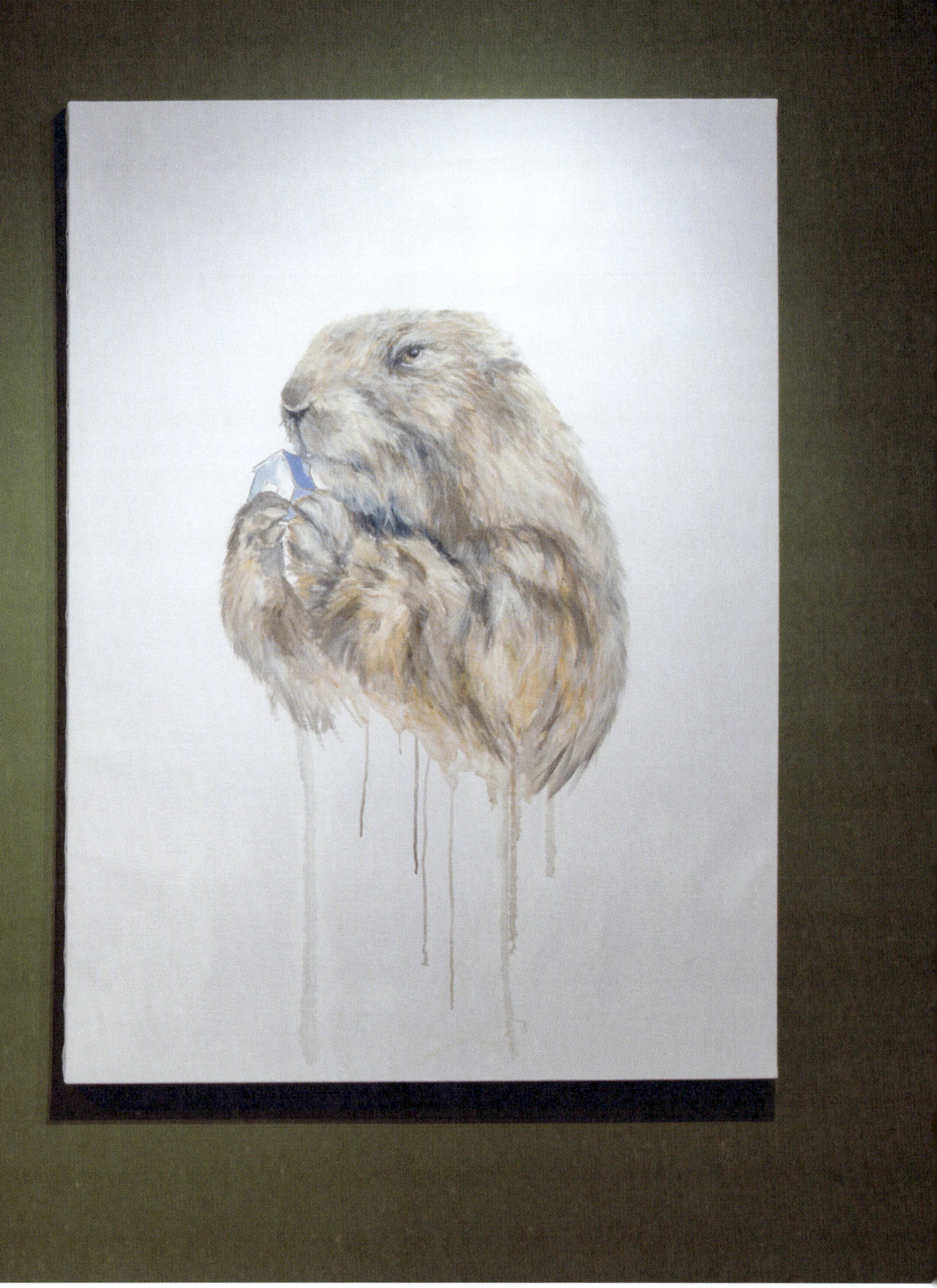

Portrait de famille 5, 2024

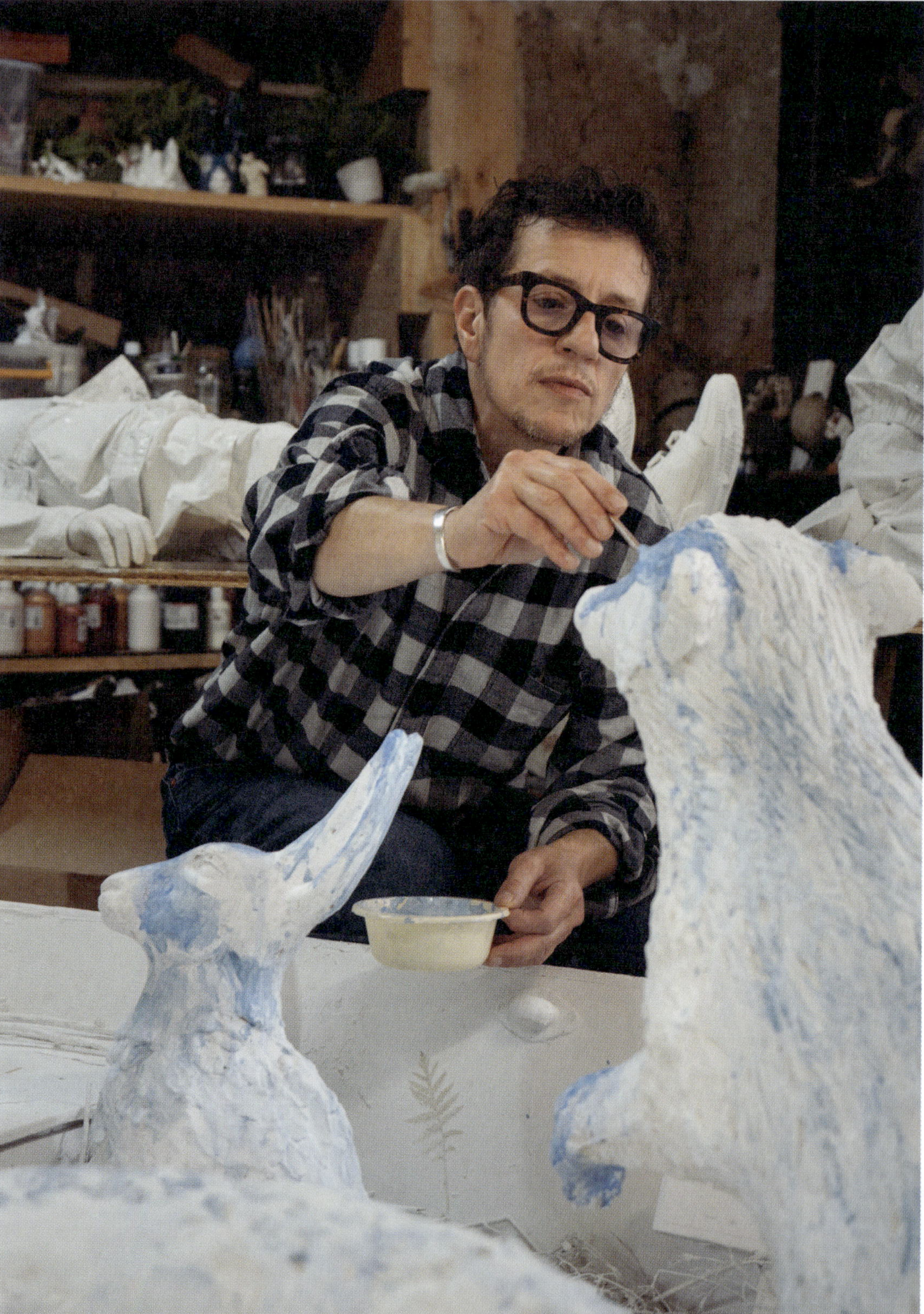

Interview between Edi Dubien and Rémy Provendier-Commenne

Rémy Provendier-Commenne   This exhibition at the Musée de la Chasse et de la Nature is your first in a Paris museum, but your work already has a substantial following.

Edi Dubien   I've been part of the art scene since 2017. I first exhibited at the Maison des Arts de Malakoff, invited by Aude Cartier, for a solo show called *Voyage d'un animal sans mesure* (journey of an immeasurable animal) and that's where I met gallery owner Alain Gutharc. My first solo exhibition in a museum was *L'homme aux mille natures* (man of a thousand characters) at the Musée d'Art Contemporain de Lyon, after having my drawings seen at the Salon du Dessin de Marseille—shown by Alain Gutharc—by Matthieu Lelièvre and Isabelle Bertolotti, the museum director.

The show at the Musée de la Chasse et de la Nature is my first exhibition in a Paris museum. It is therefore a very special exhibition for me, in a very special place, steeped in history, and I'd like to thank the François Sommer Foundation and the museum for giving me this opportunity. Inititally it felt strange to exhibit in this museum; I'm not particularly in favor of hunting, but at the same time I've naturally found my place there. This museum seems to me frozen

in time, it deals with so many other themes, with a lot
of poetry and also a lot of love.

This museum is a delight for me because I find spaces
where I can slip in my symbols, my wishes, my words
of love and life. It's like a restorative journey, the rare
empty spaces become immense. They open up and
there are so many of them.

RPC **It's as if this exhibition already existed somewhere?**

ED Yes, absolutely, and we just had to imagine it and
discuss it, think about it, you and me. It's as if part
of my work had been conceived for this place and this
exhibition. I didn't make it up. The boar with the tutu
has been around for a long time. In fact, I'd already
been preparing this exhibition in my head for a very
long time. Yes, yes, it was a given. Look at the deer with
the houses! The drawing was already made. The kisses,
they're there. The tutu, the dog room, they were already
made. The boat, as I told you earlier, had already been
painted, already drawn. I dreamed of doing it in 3D.
It's done. The figure lying down with the rebirth,
that was already done. Of the drawings, everything
was already ready, very ready. The works were perfectly
suited for this museum.
I've always loved the transitions, the seasons, the river,
it's like a positive shift. In the boat on the museum's
ground floor, there's the cycle of life that crosses time,
following the flow of water. I represented it with the
little dinosaur and the other animals until the present.
I am the boy. The boy cries from sadness, giving birth
to wonders that revive the living. It's a resilience,
a transformation, a way for me to shed light
on the fragile and turn fragility into strength.

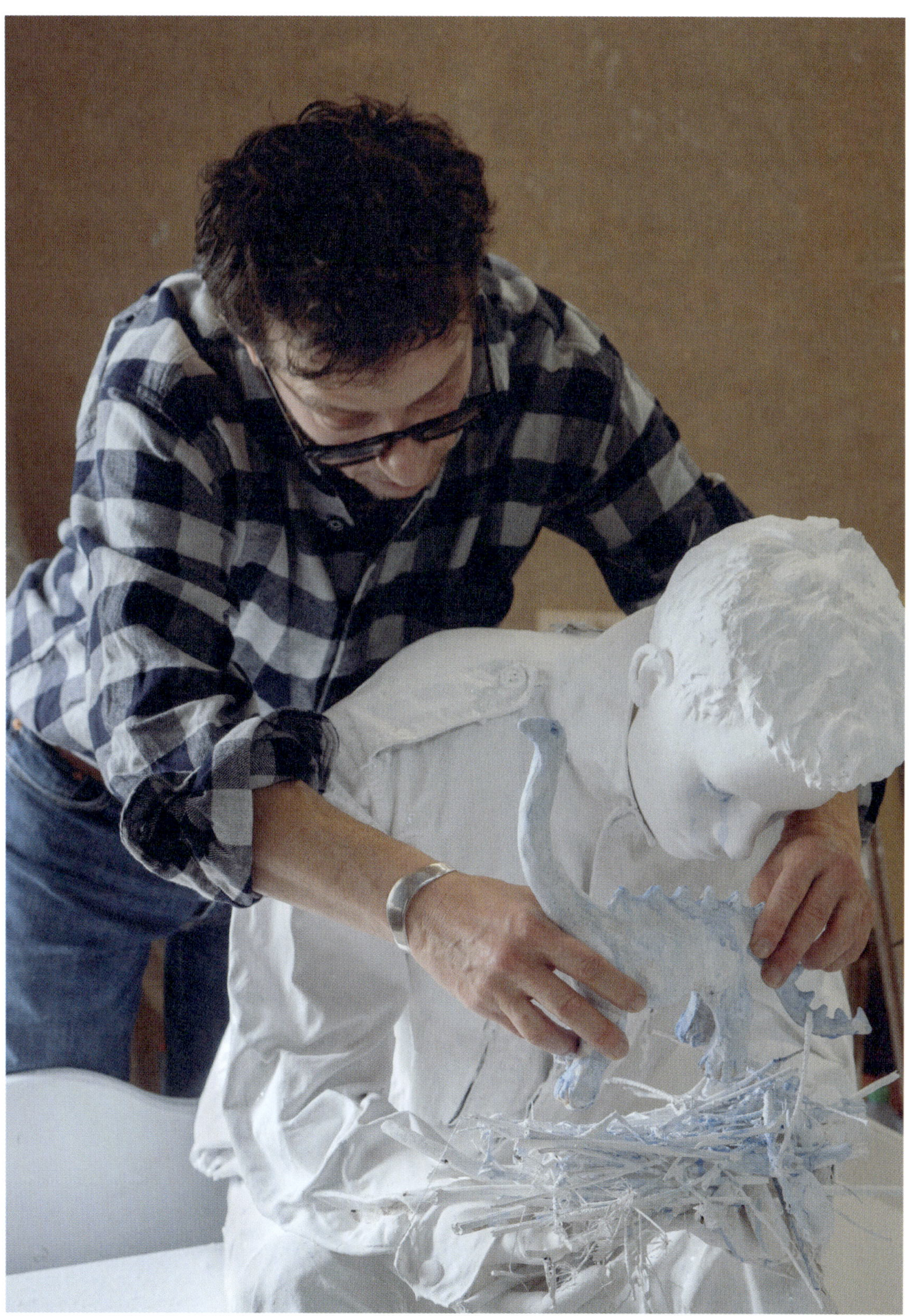

RPC There is precisely something present in this boat
and in other works, something very strong: a tear.

ED The tear, it is not simply "I'm crying". They are
born of emotion, but they are also water, a liquid.
Regarding the boat, they fill it symbolically. It's linked
to animals, like blue, the color of tears. They bear an
imaginary, a dream, but also a thought: humans think
about what happened to the dinosaurs and what
might come to pass tomorrow. It embodies a thought,
an intention. It's like ex-votos and magical thinking.
My work is about this: breathing new life into animals,
breathing new life into life. As in an ex-voto, death
is not definitive, it is transformed. It's the power
of magical thinking, symbolized by the tear.
That's why, when I say "crying toads", it can come
unconsciously from *Donkeyskin*, from the witch who
spits toads. But there's also "crying rabbits", in other
words, in this blue tear above this little rabbit, there's
the will to save it, to bring it to life through tears,
through thought. These are protective, life-giving
tears, more than tears of sadness.

RPC For this exhibition, there are a lot of new drawings,
a practice you consider essential. Let's talk about the path
that led you to drawing.

ED I started taking photos at 13, I wanted to be a war
photographer to denounce violence and abuse.
At the same time, I started sculpting, painting came
later when my best friend died. I've always practiced
drawing, I've always alternated media like breathing.
With my transition, everything clicked and I felt free
to exist.

And that's when I started drawing a lot, I wasn't afraid
anymore.

Making images and settings that are sometimes
improbable helps create a style of writing that allows
a certain fluidity, to introduce something vivid and
very precise into the emotion I want to evoke. I love
Dürer's engravings and drawings. I like the head-on
approach of the image.
Every morning, I get up at 6 a.m. to go to the studio:
I start drawing, I already know what I'm going to do,
I've thought about it and I visualize it. Nothing is done
at random. Everything has a meaning. Everything is
connected. These are associations of images, feelings,
sensations, contrasts and perceptions.

RPC We can't hide behind a drawing.

ED Indeed, I show myself, I've hidden enough as it is.
I want to live in full daylight. Why hide? I want to say
things. My voice was so often silenced.

I wrote poems when I was very young. Not a diary,
poems, up to the age of 14, I still have them. I managed
to save them because I had to hide them. It was
important not to let my parents find out about my
poems, so a friend of mine kept them at her place.
At home, there was no room for creativity. When I used
to draw, my mother used to tell me it was crap.
Once, I traced a drawing and I was proud, I was five
years old, but she saw through the trick and I had
to stop experimenting if I wanted to please her.
Or find others.

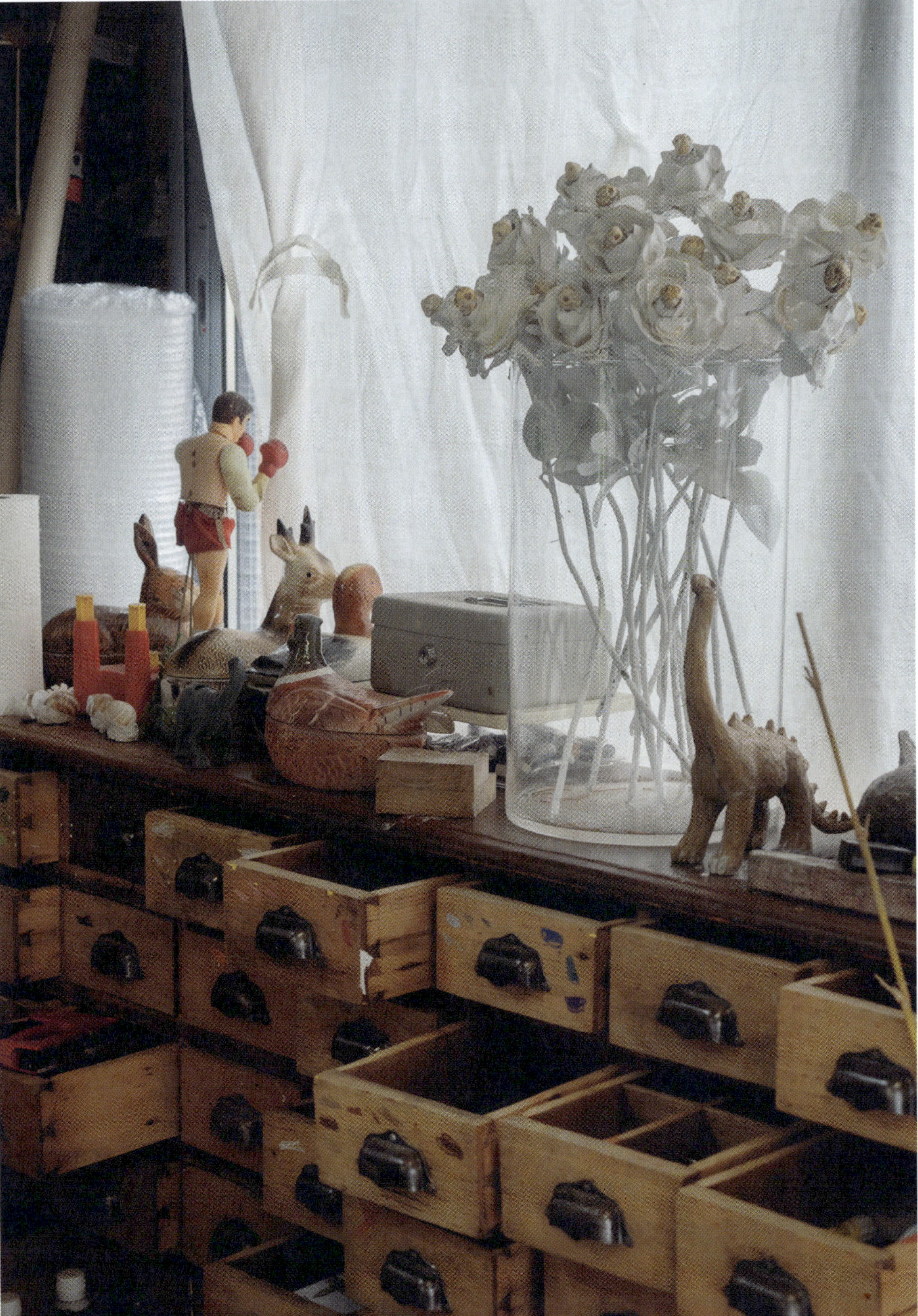

RPC What was your relationship to art when you were
younger? Did your parents give you an artistic or cultural
education?

ED I've always wanted to do what I do today. As I said,
I started with photography: I must have been
12, I remember the photos of tomatoes at my
grandmother's, she'd let them ripen, they were red,
orange and green. I can still see the fog that enveloped
this small village in Auvergne. I also spent my days
walking around Paris and taking photos.
Then, as a teenager in my bedroom, I started making
small installations that I would take photos of.
At home, there was a painting book that belonged
to my mother. I must have been small, and when
I opened it, I came across *The Anatomy Lesson
of Dr. Nicolaes Tulp* by Rembrandt, it frightened me.
I think my initial steps were in churches.
The paintings and frescoes were like a comic strip
for the child I was. It was quite surreal, but I thought
it was beautiful.
I didn't go to school much and I was kicked out
of accounting school because I was reading
Baudelaire behind my keyboard.

RPC Was the work your mother did beautiful?

ED I didn't like everything, but I did like her Pinocchio,
which strangely enough she drew several times.
So later I drew him again, but this time cross-dressed.
She copied a lot of Walt Disney characters.
I subsequently drew inspiration from it and played
with it in a more contemporary way. Like Bambi who
I put in makeup.

145

ED   But my favorite when I was a child was Colargol
      (Jeremy the bear). I drew him later, this little bear
      who wanted to sing like a bird.
      Even now, I love learning, understanding and
      improving. Nothing is ever locked-in, otherwise
      it would be terribly sad. I could never be satisfied with
      repeating the same thing, because if my work didn't
      evolve, I wouldn't want to do it anymore. That's why
      I work so hard to learn. It's like life: art has to move
      forward, ask new questions and never get stuck in
      the past. Work that stays the same for 10 years is dead
      work to my mind. Yet I love life.

**RPC   And your connection with nature comes from your
      childhood in the Auvergne, from your grandmother,
      is that right?**

ED   Yes. I grew up observing nature all around me. An only
      child until I was 10, I spent a lot of time alone with my
      dog Oscar, a big black Belgian Shepherd. He was my
      pal, my first strong bond with animals. I had a powerful
      connection with him, we were going through the same
      thing. In Auvergne, I had a world of my own, a space
      of total freedom. My wealthy parents had enrolled me
      in religious schools in Paris, which, as a child already
      aware of my trans issue, was a source of anxiety.
      But in Auvergne, things were different. I was back in
      the wilderness: foxes, fields, skinned knees, uncombed
      hair. My childhood memories, especially with my
      grandmother, are very happy and deeply emotional.
      It was this attachment that prompted me to look for a
      country house. That's where it all began, and my stays
      in Auvergne have sustained me throughout my life like
      restorative memories. Having lived through periods of
      abuse, Oscar, my dog, and I shared a deep bond, which

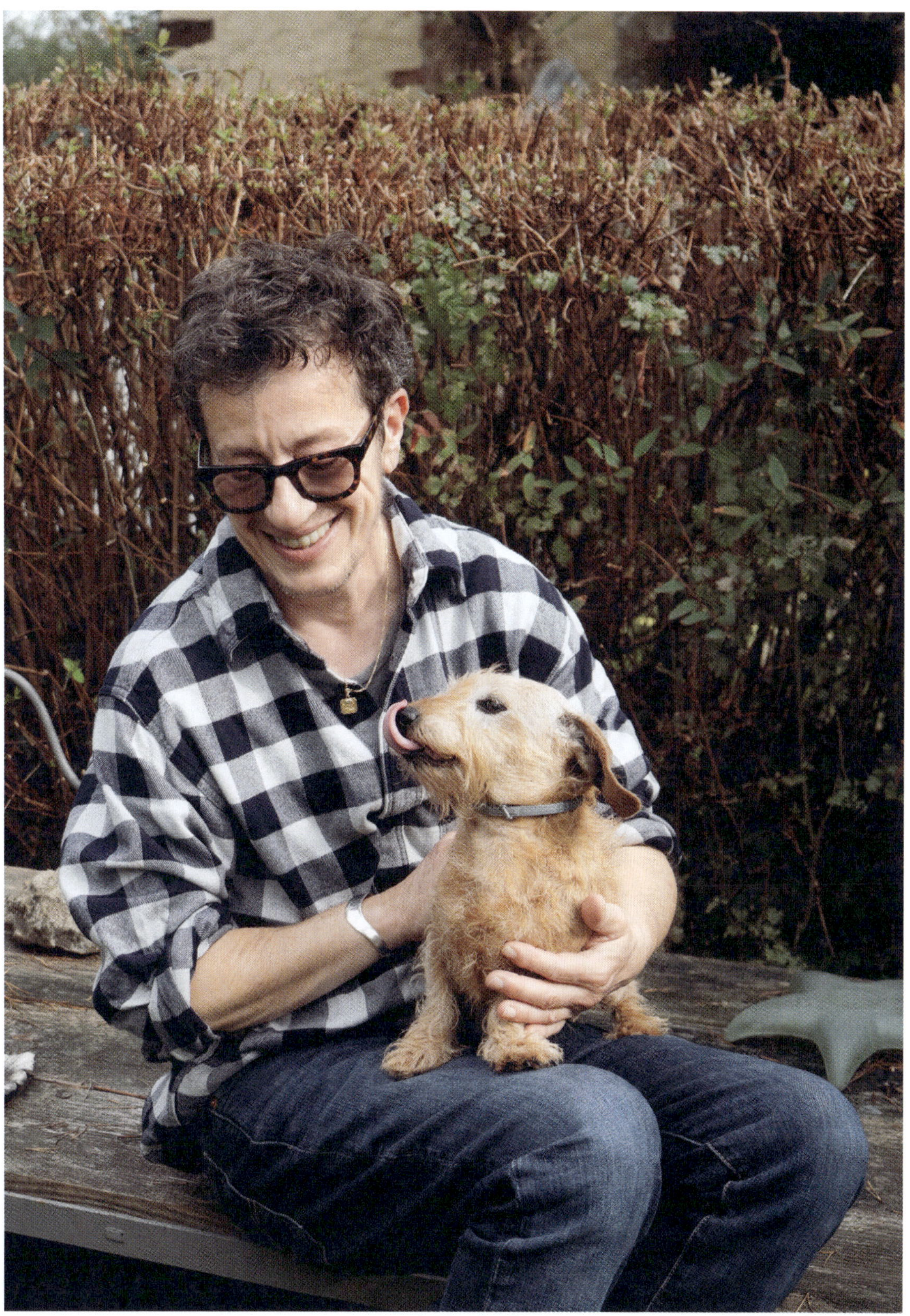

enabled me to develop empathy for the most fragile
and vulnerable beings. Through them, I find resonance
with my own trajectory, my strength, but also my
sensitivity. Fragility has to become a strength.
Nature is violent, of course, but it doesn't destroy itself.

**RPC I know that you yourself are involved in animal
protection, that you are particularly sensitive to child
protection, that you are very protective.**

ED   Yes, and I'm the same way in my work. I get messages
across and I put a lot of visibility into defending this
animal life which is ours. I'm a member of the Ligue
de Protection des Oiseaux (league for the protection
of birds - LPO France), and even if I don't always have
the time to take part in field work, I take action at
home, where fields and hedges, as well as ponds,
are there for them, they are little treasures. I'm careful.
My work, if looked at closely, is not just a celebration
of nature and animals. It's about repair and exchange.
If you look at my drawings, the flowers, animals
and boys are there to denounce something, what's
going wrong or what's going right, it's a language.
I scavenged a lot of old photos for my work, of war
children, on which the symbolism of flowers, insects,
ferns and animals was there to mend them, to give
them new life. What I do is shift time, shift situations,
I erase the unthinkable. I give life back to life,
for a moment of sweetness.

**RPC Today, you live in the Loir-et-Cher region. Was it a choice
to get closer to the countryside and nature?**

ED   Yes. I'd had enough of Paris, which was no longer
the city I'd known. I grew up in a Paris of another era,

with its little grocery stores where bottles of milk
were lined up in front of the stores. Simple and lively
places. Then, as I spend most of my time in my studio,
I thought that if I was going to have a workspace,
it might as well be in the countryside, with land
and a connection to nature. I recreated a bit of my
childhood there: simple things, objects like vintage
flowerpots that remind me of my grandmother.
But my soul is still that of a Parisian, with my heart
in Auvergne.

RPC   **Did this immersion in nature, away from the oppressive
atmosphere of everyday life, help you to shape yourself?**

ED   I started taking care of nature and realized that
by taking care of nature, I was taking care of myself.

RPC   **Do you see in these characters a little of the person who
struggles in the face of ecological threats?**

ED   There's no sadness, he's not destitute. Rather, it's
a zest for life, an understanding, an attentiveness
to the world. The boy in my work is never sad, quite
the contrary: he seeks to right situations, either by
denouncing them or by passing on energy, light and
a great deal of empathy.

RPC   **And what do you do with these animals in your drawings?**

ED   I show them first, I give them a voice, I give them
visibility. I speak as much of them as of us, and of this
bond that needs to be reestablished and protected,
which most of us have forgotten.
It's a part of us, I give them their space.
I also use this opportunity to denounce a world

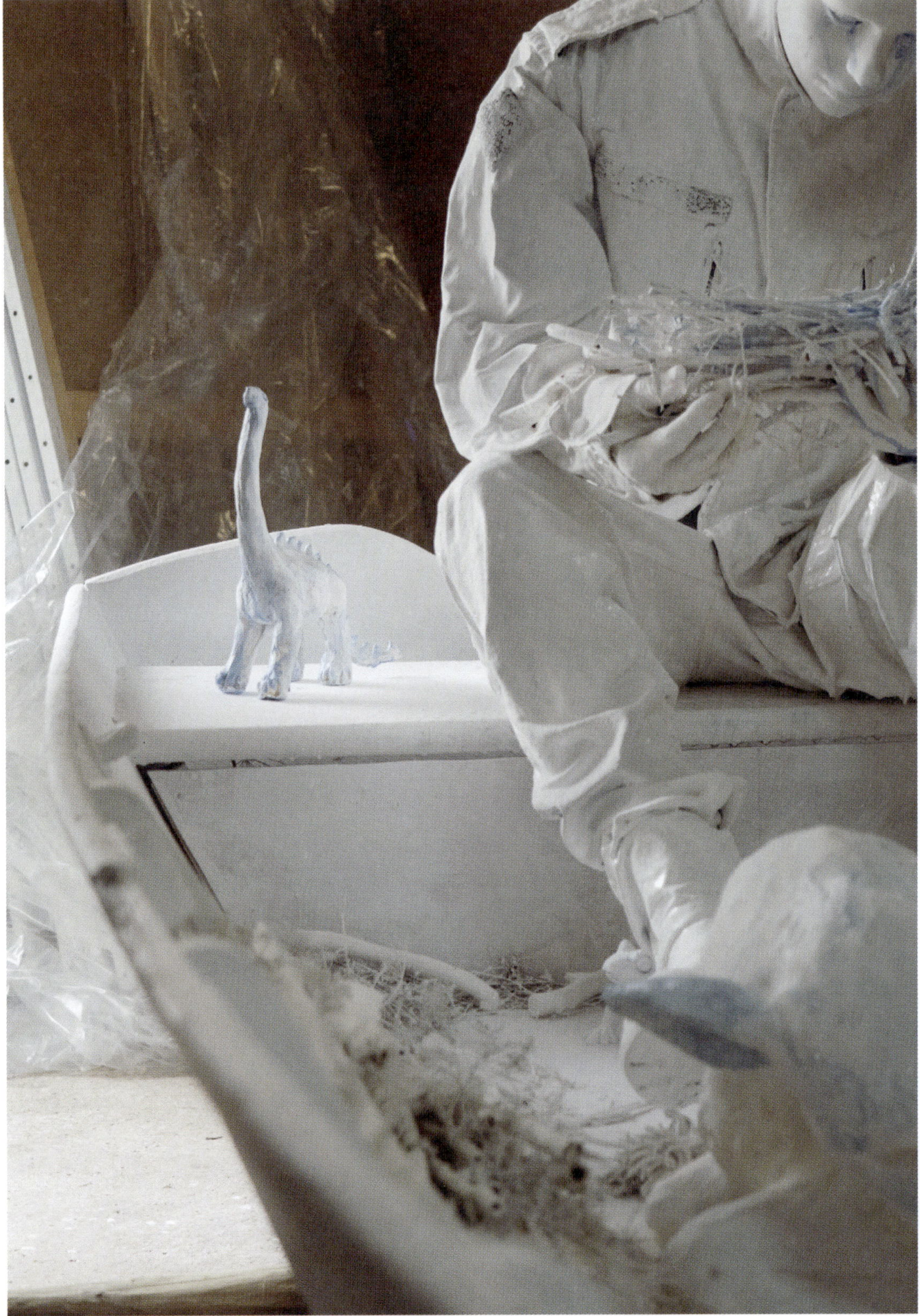

that is violent towards the weakest. The squirrel
is holding high-heeled shoes, a way of questioning
and shedding light on women's roles. The wild boar
is king, the marmot has a house, which speaks of
their threatened spaces. The hare with its dragonfly,
or the badger with its ladybug, which could finally
bring it good luck, is a way of revealing the vulnerable.
On what we want to make vulnerable in order
to dominate it. It's another way of shedding light
on what we don't want to see.
I have chosen animals that come around the house
for the most part, like foxes, deer, badgers...
and squirrels, of course. These are animals that
are often seen. They're part of the family, my
family, they're my sisters and brothers, my fathers
and mothers. My children.

RPC It's a bit like the deer in the deer and wolf room,
the installation of little resin houses on the taxidermied
deer, there's always this idea of the animal's role.

    ED Yes, and these houses are also clouds, perhaps
childhood memories. Is this the childhood home?
Or is it a human's space? It's a way of shedding light
on the role of animals before it becomes a mere
memory, it's a way of thinking about it. These houses
are pierced, but the light shines through.
It's an opening to illuminate things, to ask questions
and, above all, to talk about them.

RPC Like the title of the exhibition and this book, *The Endless
Glimmer?*

    ED *The Endless Glimmer*, that's what I've always strived
to do. Illuminate, enlighten myself. It's a way of

reaching out to others, to ourselves. To make things
shine. It's against obscurantism. Light is life. We must
always light up ourselves, others and the world around
us. This title also symbolizes my desire to highlight
love, animals, our relationship with others and our
environment, the world and ourselves. This title also
symbolizes my desire to shed light on love, animals,
our relationship with others and our environment,
the world, ourselves. The world moves too fast, and
people are divided into groups. I don't want to belong
to any one of them. I want to stay free, learn from
everything. Freedom means being able to evolve and
change, or at least to think things through, and that's
why my work evolves too. Dark times, not what we
want. It's necessary to always recall the importance
of light, freedom and desire. And with this exhibition,
I want to convey a message of hope… "It's high time
to rekindle the stars," as Apollinaire said.

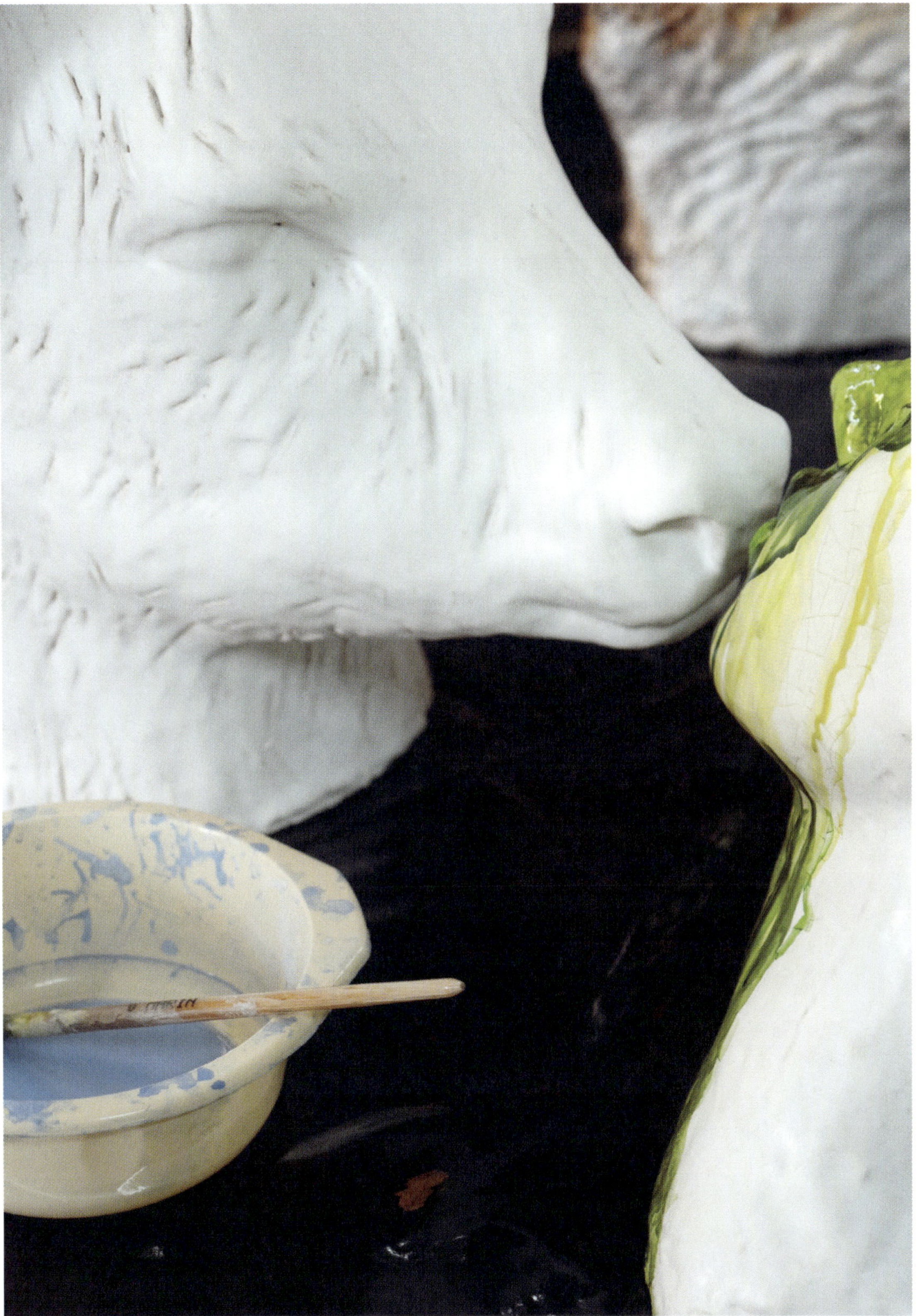

Edi Dubien

Edi Dubien explores the social, psychological and
emotional constructs that diverge from normative
discourse and imposed life patterns. Flora and fauna,
the main motifs of his drawings and watercolors, are used
to portray individuals– from children to adults–reduced
to silence by the violence of a society that disregards both
diversity and the environment. Through a perceptive
dialogue between people and nature, Edi Dubien's work
raises awareness of the importance of self-acceptance
in all its diversity, and of respect for others.

Born in 1963 in Issy-les-Moulineaux, Edi Dubien lives
and works between Paris and his farm in the Loir-et-Cher
countryside.
Edi Dubien has experienced two births: the first in 1963,
and the second on June 23, 2014, when his civil status was
modified allowing him to live and be recognized by society
as a man.
Self-taught, never having attended art school, Edi Dubien's
work addresses not only his own personal journey,
but also reflections on the world, its catastrophes,
its successes and its potential.
His first major retrospective, *L'homme aux mille natures*,
was presented in 2020 at Musée d'Art Contemporain
de Lyon. In 2024, he returned to Lyon for the Biennale,
where he presented a series of works at Les Grandes
Locos, at the B metro station–Gare Part-Dieu and
at the Musée Gallo-Romain de Saint-Romain-en-Gal
(until January 5, 2025).

Captions

Series of untitled drawings, Watercolor, pencil, ink, variable sizes
Résistant, Acrylic and pencil on canvas, 300 × 200 cm, 2024
Traverser le temps, Boat, plants, slip, plaster, resin, acrylic, 420 × 135 × 120 cm, 2024
Untitled drawings, Watercolor, pencil, ink, variable sizes
Je serai le plus beau pour aller danser, Tulle, 2024
Réincarnation, Plaster, slip, resin, 160 × 42 × 63 cm, 2024
Amulette, Earthenware, slip, rope, variable sizes, 2024
Cachette, Earthenware, 30 × 30 × 28 cm, 2024
Pleurer des lapins, Acrylic, slip, resin, plaster, 83 × 72 × 42 cm, 2024
Romance 2, Earthenware, 34 × 47 × 30 cm, 2024
Romance 1, Earthenware, 37 × 33 × 52 cm, 2024
Pleurer des crapauds, Acrylic and ink on canvas, 195 × 114 cm, 2017
Face à face, Watercolor, pencil, ink, drawing mounted on canvas, 220 × 130 cm, 2024
Dans nos maisons transpercées, Resin, slip, variable sizes, 2024
Je t'aime moi non plus, Roses, resin, engobe, earthenware, 2024
À nos amours, Earthenware, 40 × 30 × 30 cm, 2024
Colliers totems, Earthenware, 2024
Mon jardin suspendu, Acrylic and oil on canvas, 225 × 175 cm, 2022
Je vous aime, Faux fur, color, 2024
Ça n'ira pas à tout le monde 1 and 2, Earthenware, high heels, 2024
Quelques mots d'amour 1 and 2, Plaster and resin, 2022
Ça n'ira pas à tout le monde 1 and 2, Earthenware, high heels, 2024
Portrait de famille 1, 2, 3, 4, 5, 6, 7 and 8, Acrylic on canvas, 130 × 97 cm, 2024
    1. *Renard et sa lavande fraîche*
    2. *Blaireau et sa coccinelle porte bonheur*
    3. *Chevreuil maquillé*
    4. *Écureuil et son talon aiguille*
    5. *Marmotte et sa maison vide*
    6. *Le raton laveur sauve qui peut*
    7. *Le sanglier roi*
    8. *Le lièvre et sa libellule*

Credits

The Musée de la Chasse et de la Nature
Inaugurated by André Malraux in the Hôtel de Guénégaud
(François Mansart's 17th century historic building) on February
21, 1967, the Musée de la Chasse et de la Nature was extended
in 2007 to the adjacent Hôtel de Mongelas (18th century).
Thanks to his renovation and extension, the museum "exposes"
the relationship between man and animal through the ages
(from Antiquity to the present day) and relies on the exceptional
collections of ancient, modern and contemporary art assembled
by the founders and constantly increased for nearly half
a century. A private museum, it has been awarded the
"Musée de France" label by the Ministry of Culture.
An inhabited museum, the home of an aesthetic collector,
the Musée de la Chasse et de la Nature, founded in 1967
by François and Jacqueline Sommer, has in recent years, under
the leadership of Claude d'Anthenaise, its curator for 23 years,
been able to shift its hunting focus to delve deeper into the
relationship between man and the animal throughout history.
The museography, which is deliberately singular, brilliantly
plays with the mixture of genres in the heart of the historic
and majestic setting of the Hôtel de Guénégaud and the
Hôtel de Mongelas combined. Since 2007, the date of the first
renovation, the temporary exhibitions have been as many
opportunities for invited contemporary artists, to take over
the premises as to dialogue with the rich and varied collections.

The François Sommer Foundation
Founded in 1964 by François (1904-1973) and Jacqueline Sommer
(1913-1993), and recognized as a non-profit organization in 1966,
the François Sommer Foundation aims to:
— to share with as many people as possible the collection
of ancient, modern and contemporary art housed in the Musée
de la Chasse et de la Nature in Paris;
— to advance knowledge of wildlife and ecosystems, by carrying
out studies in the areas it manages in France and Africa,
or by funding scientific research programs in France and Europe;
— to contribute to the ongoing search for a harmonious
balance between the conservation of nature in all its forms
and the promotion of sustainable, responsible hunting.

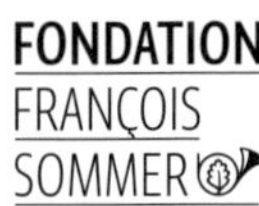
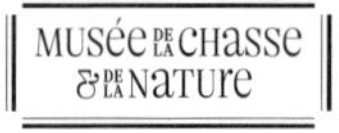

Captions

Series of untitled drawings, Watercolor, pencil, ink, variable sizes
Résistant, Acrylic and pencil on canvas, 300 × 200 cm, 2024
Traverser le temps, Boat, plants, slip, plaster, resin, acrylic, 420 × 135 × 120 cm, 2024
Untitled drawings, Watercolor, pencil, ink, variable sizes
Je serai le plus beau pour aller danser, Tulle, 2024
Réincarnation, Plaster, slip, resin, 160 × 42 × 63 cm, 2024
Amulette, Earthenware, slip, rope, variable sizes, 2024
Cachette, Earthenware, 30 × 30 × 28 cm, 2024
Pleurer des lapins, Acrylic, slip, resin, plaster, 83 × 72 × 42 cm, 2024
Romance 2, Earthenware, 34 × 47 × 30 cm, 2024
Romance 1, Earthenware, 37 × 33 × 52 cm, 2024
Pleurer des crapauds, Acrylic and ink on canvas, 195 × 114 cm, 2017
Face à face, Watercolor, pencil, ink, drawing mounted on canvas, 220 × 130 cm, 2024
Dans nos maisons transpercées, Resin, slip, variable sizes, 2024
Je t'aime moi non plus, Roses, resin, engobe, earthenware, 2024
À nos amours, Earthenware, 40 × 30 × 30 cm, 2024
Colliers totems, Earthenware, 2024
Mon jardin suspendu, Acrylic and oil on canvas, 225 × 175 cm, 2022
Je vous aime, Faux fur, color, 2024
Ça n'ira pas à tout le monde 1 and 2, Earthenware, high heels, 2024
Quelques mots d'amour 1 and 2, Plaster and resin, 2022
Ça n'ira pas à tout le monde 1 and 2, Earthenware, high heels, 2024
Portrait de famille 1, 2, 3, 4, 5, 6, 7 and 8, Acrylic on canvas, 130 × 97 cm, 2024
    1. *Renard et sa lavande fraîche*
    2. *Blaireau et sa coccinelle porte bonheur*
    3. *Chevreuil maquillé*
    4. *Écureuil et son talon aiguille*
    5. *Marmotte et sa maison vide*
    6. *Le raton laveur sauve qui peut*
    7. *Le sanglier roi*
    8. *Le lièvre et sa libellule*

Credits

Pages 1 to 137 : Photographs © Aurélien Mole, 2024
Pages 138 to 153 : Photographs © Lara Al-Gubory, 2024

Pages 96 and 98: © Laurie Karp
Pages 102 and 105: © ADAGP Paris, 2025, for works by Philippe Cognée
Pages 105: © Dewar & Gicquel
Pages 106 and 107: © ADAGP Paris, 2025, for works by Corinne Borgnet
Page 106: © Jean-Luc Chapin
Pages 106 and 107: © ADAGP Paris, 2025, for works by Franck Evennou
Pages 106 and 109: © ADAGP Paris, 2025, for works by Françoise Pétrovitch
Pages 108 and 109: © ADAGP Paris, 2025, for works by André Arbus
Page 113: © ADAGP Paris, 2025, for works by Rebecca Horn
Pages 112, 113 and 119: © ADAGP Paris, 2025, for works by Luzia Simons
Page 113: © ADAGP Paris, 2025, for works by Vincent Dubourg
Page 125: © Jeff Koons
Page 131: © ADAGP Paris, 2025, for works by Eva Jospin
Pages 130 and 131: © Benjamin Graindorge

The Musée de la Chasse et de la Nature
Inaugurated by André Malraux in the Hôtel de Guénégaud
(François Mansart's 17th century historic building) on February
21, 1967, the Musée de la Chasse et de la Nature was extended
in 2007 to the adjacent Hôtel de Mongelas (18th century).
Thanks to his renovation and extension, the museum "exposes"
the relationship between man and animal through the ages
(from Antiquity to the present day) and relies on the exceptional
collections of ancient, modern and contemporary art assembled
by the founders and constantly increased for nearly half
a century. A private museum, it has been awarded the
"Musée de France" label by the Ministry of Culture.
An inhabited museum, the home of an aesthetic collector,
the Musée de la Chasse et de la Nature, founded in 1967
by François and Jacqueline Sommer, has in recent years, under
the leadership of Claude d'Anthenaise, its curator for 23 years,
been able to shift its hunting focus to delve deeper into the
relationship between man and the animal throughout history.
The museography, which is deliberately singular, brilliantly
plays with the mixture of genres in the heart of the historic
and majestic setting of the Hôtel de Guénégaud and the
Hôtel de Mongelas combined. Since 2007, the date of the first
renovation, the temporary exhibitions have been as many
opportunities for invited contemporary artists, to take over
the premises as to dialogue with the rich and varied collections.

The François Sommer Foundation
Founded in 1964 by François (1904-1973) and Jacqueline Sommer
(1913-1993), and recognized as a non-profit organization in 1966,
the François Sommer Foundation aims to:
– to share with as many people as possible the collection
of ancient, modern and contemporary art housed in the Musée
de la Chasse et de la Nature in Paris;
– to advance knowledge of wildlife and ecosystems, by carrying
out studies in the areas it manages in France and Africa,
or by funding scientific research programs in France and Europe;
– to contribute to the ongoing search for a harmonious
balance between the conservation of nature in all its forms
and the promotion of sustainable, responsible hunting.

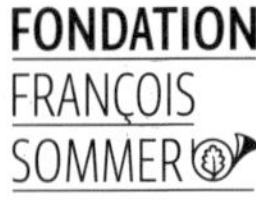

The Endless *Glimmer*

Exhibition curator
Rémy Provendier-Commenne,
Head of collections,
Musée de la Chasse et de la Nature

Publishing direction
David Desrimais

Editorial coordination
Lisa Valentin

Graphic design
Emma Zampieri – Studio JBE

Translation
Monique Gross

Photoengraving
IGS-Print

Typefaces
Faune (Alice Savoie, Cnap)
Corsario (Felix Braden, Floodfonts)

Acknowledgements by Edi Dubien
Special thanks to Thomas Jolly.
Special thanks to Remy Provendier-
Commenne for his invitation.
I would like to thank my assistant
Regine Civelli and my gallery Alain
Gutharc and Avelino Abarca.
I would also like to thank Benjamin
Simon, Françoise Fesneau and
the entire team at the Musée de
la Chasse et Nature, the François
Sommer Foundation, its Chairman,
Henri de Castries, and its Managing
Director, Alban de Loisy.
Thanks to Jean-Claude Fourmont.
**Acknowledgements by Musée
de la Chasse et de la Nature**
The François Sommer Foundation
and Musée de la Chasse et de la
Nature teams: Henri de Castries,
chairman; Alban de Loisy, *general
manager*; Laurence Amatu,
Valérie Bleuze, Béatriz Quiterio,
administration; François Chemel,
Quentin Ebrard, Benjamin Simon,
communications; Jean-Marie Alcaraz,
Denis Lemaire, Vicente Gregori,
technical team; Gaëlle Le Page,
iconography and documentation;
Zoé Schocké, *artwork supervision*;
Françoise Fesneau, *secretary*; Cécile
Van der Meersch, Manon Hoarau,
public services; Agence DPSA,
security; passages [...], *graphic
design*; Médicis, *signage production*;
ATS, *banner printing*; Imprimerie
Moutot, *communication support
printing*; Pierre Frey, *wallpaper and
fabric printing*; Françoise Perronno,
Jean-Philippe Quesnot, Philippe
Boissel, Valentin Briffaut, *hanging*
The Musée de la Chasse et de la
Nature joins Edi Dubien in thanking
Alain Gutharc and Avelino Abarca,
Régine Civelli, as well as Philippe
Gautier for his loan and all those
who contributed to the success
of this exhibition.

Acknowledgements by JBE Books
Aure Bergeret, Mathieu Cénac,
Pierre-Édouard Couton,
Didier Desrimais, Benjamin Hélion,
Damien Jacq, Benjamin Lanot,
Olivia de Smedt

Printed in Lithuania
Legal deposit: January 2025

90 rue de la Folie-Méricourt
75011 Paris
jbe-books.com

ISBN 978-2-36568-111-7

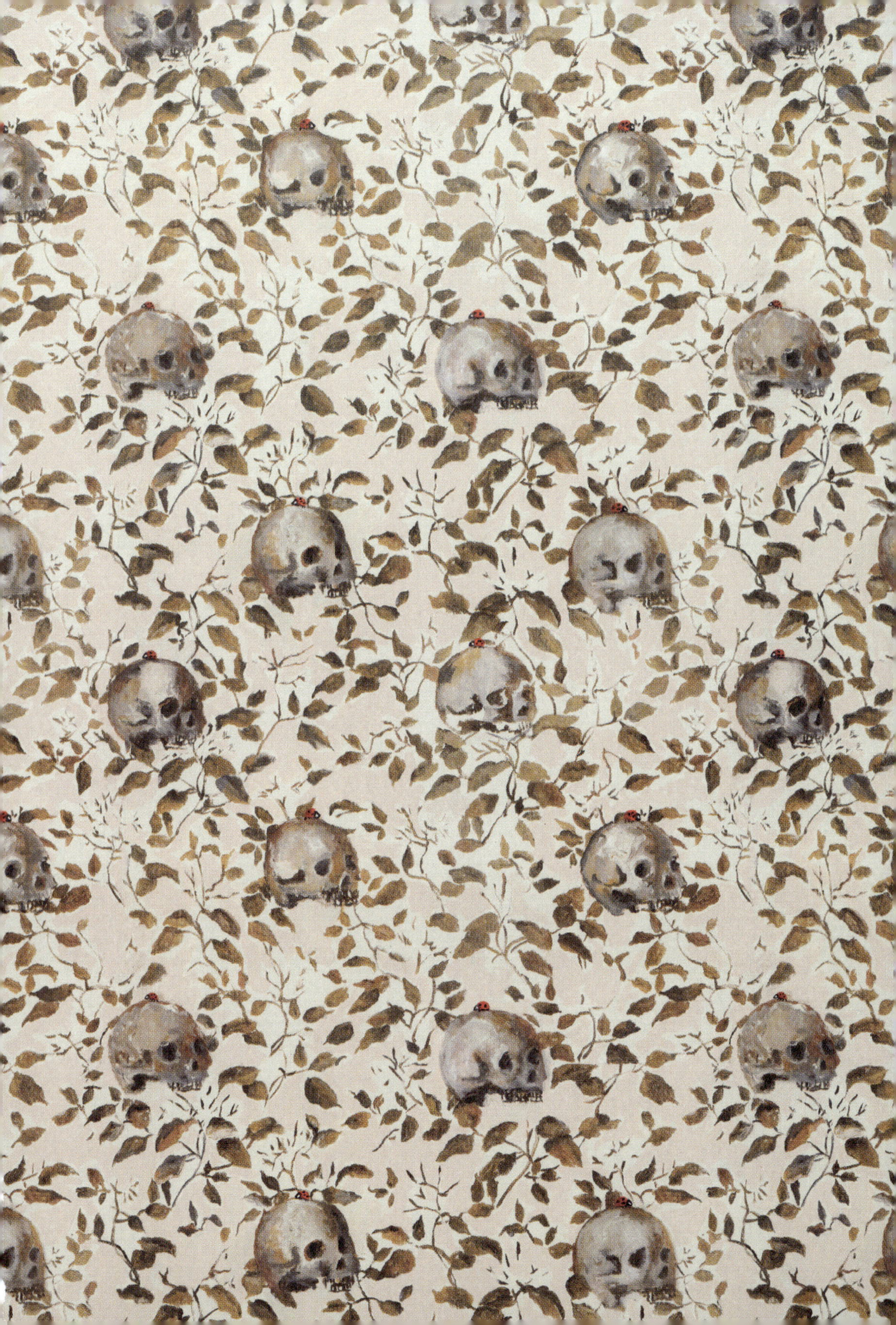

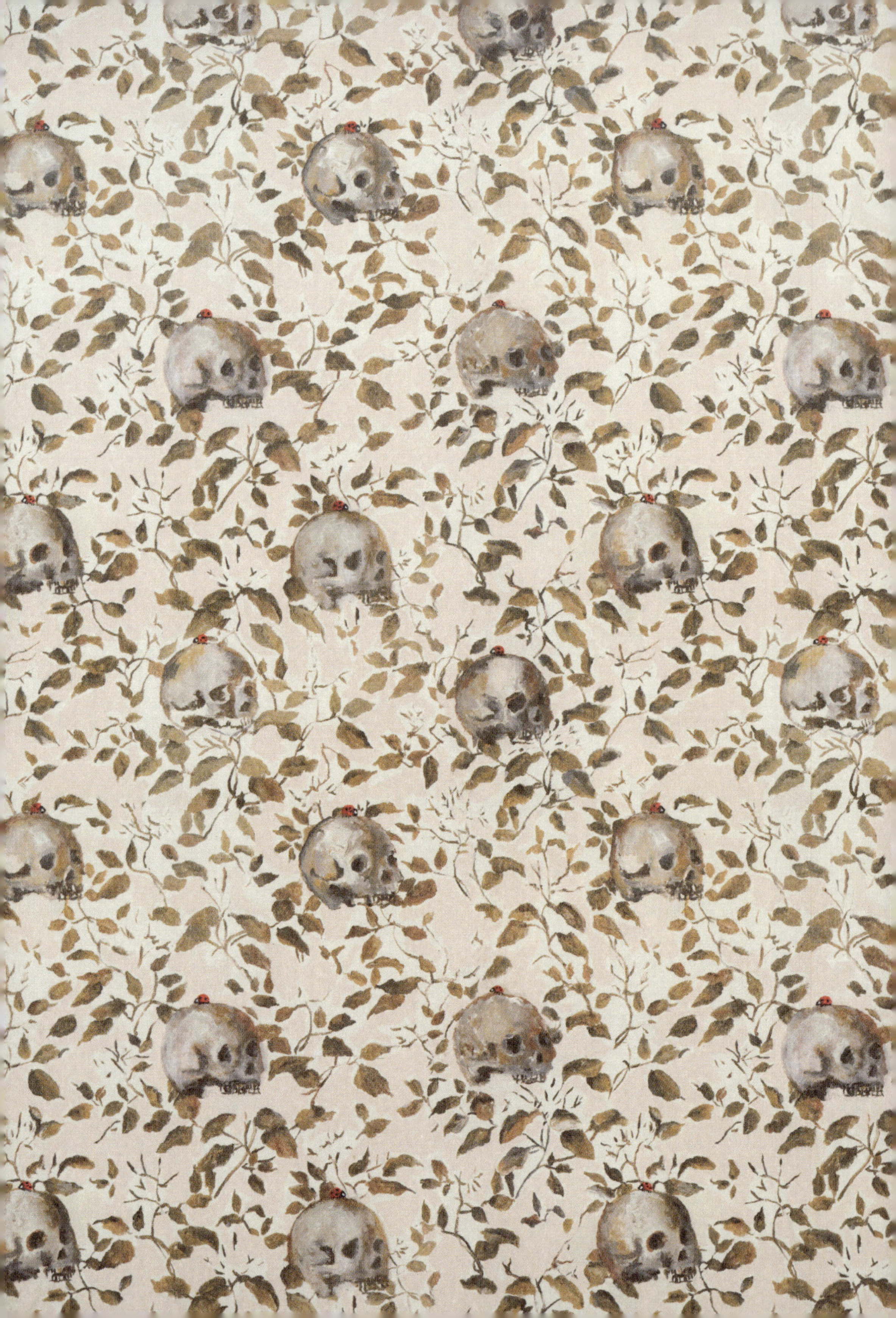